Conquest by Law

Conquest by Law

How the Discovery of America Dispossessed Indigenous Peoples of Their Lands

LINDSAY G. ROBERTSON

OXFORD

UNIVERSITY PRESS

2005

11-22-2005
LAN
$29.95

OXFORD
UNIVERSITY PRESS

Oxford University Press, Inc., publishes works that further
Oxford University's objective of excellence
in research, scholarship, and education.

Oxford   New York
Auckland   Cape Town   Dar es Salaam   Hong Kong   Karachi
Kuala Lumpur   Madrid   Melbourne   Mexico City   Nairobi
New Delhi   Shanghai   Taipei   Toronto

With offices in
Argentina   Austria   Brazil   Chile   Czech Republic   France   Greece
Guatemala   Hungary   Italy   Japan   Poland   Portugal   Singapore
South Korea   Switzerland   Thailand   Turkey   Ukraine   Vietnam

Published by Oxford University Press, Inc.,
198 Madison Avenue, New York, New York 10016

www.oup.com

Oxford is a registered trademark of Oxford University Press

Library of Congress Cataloging-in-Publication Data
Robertson, Lindsay Gordon.
Conquest by law: how the discovery of America dispossessed
indigenous peoples of their lands / by Lindsay G. Robertson.
p.   cm.
Includes bibliographical references.
ISBN-13 978-0-19-514869-5
ISBN 0-19-514869-X
1. United Illinois and Wabash Land Companies—Trials, litigation, etc.
2. Indians of North America—Land tenure—United States—History.
3. Indians of North America—Land transfers—History. 4. Land titles
—Illinois—History. 5. Land titles—Indiana—History. 6. United States
Supreme Court—History. 7. Constitutional history—United States. I. Title.
KF228.U5R63 2005
346.7304'32'08997—dc 22   2004022795

9 8 7 6 5 4 3 2 1

Printed in the United States of America
on acid-free paper

To my family,
and in memory
of our cousin,
Stephen Roberts Johnson

ACKNOWLEDGMENTS

During the fourteen years I have been engaged in this project, I have become indebted to many people. Jasper and Lindsay Brinton deserve first mention for the reasons stated in the preface. It is fair to say that, without them, this work would not have been possible. Indeed, the Brinton family, especially Judge Jasper Yeates Brinton, merit thanks collectively for preserving the Illinois-Wabash papers over almost two hundred years. Three members of the University of Virginia faculty also deserve special mention. Charles McCurdy of the Corcoran Department of History and the School of Law provided support and guidance from the project's inception, and indeed throughout my education as a legal historian. Peter Onuf of the Corcoran Department of History offered the same during my doctoral studies in the history of the early republic. Richard Merrill of the School of Law was a continuing source of inspiration and support. I am also indebted to my wonderful editors, Dedi Felman, Michele Bové, and Chris Dahlin, and to Ed Ayers, Richard Bartley, Al Brophy, Barry Cushman, Vine Deloria Jr., Paul Gilje, Rob Griswold, Katheleen Guzman, Sid Harring, Taiawagi Helton, Owen Hughes, Matthew Kelly, Margaret McFarland, Brad Morse, John Robertson, Michael Scaperlanda, Nelson Simon, Alice Stanton, Rennard Strickland, Rick Tepker, Will Thomas, and Roger Thompson, all of whom have read the manuscript in whole or in part and given me the benefit of their comments. My thanks are owed as well to numerous individuals who helped guide my on-site research efforts, especially Richard Day, historian at the Indiana Territory State Historic Site; Charles Hobson, editor in chief of the Papers of John Marshall; and the staffs of the Vincennes University Library, the Indiana Historical Society, the Indiana State Library, the Illinois Historical Society, the Illinois State Library, the Historical Society of Pennsylvania, the Virginia State Library, the Virginia Historical Society, the American Jewish Historical Society at Brandeis University, Alderman Library at the University of Virginia, the University of Virginia Law Library, Van Pelt Library at the University of Pennsylvania, the University of Pennsylvania Law Library, the University of Oklahoma Law Library, the Library of Congress, McCabe Library at Swarthmore College, the Maryland Historical Society, the Historical Society of Frederick County, Maryland, the Papers of John Marshall, the British Library, the British Public Record Office (Kew and Chancery Lane), and the National Library of Scotland. I am also grateful to Richard Dunn and the Philadelphia Center for Early American Studies (now the McNeil Center) for providing me office space and funding over two years in Philadelphia as a research and visiting fellow. Several organizations, including the National Trail of Tears Association, the Federal Bar Association Indian Law Section, and the Sovereignty Symposium, have given me much appreciated opportunities to speak on the substance of my findings, as well as useful feedback. My students at the University of Oklahoma College of Law, the University of Virginia School of Law, and the George Washington University National Law Center have offered the same for the past fourteen years. Special thanks are owed to Claudia and Jake Jacobs of Mount Carmel, Illinois, with whom I spent a delightful evening searching for the remains of William M'Intosh's house at the Grand Rapids of the Wabash; to John and Catherine Leiner, who provided me shelter and company when researching in Indiana and Illinois; to my research assistants, Kristi Covey, Stephen Butler, Huma Yasin-Yunus, Doug Wallace, and Geoff Jennings (who suggested the title); to Melissa Adamson, Dawn Tomlins, and Misty Akins; to Curtis Berkey, for his upbeat encouragement; to Giovanna Gismondi Luis, for her counsel and support; and to Polly, James C., Preston, Eliza, and John Robertson, for their apparently inexhaustible patience.

PREFACE

Perhaps no event in the modern era has been more profoundly consequential than the European "discovery" of the Americas. When Columbus landed in what he thought was the Indies, none could have foreseen the rapid conquest of the great indigenous empires in Mexico and Peru, the huge influx of Europeans, the subjugation of indigenous populations, or the rise of the new European-founded states of the Western Hemisphere. The discovery of the Americas forced Europeans to adapt their traditional worldview to accommodate the Columbian landfall. For political and cultural reasons, the intellectual structure they ultimately applied to define the terms of their relationship to this "new world" was legal. Over a succession of generations, Europeans devised rules intended to justify the dispossession and subjugation of the native peoples of the Western Hemisphere. Of these rules the most fundamental were those governing the ownership of land. This book sets forth the troubling and hitherto unknown history of how the descendants of European colonizers shaped these rules to seize title to indigenous lands in the United States.

In this country and, to a great extent, in other former British colonies, the legal rule justifying claims to indigenous lands discovered by Europeans traces to the 1823 decision of the Supreme Court of the United States in

Johnson v. M'Intosh. Johnson contained the "discovery" doctrine, which answered the question: What rights did Europeans acquire, and indigenous peoples lose, upon the discovery of the New World? The answer, according to the Court, was ownership of all discovered lands. Discovery converted the indigenous owners of discovered lands into tenants on those lands. The underlying title belonged to the discovering sovereign. The indigenous occupants were free to sell their "lease," but only to the landlord, and they were subject to eviction at any time. More than 180 years later, the discovery doctrine is still the law.

The importance of *Johnson v. M'Intosh* to the property rights of indigenous and nonindigenous peoples in the former British colonial world has led numerous scholars and practitioners to attempt to ferret out its meaning. In the past two decades, more than 750 articles and several books have cited the opinion.[1] For the most part, the authors seek to establish doctrinal and intellectual antecedents of the opinion or to illuminate qualifications imposed by subsequent decisions.[2]

This book, in contrast, began more than a decade ago as an article intended to provide context for the case of *Johnson v. M'Intosh* by identifying the participants and establishing the litigation history. I had no expectation that I would reach any revolutionary, or even surprising, conclusions, only that I might provide some background to make the decision more accessible. In the summer of 1991, however, while engaged in archival research, I had a serendipitous experience that profoundly altered the project's course. In the card catalogue at the Historical Society of Pennsylvania, I found a brief reference to a deaccessioned collection of documents relating to the United Illinois and Wabash Land Companies, the effective plaintiffs in *Johnson v. M'Intosh.* I asked the reference librarian where these documents were, and after researching for a short while she determined that they had been reclaimed years before by the donor, who lived in England. On a hunch, I asked if the documents had been sent directly to England or reclaimed by a local person. This she kindly checked into as well, ultimately determining that they had been collected by the donor's son, for whom she had a name and old address. I found a public telephone and a few minutes later was speaking with Jasper Brinton, the donor's son, who told me that, after he had reclaimed the documents, his father told him to keep virtually all of them. He very kindly offered to show them to me, and I gratefully accepted. When I arrived at his home outside Philadelphia, he took me to a large trunk in his basement. I had no idea what sort of documents he had, or how many, and when he opened the trunk I was stunned. Jasper Brinton's great-great-great grandfather, John Hill Brinton, was the last secretary of the United Illinois and Wabash Land Companies. In the trunk were the Companies' complete corporate records, compiled over more than fifty years—hundreds of documents (some in code, with the key to the code included) never cited by scholars. I spent the next two days as the guest of Jasper and Lindsay Brinton reading the documents. By the time I finished I had the first part of a hugely troubling story. Ten years would pass before I had the whole of it.

This book is the first complete account of the history of *Johnson v. M'Intosh*. The story it tells is unsettling. *Johnson* was a collusive case, an attempt by speculators in Indian lands to take advantage of since-closed loopholes in the early federal judicial system to win a judgment from the Supreme Court recognizing their claim to millions of acres. To achieve this the speculators brought onto their payroll many of the leading figures of the early republic, including former congressman Robert Goodloe Harper, Daniel Webster, first secretary of the navy Benjamin Stoddert, and General William Winder, the lawyer who represented William M'Intosh, the Companies' *Johnson* opponent, before the Supreme Court. Their efforts might well have succeeded had not Chief Justice John Marshall been guided by his own interests at the time the case finally came before him. Marshall saw *Johnson* as a vehicle for removing an obstacle standing between his former colleagues in Virginia's Revolutionary War militia and bounty lands promised them in western Kentucky. To resolve an ongoing dispute over title to these lands, Marshall incorporated the discovery doctrine into his opinion in the *Johnson* case, converting what might have been a one-paragraph decision into one comprising more than thirty-three pages. Traveling far beyond the question presented in a case was typical of Marshall, was contemporaneously criticized, and, as a method of adjudication, is excused today largely because scholars have on the whole sympathized with Marshall's perceived ends. In the case of *Johnson*, as the chief justice himself came to realize, traveling beyond the question presented was a tragic mistake.

Marshall's incorporation of the discovery doctrine into the *Johnson* opinion led to political catastrophe for Native Americans. To Marshall's distress, Georgians seized on the doctrine as justification for the passage of an act imposing Georgia law on the Cherokees. This action inspired Congress to pass the Indian Removal Act of 1830, and the forced migration of the eastern tribes began. When the legitimacy of the doctrinal theory underlying these acts came before the Court in *Worcester v. Georgia* in 1832, Marshall repudiated the discovery doctrine, but by then it was too late. Marshall's death in 1835 and the filling of the Court with Andrew Jackson's appointees prevented the securing of this repudiation, and the United States has inherited a legal regime dependent on their subsequent politically driven resurrection of a wrongly decided, collusive case. Perhaps even more troubling, other former British colonial states have imported the doctrine, establishing it as a baseline for indigenous relations throughout the English-speaking world.

I have four aims in this book. First, having had access to a wealth of previously unknown primary materials, I seek to explain the meaning of *Johnson v. M'Intosh* and the discovery doctrine by illuminating in detail the history of the case's prosecution and placing its resolution in legal and political contexts. My goal is not to demonstrate doctrinal and intellectual parallels over time, but to establish just what was on the minds of the participants in the case at the time it was crafted, pleaded, argued, and decided. By understanding the case in context, one arguably acquires a better sense of how the decision ought now to be interpreted and applied.

My second aim is to expose the process of judicial lawmaking in the early republic. The legal system in which the Marshall Court rendered *Johnson v. M'Intosh* and, indeed, all of its other great decisions was very much in process of formation, not least jurisdictionally. The history of the *Johnson* litigation well illustrates the ethical and political consequences of this circumstance: collusion, fabrication, and manipulation of pleading rules were integral to the litigation, as the plaintiffs' attorneys aggressively sought to turn deficiencies in the system to their clients' advantage.

My third aim is to encourage two modest reconceptualizations. First, some scholars have tended to present some of our early jurists, especially John Marshall, as more or less consistently prescient and wide-ranging in their thought. The discovery doctrine, for example, is commonly seen as Marshall's attempt to craft a rational scheme for land acquisition in the United States. While I do not entirely disagree with the conclusions reached by these scholars, it seems to me that in some instances they may ask too much of their subject. After all, Marshall had a lot on his plate: in addition to authoring Supreme Court opinions, he had circuit riding obligations, a family to support, and a social life to enjoy. The *Johnson* opinion was issued eight days after argument closed, and Marshall drafted the opinion while listening to argument in other cases and engaging in other life activities. I think the rather more prosaic explanation for the opinion that follows is likelier given these realities. Second, there has been an occasional tendency in the historiography of Anglo-indigenous relations during the early republican period to characterize federal policy as consistently knowingly duplicitous. Without intending to suggest that this was never true, I do not believe *Johnson* fits this model. Instead, I think the opinion offers an instructive picture of how intelligent people can sometimes unthinkingly create catastrophic problems they find themselves powerless to fix.

In this vein, my final aim is to encourage a reassessment of the jurisprudential legacy of *Johnson* in light of its procedural and political history. I believe that the Court viewed *Johnson* as a relatively insignificant decision when rendered and that the case achieved landmark status as a result of political circumstances unrelated to its origins. *Johnson* became essential to Indian removal. When John Marshall attempted to kill the heart of the opinion, Andrew Jackson's Supreme Court appointees revived it. The removal policy itself has since been excoriated. Consequently, what we now embrace is a repudiated rule revived to support an excoriated policy. Perhaps it is time to rethink this.

A final word about the book's focus. Despite the fact that the legacy of the *Johnson v. M'Intosh* litigation is felt most acutely by indigenous peoples, the history of the litigation was dictated almost entirely by European Americans. Indigenous peoples seldom appear in the following narrative. I hope their absence will underscore the extent of their effective disfranchisement in the judicial conquest of Native America.

87.35   77.35   67.

55

NEW
SOUTH WALES

P. Mourning   Bear I^s   C. Jones
The Cubbs
Equan B.   JAMES
R. Kikikonan   Viners I.   Stade R.
Albany R.   Westons   LA
Canuco R.   Charlton I.   Rupert R.   ESKIM
North P.   Com   Fort F. Rupert   NE
R.   Frenchmans R.   L. Mistas Sins
Madvey R.

50

CANADA   Tadousac

Upper
or Lake
Superior   ADIRONDAKS   Quebec
Richlingham   Trois Rev.
L. Hurons   Montreal
NEW ENGLAND
45   Falmouth
Casko L.
L. Ontario   Portsmo outh
Niagara   Boston   C. Cod
Le Detroit   Albany   New London   L. Nant.
L. Erie   Milford   Martha's
Illinois L.   New York   Vineyard
Philadelphia   Long I.
40   VIRGINIA   Shrewsbury
Burn gat
Wood R.   Anna polis   C. May
Walkers Settlement   Delaw. B.
CHERAKEES   Williams bur   Henlopen
James Town   Okatanquion
CHIKASAWS   Roano   Chingoteak
35   CAROLINA   C. Charles
TOULSIANA   Cheasepeak B.
CREEK   Kuratuk Inlet
Bath Town   Roanoke Inlet
C. Hattaras
CHACTAWS   GEORGIA   Beaufort   Okakok Inlet
C. Lookout
NA   O. Fear
Charles T   C. Cartaret
Helena Sound
CREEK   Port Royal
R. Iberville   St Simons R.
FLORIDA   St Johns R.
St Augustin
C. Racondide   Eutalia I.
B. Apalache   Mosquitos
30
C. Canaveral

An
Accurate Map
of the
BRITISH EMPIRE
in
N^th AMERICA
as settled by
the Preliminaries in
1762.

7o   Longitude   West from Ferro   6o   5o

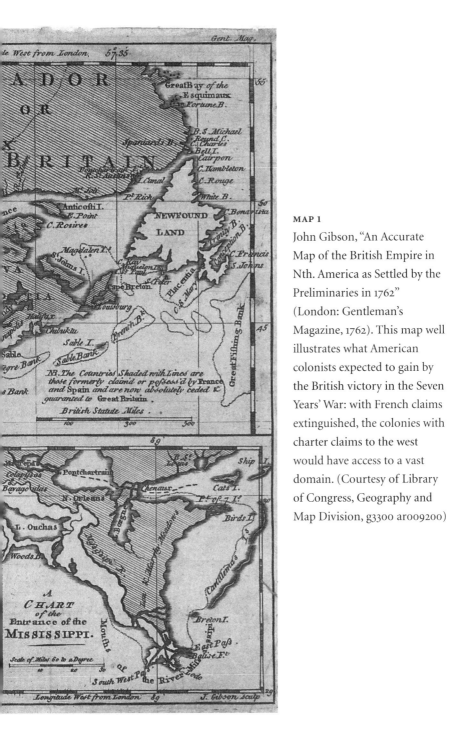

MAP 1

John Gibson, "An Accurate Map of the British Empire in Nth. America as Settled by the Preliminaries in 1762" (London: Gentleman's Magazine, 1762). This map well illustrates what American colonists expected to gain by the British victory in the Seven Years' War: with French claims extinguished, the colonies with charter claims to the west would have access to a vast domain. (Courtesy of Library of Congress, Geography and Map Division, g3300 ar009200)

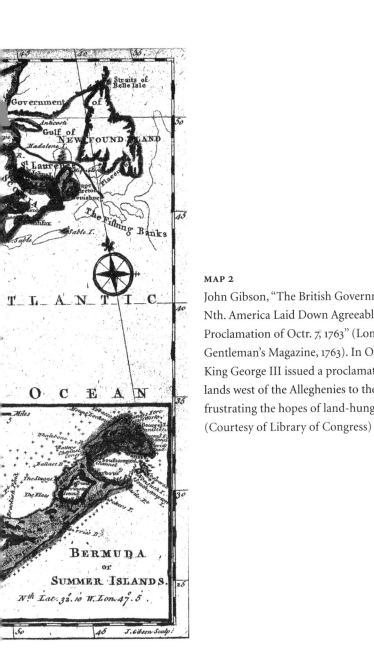

MAP 2

John Gibson, "The British Governments in Nth. America Laid Down Agreeable to the Proclamation of Octr. 7, 1763" (London: Gentleman's Magazine, 1763). In October 1763, King George III issued a proclamation reserving lands west of the Alleghenies to the Indians, frustrating the hopes of land-hungry colonists. (Courtesy of Library of Congress)

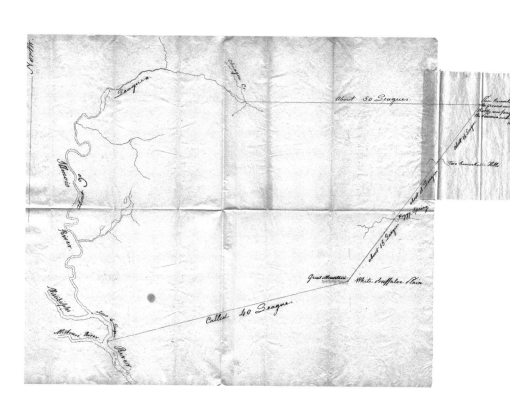

MAP 3

The upper Illinois purchase. This and the three maps that follow (Maps 4–6)
show the Illinois Company purchases of 1773 and the Wabash Company
purchases of 1775. The maps are 1805 copies of those submitted to the
Vincennes land commissioners. (Maps 3–6 courtesy of Jasper Brinton)

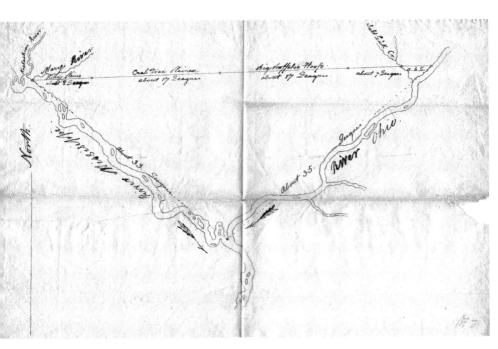

MAP 4

The lower Illinois purchase.

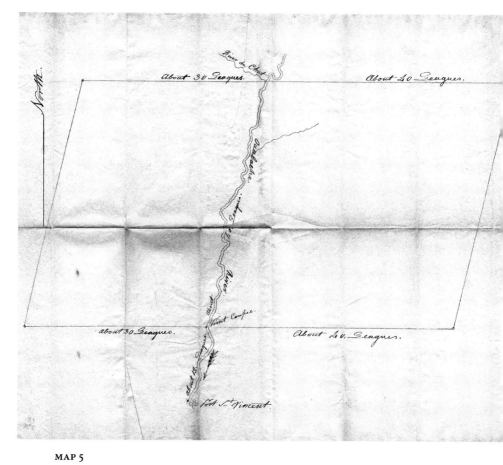

MAP 5

The upper Wabash purchase.

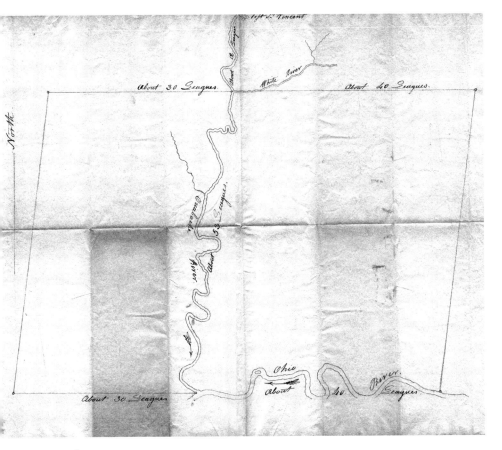

MAP 6
The lower Wabash purchase.

CONTENTS

Conquest by Law

CHAPTER 1

The Illinois and Wabash Land Companies

Purchases and Petitions

On a cold Friday evening, February 14, 1823—St. Valentine's Day—a group of about thirty lawyers and judges gathered at the White House in Washington, D.C., for a supper hosted by President James Monroe. Scuppernong and Constantia wines flowed freely, as did extravagant conversation. Guests debated the hotly contested presidential race, the first in the history of the new republic to attract a field of credible candidates. Andrew Jackson, William Crawford, Henry Clay, and the ultimately successful John Quincy Adams all vied for the honor of succeeding Monroe. Henry Clay, who was at the dinner, assured all who cared to know that the "miserably cold" rooms in the Executive Mansion would be "better warmed during his tenure." Others in attendance, including Robert Goodloe Harper, former congressman from South Carolina and now a Baltimore attorney, no doubt spoke more about the important cases they would soon argue at the new term of the Supreme Court. Of this group, none topped young Henry Murray of Annapolis, Maryland, who during the evening boasted of being in Washington to argue a case in which "seven[ty] millions of acres of land are in controversy, . . . more land," it occurred to another attendee, "than all England."[1]

The case was *Johnson v. M'Intosh*, and to its advocates, from the beginning, it was all about land: 43,000 square miles of lush, rolling farmland commanding the junctures of four major river systems in Indiana and Illinois.[2] On the day following the White House dinner and for two days thereafter, Harper, Murray, Daniel Webster, and Baltimore attorney William Winder urged five justices of the Supreme Court of the United States to recognize their clients' title to lands within this massive domain. In the process, and completely incidentally, the attorneys and Court together created a legal doctrine that answered a profound and fundamental question: What legal rights did Europeans acquire—and indigenous peoples lose—by virtue of the European "discovery" of America? It was a question, as Francis Walker Gilmer would say, "as wide as the horizon—& new," yet it was answered with virtually no sense of depth of impact.[3]

This is a story of unintended consequences, of the way a spurious claim gave rise to a doctrine intended to be of limited application, which itself gave rise to a massive displacement of persons and the creation of an entire legal regime. In *Johnson v. M'Intosh*, the Supreme Court announced the so-called discovery doctrine, which provided that, upon discovery of the continent, European sovereigns acquired title to all discovered lands, while indigenous peoples retained only an "occupancy" right that could be transferred only to the same discovering sovereigns. Throughout the United States, the American political descendants of these discovering sovereigns overnight became owners of lands that had previously belonged to Native Americans. The indigenous owners were converted into tenants on their lands and denied the right to sell their "leases" on the open market. Nine years later, in what should have been another landmark discovery doctrine decision, *Worcester v. Georgia*, the majority of the Court rejected this doctrine in favor of a formulation rerecognizing indigenous ownership. Unfortunately, by then it was too late. Various factors, including the death of Chief Justice John Marshall, facilitated a politically driven revival of the discovery doctrine in the years immediately following *Worcester*, and the doctrine still continues to be recognized and applied by courts in the United States. This book is the story of the doctrine's creation, repudiation, and revival and an argument for its fundamental reconsideration based on substantive flaws and profound procedural irregularities.

It is also a story about contradictions: about American colonists heroically fighting to throw off the yoke of British oppression, in part to satisfy rather unheroic hunger for indigenous lands; about the ease with which lawyers could employ collusion and untruth to further litigation aims in a federal republic committed to virtue; and about a Supreme Court determined to safeguard private property rights yet capable in a single opinion of dispossessing tens of thousands. Lastly, it is a story about a nation in its infancy, with a judicial process rife with holes, serious unresolved constitutional questions of just who would be in control—the states or the federal government, the Supreme Court or Congress—and no shortage of people eager to exploit these uncertainties for private gain.

The story is neither simple nor brief.

Imperial Dissolution and the Illinois and Wabash Land Purchases

The claim in *Johnson v. M'Intosh* arose fifty years before its final resolution, in a time of almost mind-numbing jurisdictional confusion, when the British Empire in North America began to break apart. Imperial dissolution was a process. In the years following the passage of the Stamp Act in 1765, the relationship between Great Britain and most of its North American colonies deteriorated to the point of political separation, effected by the Declaration of Independence in 1776 and secured by eight years of war. Between 1765 and 1776, jurisdictional lines blurred, political allegiances wavered, and economic networks fragmented.

Well-funded groups of land speculators armed with tenuous legal authority poured political capital and cash into the vacuum created by these disturbances in the hope of winning huge profits from the turmoil. Land was abundant in North America, and the growing population promised a lucrative market. Among the most attractive targets for speculators was Indian tribal land, much of which was lush, expansive, and cheap.

Initially, it was not easy for speculators to lay legal claim to tribal land. France and numerous Indian nations had successfully kept British settlers confined to lands east of the Allegheny Mountains until 1763, when Britain expelled France from North America at the end of the Seven Years' War.

British colonists thereafter clamored for the right to cross over the mountains to acquire Indian lands. The British Crown, however, was determined to provide no new pretext for war, and to the disgust of most British colonists decided to preserve the mountains as a barrier to settlement.

Many of the colonies had royal charter claims to various parts of these lands; the colony of North Carolina, for example, by its original royal charter included all the lands that would become the state of Tennessee. The Crown expected that well-connected colonists would seek grants, called "patents," establishing title to the transmontane lands from their colonial governors. At the same time, the Crown expected that numerous less well-connected colonists would simply head west to buy or seize lands directly from the Indians without benefit of colonial government sanction.

To arrest all these possibilities, on October 7, 1763, King George III issued what would prove, from an American vantage, the most controversial proclamation of his reign. The Proclamation of 1763 declared the lands west of the Allegheny Mountains to be reserved for the use of the Indians; barred colonial governors from authorizing surveys or issuing patents establishing title to these lands; forbade individual colonists to purchase, settle, or take possession of any of them without a license from the Crown; and ordered squatters to leave immediately.[4] The Crown claimed a "preemption" or "preemptive" right to these lands (i.e., an exclusive right to purchase, whenever the Indian owners should be willing to sell). East of the mountains, the Crown's governors and commanders in chief were authorized to exercise the preemption right to purchase Indian lands on the Crown's behalf, but west of the mountains, the right belonged to the Crown alone. Neither colonial governors nor individual colonists had any right to claim title to Indian lands west of the mountains. The Proclamation of 1763 was the first of many British moves that would lead to the American Revolution.

Most colonists loudly protested the proclamation, viewing it as an unconstitutional denial of access to lands they had fairly won by defeating the French in the Seven Years' War. However, not all viewed it in a negative light. Proscription of unlicensed purchases of Indian lands was a fact of life in the eastern colonies. Colonial legislatures had long prohibited such individual purchases within their boundaries, ostensibly to preserve the peace.

To the extent these statutes had been enforced, one of their principal effects had been to limit the pool of potential acquirers of Indian lands to those sufficiently well connected either to obtain a license to purchase or to receive a patent or grant of title once the lands had been purchased by the colonial government. The royal proclamation narrowed even further the number of potential acquirers of Indian lands; by decreasing the odds of successful acquisition, the royal proclamation increased the potential return. Few British North Americans, of course, were sufficiently well connected to obtain that coveted Crown patent, which required access to power in London. But the proclamation would keep many purchasers out of the market, and crafty speculators might find a way around it.

One such speculator was Pennsylvanian William Murray, western agent for David Franks and Company, a prominent Philadelphia trading firm.[5] Murray, as others, was convinced that the proclamation's prohibition of individual land purchases from Indians was bound to be repealed, given how offensive it was to most colonists. What he needed was some means to create the impression that the repeal had in fact already occurred, some document he could present to British military officers west of the mountains to forestall their interfering with negotiations with the tribes. In the end, he hit what appeared to be pay dirt. Although the circumstances remain somewhat murky,[6] sometime prior to the spring of 1773 Murray obtained an altered copy of an opinion issued in 1757 by Charles Pratt, Lord Camden, then England's attorney general, and Charles Yorke, then solicitor general. It related to the right of the British East India Company to purchase land directly of "the Mogul or any of the Indian princes or governments." The British East India Company had requested the opinion because of logistical difficulties in obeying a requirement that it obtain the approval of a distant Crown prior to acquiring lands in India. The opinion helpfully provided that the king's "Letters Patent" were *not* necessary for lands "acquired by treaty or grant from the Mogul or any of the Indian Princes or Governments, . . . the property of the soil [i.e., title to the property] vesting in the Company." The altered transcription that came into Murray's hands omitted the reference to "the Mogul" and substituted for "the Company" "the grantee."[7] According to the modified Camden-Yorke opinion, the Crown's patents were not necessary to convey title to lands purchased from

"Indian princes." This had the effect of shifting the locus of the lands subject to the opinion from South Central Asia to North America. If one believed that the Camden-Yorke opinion had been issued after the proclamation, as Murray was prepared to intimate, it might be read to supersede the Crown's prohibition of individual purchases west of the Allegheny Mountains.

Thus, from a scheme hatched on the eve of the Revolution and predicated on fraudulent legal authority, was born the land speculation that would give rise to the *Johnson v. M'Intosh* litigation. Armed with the Camden-Yorke opinion, Murray solicited from David Franks, his London partners, and thirteen other Pennsylvania merchants—hastily organized as the Illinois Company—financial backing for a large Indian land purchase west of the mountains.[8] It was a grand gamble, dependent on no one's looking too closely, a circumstance increasingly likely in the disintegrating political climate.

Leaving Philadelphia in the spring of 1773, Murray stopped at Pittsburgh, then continued west.[9] Before June 11, he arrived at Kaskaskia, the principal British military outpost on the Mississippi. After presenting the Camden-Yorke opinion to commanding officer Hugh Lord, he declared his intention to make a purchase of Indian land. Lord was mystified. Camden-Yorke did indeed appear to authorize the purchase Murray proposed. Nevertheless, it said nothing about settlement, which had also been proscribed by the proclamation. Accordingly, Lord informed Murray that although he might be free to buy land from the Indians, he would not be allowed to settle any lands acquired from them.[10]

Murray thereafter met at Kaskaskia with members of the various Illinois tribes. On July 5, 1773, a group "effectually representing all the tribes of the . . . Illinois Indians" executed a deed poll (i.e., a deed executed by only one party) conveying to the members of the Illinois Company two enormous tracts comprising approximately 23,000 square miles located at the junctures of the Mississippi with the Illinois and the Ohio, key channels for the northwestern fur trade.[11] On September 10, Murray had the deed poll recorded in the office of the local notary.

News of Murray's activity was communicated to the British government in London, where it came quickly to the attention of William Legge, second

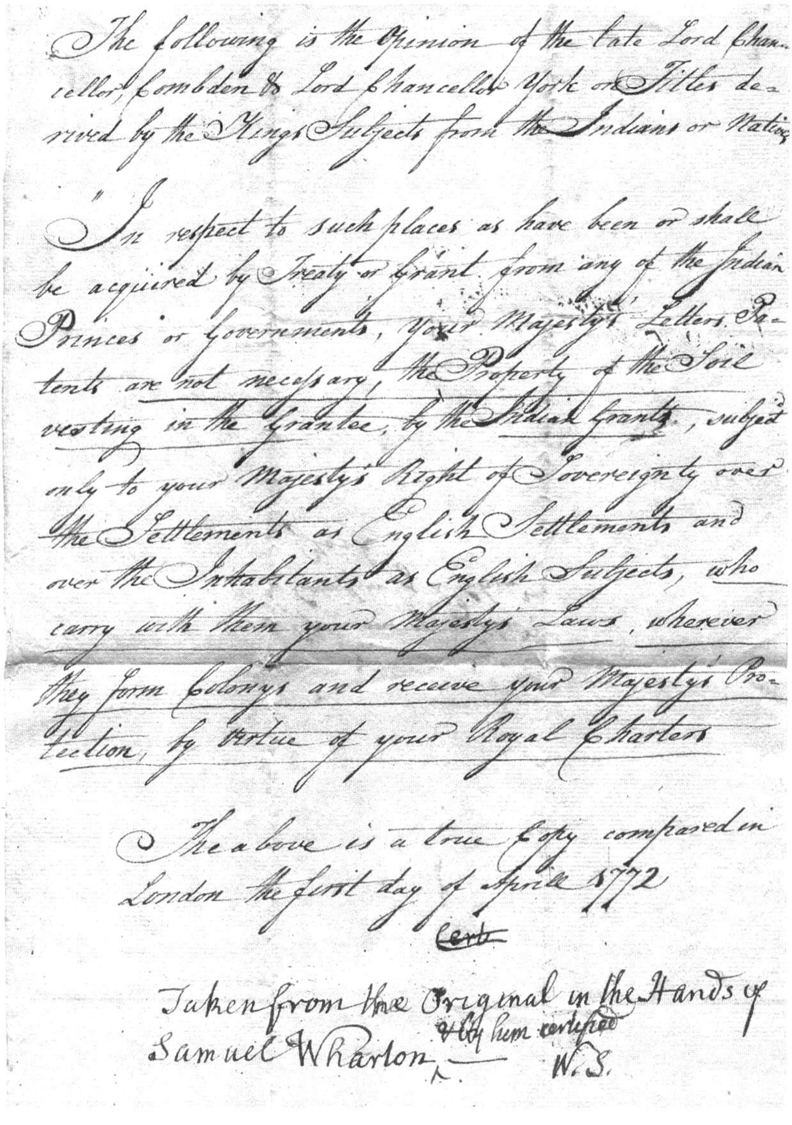

The following is the Opinion of the late Lord Chancellor Combden & Lord Chancellor York on Titles derived by the Kings Subjects from the Indians or Natives

"In respect to such places as have been or shall
be acquired by Treaty or Grant from any of the Indian
Princes or Governments, your Majesty's Letters Patents are not necessary, the Property of the Soil
vesting in the Grantee, by the Indian Grants, subject
only to your Majesty's Right of Sovereignty over
the Settlements as English Settlements and
over the Inhabitants as English Subjects, who
carry with them your Majesty's Laws, wherever
they form Colonys and receive your Majesty's Protection, by Virtue of your Royal Charters

The above is a true Copy compared in
London the first day of April 1772

Cert

Taken from the Original in the Hands of
Samuel Wharton & by him certified
W. S.

FIGURE 1

"The opinion of the late Lord Chancellor Cambden & Lord Chancellor York on Titles derived by the King's Subjects from the Indians or Natives." The Camden-Yorke opinion provided a means for the Illinois and Wabash Companies to circumvent the prohibition of unlicensed purchases of Indian lands in the Proclamation of 1763. This is the Companies' copy of the opinion, attested as genuine by shareholder William Smith. (Courtesy of Jasper Brinton)

Earl of Dartmouth and British secretary of state for North America. Dartmouth, forty-two years old and a year into his position, was committed to the preservation of peace on the frontier and to the administration of the prime minister, his half-brother, Lord North, both of which the news threatened. Dartmouth feared Murray's purchase would antagonize the Indians and provoke a new war. Moreover, he refused to believe the Camden-Yorke opinion genuine. Against a rapidly deteriorating political backdrop—on December 16, 1773, Bostonians disguised as "Mohawk braves" dumped duty-laden tea into Boston Harbor—Dartmouth instructed British General Frederick Haldimand, the ranking officer in North America, to declare the purchase illegal and assist Hugh Lord in preventing settlement.[12] Acting on these orders, Haldimand issued a proclamation on March 10, 1774, declaring "void and fraudulent" Murray's and any other purchases of Indian lands reserved by George III under the Proclamation of 1763.[13] He also instructed Lord to delete from the public notary's register any proceeding relating to purchases already made and to declare publicly that they were invalid.[14]

In ordinary times, this would have been enough. In the spring of 1774, however, the Empire was breaking apart, and among the earliest casualties of dissolution was clarity of jurisdiction. The colony of Virginia had a claim under its royal charter to the lands Murray had purchased from the Illinois Indians. The Crown having expressly denied the claim, on April 19, 1774, Murray and the Illinois Company addressed a petition to Virginia's royal governor, Lord Dunmore, acknowledging Virginia's authority over the lands north of the Ohio River and asking Dunmore to attempt an appeal.[15]

Dunmore, a year younger than Dartmouth, was sitting on a powder keg. Appointed Virginia's governor in 1771, he quickly came into conflict with the colony's legislative assembly, which included many soon to be prominent revolutionaries, among them Thomas Jefferson and Patrick Henry. In the spring of 1773, a year before Murray arrived with the Illinois petition, the assembly had established the first colonywide committee of correspondence to coordinate resistance to Britain. The Boston Tea Party followed eleven months later. In March 1774, the British Parliament closed the Port of Boston effective June 1, although the news would not reach Virginia until May. When Murray presented his petition to Dunmore in Williamsburg, the capital, the assembly was out of session, but they were scheduled to reconvene in two weeks. Dunmore faced the very real possibility that his days as governor were numbered, and this may have increased his enthusiasm for the offer Murray was prepared to make.

Royal governorships were profit-making appointments. In Virginia, the easiest profits came from land speculation. The Proclamation of 1763 barred Dunmore from granting lands west of the mountains to anyone, including himself and his family and friends. Murray's petition, however, suggested a way around that problem: direct Indian purchase on the authority of Camden-Yorke. Murray offered Dunmore a chance to join in by accepting for himself and his son, John, membership in a new Wabash Land Company, to be organized for the purpose of making another large purchase on the authority of Camden-Yorke in the Illinois country along the Wabash River, at the boundary of what would become the states of Indiana and Illinois.[16] Dunmore accepted and, three weeks later, wrote to Dartmouth recommending that the Crown not oppose the Illinois Company's title to the lands purchased from the Illinois Indians, on the grounds that speculation could not be arrested and that these speculators, at least, were generally law-abiding.[17]

Dartmouth would have none of it.[18] Indeed, the British government was even then in process of withdrawing the western lands north of the Ohio River, including the Illinois Company lands, entirely from English North America. In June 1774, Parliament passed the Quebec Act, attaching these lands to the Province of Quebec, a French colony that Britain had acquired at the end of the Seven Years' War.[19]

The Quebec Act, which also restored French civil law in the province, was intended to drive a wedge between French Canadians and colonists to the south, but it did so at a cost of further aggravating Virginians. In September, Virginians took their anger to Philadelphia, where, with representatives from the other aggrieved colonies, they convened the First Continental Congress. Seven months later, the colonies and Britain were at war.

Murray, meanwhile, set about organizing the new company for his second major acquisition. The Wabash Company, formed for the purchase on the Wabash River, was recruited mainly from wealthy Marylanders and included Dunmore and his son.[20] On October 18, 1775, acting through an agent, French merchant Louis Viviat, Murray and the Wabash Company

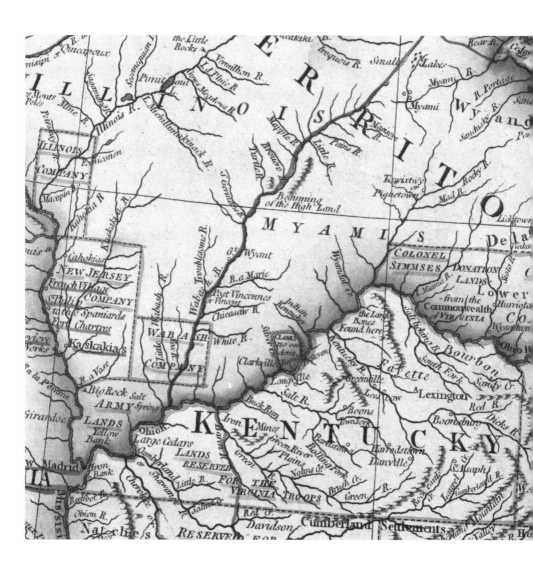

Detail, William Faden, "The United States of North America with the British Territories and those of Spain according to the Treaty of 1784" (London, 1793). The upper Illinois and lower Wabash tracts are approximately delineated in the lower left. The "New Jersey Company" lands located between the Illinois and Wabash tracts were the subject of an abortive speculation attempt engineered by George Morgan. The "Army Lands" indicated at the juncture of the Ohio and the Mississippi were designated in 1787 for eventual bounty distribution by the United States but were abandoned in 1796 in favor of lands in Ohio the Indian title to which had been acquired the previous year. Kaskaskia lies just to the east of the Mississippi north of its confluence with the Ohio. Vincennes lies north of the lower Wabash grant on the east side of the Wabash. William M'Intosh's house at the Grand Rapids of the Wabash (see chapter 2) was sited on the west side of the Wabash opposite its confluence with the White. The Virginia military bounty lands (see chapter 4) are identified in the southwestern corner of Kentucky. The militia lands lay to the west of the Tennessee River, here called the Cherokee. (Courtesy of Library of Congress) purchased from members of the Piankashaw tribe two vast tracts along the Wabash River north and south of Vincennes, a French settlement that later would serve as the capital of the Indiana Territory.[21] On December 5, the deed poll was recorded in the office of notary Louis Bomer at Kaskaskia. These lands, as well as the Illinois lands, were rich and strategically sited. Assuming both titles held, Murray and his companies would control the transportation routes for the greater part of the northwestern fur trade.

Petitions for Recognition of Title, 1775–1784

To hold, however, both titles needed legal sanction from some government with a creditable claim to jurisdiction over the lands. Murray had already unsuccessfully sought Crown approval of the Illinois purchase, via Dunmore. On June 8, 1775, four months before the Wabash purchase, rebellious colonists forced Dunmore to flee Williamsburg. On July 17, Virginia's new revolutionary government, the Virginia Convention, convened in Richmond. In November, shortly before the Wabash deed was recorded in Kaskaskia, two petitions were submitted to the Convention by disgruntled purchasers from another land speculation company, the Transylvania Company, that had also purchased Indian lands west of the mountains in reliance on Camden-Yorke.[22] The Transylvania lands, like the Illinois and Wabash lands, lay within Virginia's boundaries under the royal charter establishing the colony. Murray decided to see how the Transylvania claim fared in Richmond. If it succeeded, he and his partners would seek recognition of title from the Virginia revolutionaries.

The Transylvania purchase had been negotiated six months prior to the Wabash purchase by Judge Richard Henderson. The lands purchased were Cherokee lands located between the Kentucky and Cumberland Rivers in what is now Kentucky.[23] Henderson, according to the complaining petitioners, was selling the lands for excessive amounts and aimed to create an independent government within the bounds of Virginia.[24] He and the other Transylvania proprietors responded by challenging the Virginia Convention's jurisdiction and arguing that in 1775 nothing in the Virginia statutes prohibited their purchase.[25]

The Convention was not about to concede jurisdiction, but the delegates had reason to be concerned by the Transylvania Company's argument that the purchase was not illegal under Virginia law. Virginia had on its books a 1705 law invalidating unlicensed purchases of lands from "tributary" Indians—Indians subject to the political power of the colony—but that was a discrete group largely confined to the Virginia tidewater.[26] The Cherokees were not tributary. It was true that the Royal Proclamation of 1763 declared such purchases void, but revolutionary Virginians were on the verge of declaring independence based in part on their belief that the Proclamation of 1763 was unconstitutional, and they could hardly rely on it to deny Henderson's claim.

The Convention first resolved to update its 1705 preemption law invalidating unlicensed purchases of tributary Indian lands: the new resolution declared invalid unlicensed land purchases "from *any* Indian tribe or nation."[27] Subsequently, the Convention, at Thomas Jefferson's prompting, incorporated the state's right of preemption of Indian lands into the commonwealth's new constitution, adopted in 1776. Next, having arrested future purchases, Virginia temporized. Three years passed before Virginia held hearings on the Transylvania claim. At their conclusion, the claim was compromised, the Virginia House of Delegates resolving that all unlicensed Indian land purchases "made or to be made" were void, but that as Henderson and company had gone to great expense in purchasing and settling the Transylvania lands, they were entitled to some compensation, ultimately fixed at $200,000.[28] This resolution was not entirely altruistic. After the compromise vote, Virginia assumed Henderson's title to the Cherokee lands, in effect retroactively designating him the state's purchasing agent. The Cherokees would not be invited to reclaim their illegally purchased lands. The $200,000 constituted Henderson's commission for arranging the sale to Virginia of the Cherokee Nation's Kentucky domain.

News of the decision to compensate the Transylvania Company was all Murray and company needed to hear. On December 28, 1778, the now united Illinois and Wabash Companies presented a joint memorial, or petition, containing a statement of facts to Virginia's governor, council, and assembly stating their intention to take possession of the lands they had bought from the Piankashaws in 1775.[29] The Illinois and Wabash lands, however, were northwest of the Ohio River in a part of the state that Virginia was considering turning over to the new federal government.[30] Recognizing the Illinois and Wabash claims would merely reduce the value of the claim Virginia planned to transfer to Congress. No benefit to Virginia would accrue from Murray's retroactive appointment as purchasing agent. The Illinois and Wabash claims would be denied. At Virginia delegate George Mason's prompting, the legislature resolved that Virginia had the exclusive preemption right to all Indian lands within its charter limits, that no persons "have, *or ever had*," a right to purchase any such lands without state license, and that all unlicensed individual purchases were, therefore, void.[31] In June 1779, this resolution became law under the title "An Act for declaring and asserting the rights of this commonwealth, concerning purchasing lands from Indian natives" (hereafter, the Declaratory Act).[32] As far as Virginia was concerned, the Illinois and Wabash claims were dead.

When Virginia rejected the Companies' claims, the Companies shifted the locus of their petitioning from Richmond to Philadelphia, where the Continental Congress was meeting. By early 1779, Virginia had become embroiled in a debate in Congress over the conditions under which it and the other large landed states, those with charter claims to huge areas of the west, should cede their western claims to the new United States. Small states without western claims, such as New Jersey, urged that if these lands were not ceded, large states like Virginia would dominate the new national government. Joining this debate, the Illinois-Wabash speculators lobbied for cession of lands by the landed states to the national government, followed by national recognition of private purchases of Indian lands within the ceded lands. The speculators presented their arguments through Maryland's congressional delegation. Maryland was small, and wealthy Marylanders, it may be recalled, constituted the bulk of the Wabash Company shareholders. By 1779, many of these shareholders held positions of great power in the state. Most prominent among these were the governor, Thomas Johnson Jr., an original Wabash Company investor, and state congressional delegates Samuel Chase and Charles Carroll of Carrollton. Moreover, Maryland's power in Congress had grown out of all proportion to its size by its refusal to sign the Articles of Confederation, the new nation's governing document, which required the ratification of all thirteen states. By January 1779, Maryland was the only state not to have signed the Articles, and the Maryland shareholders eagerly exploited this position.[33]

On January 6, 1779, the Maryland delegation laid before the Continental Congress a declaration that Maryland would not sign the Articles of Confederation unless the western land claims of the landed states, including Virginia, were ceded to the states collectively and all grants, surveys, and purchases made to, for, or by individuals before the Revolutionary War were validated.[34] George Mason, well aware of the influence the Illinois and Wabash Companies had in Maryland, was livid. "Do you observe the care Governor Johnston [sic] . . . has taken to save this Indian purchase?" he wrote to congressional delegate Richard Henry Lee.[35] Virginia responded to Maryland's declaration by moving in Congress that the Articles be adopted with fewer than thirteen states as signatories.

There the matter sat for two years, when, on January 2, 1781, the Virginia legislature passed resolutions agreeing to cede the state's claims to territory north of the Ohio on condition that all lands not set aside as compensation for military veterans were considered a common fund for the use of members of the Confederation and that all royal grants and private purchases of land from the Indians were invalidated.[36] One month later, the Maryland legislature, under pressure from the French and concerned about the military vulnerability of the state's lengthy coastline, finally directed the state's delegation to sign the Articles.

Hoping to seize some benefit before Maryland's leverage essentially evaporated, the Illinois and Wabash Companies hastily submitted to Congress a memorial, including a petition and statement of facts, setting out the basis for their claim and offering to settle for less than the full value of the land.[37] It was too late. On November 3, the committee to which the memorial had been referred recommended its rejection, principally on the grounds that the predicate purchases had been made "without any public treaty or other proper act of notoriety" and "without licence of the then government or other public authority, . . . contrary to the common and known usage in such case established." In addition, the committee found the Illinois deed poll deficient, in that "one of the [tracts purchased from the Illinois, as described in the deed poll] . . . contains only a number of lines without comprehending any land whatever," and speculated that the Companies might have purchased from the wrong Indians, as "the Six Nations [of the Iroquois Confederacy] and their tributaries claim the same lands, in opposition to the Indians conveying the same in the deeds to said Companies."[38]

Meanwhile, Maryland continued to fight acceptance of Virginia's terms for the cession of lands, even as it supported the cession itself. In June 1783, Congress voted to accept Virginia's offer if Virginia would cede without Congress guaranteeing Virginia's title to its remaining land and remove the condition that all royal grants and private land purchases from the Indians in the ceded territory be declared invalid.[39] On the latter, Congress argued that it would be "improper" for it to declare the purchases invalid and that, in any event, the "common fund" condition—the provision that all lands not set aside as compensation for military veterans were to be considered a common fund for the use of members of the Confederation—was "sufficient on this point."[40] With this assurance, the Virginia Assembly agreed to drop the two conditions, and on March 1, 1784, Congress accepted the cession.[41]

With the acceptance of the Virginia cession, the question of jurisdiction over the lands purchased by William Murray in 1773 and 1775 had finally been settled in favor of Congress. Moreover, the Companies' claim had seemingly been denied, at least implicitly, by the inclusion of the "common fund" condition. Nevertheless, because the language was arguably ambiguous, the speculators well situated and aggressive, and the political system immature, some, including George Mason, prime mover behind Virginia's Declaratory Act of 1779, feared that the "common fund" condition would not be a "sufficient bar to Congress against confirming the claims under Indian purchases," that despite the condition, the speculators would find a way to persuade Congress to recognize the Illinois and Wabash claims.[42] Within six years, the speculators came close to proving Mason correct.

Petitions for Recognition of Title, 1784–1801

The terms of the Virginia cession directed that the western lands "should be a common fund for the use and benefit of" the confederated states. "Fund" was meant literally: after the cession of Virginia's claim to jurisdiction, the lands were to be liquidated by the United States to retire the national debt.[43] Jurisdiction alone, however, would not authorize the United States to sell the western lands. The United States had first to hold title to them. Title might be acquired in any of three ways. If the lands were already owned by another, title might be acquired by purchase or conquest; if they were vacant, title might simply be asserted. After a brief series of abortive attempts to claim title to some of these lands by right of conquest (discussed more fully below), the Continental Congress on May 20, 1785, declared its intent to sell only those lands the title to which had been purchased.[44] Congress then appointed a series of agents to begin negotiations with the Indians.

Adoption by the United States of the purchase policy restored to the Illinois and Wabash Companies some of the leverage they had lost when Maryland signed the Articles of Confederation. The reason was simple: congressional commitment to purchase title *to* Indian lands did not necessarily mean that Congress would feel obliged to purchase such title *from Indians*. If the Piankashaw and Illinois Nations did not dispute the Companies' title and the price was right, Congress might agree to purchase title to the lands acquired in 1773 and 1775 from the speculators. Even if the Indians did protest, the Companies and Congress might still strike a deal if the Companies offered better terms.

The Continental Congress ceased to exist with the ratification of the U.S. Constitution in 1789, but the purchase policy continued. In 1790, the policy was strengthened (and the market narrowed) by the passage of federal legislation, the Trade and Intercourse Act, prohibiting anyone other than the federal government from buying Indian lands.[45] In the fall of 1791, however, well before purchasing agents from the new federal Congress had ventured far enough into the Illinois country to begin the acquisition of title to the lands the Companies claimed, a U.S. military disaster at the hands of allied tribes on the Wabash River made the price of acquisition from the Piankashaws and Illinois Indians seem likely to be very great indeed, despite the elimination of potential competing purchasers. On November 4, U.S. General Arthur St. Clair's command was decimated by a force under Little Turtle of the Miamis.[46] The Companies eagerly and decisively moved to take advantage of the setback this defeat promised to the government's plan to purchase Indian lands from the tribes. On December 13, the morning after President George Washington's announcement of the defeat, the Illinois and Wabash Companies presented to the House of Representatives a brief memorial, "praying to be permitted to exhibit the titles of the Companies to certain Western lands, purchased by the said Companies, under the sanction of lawful authority; and also to make certain proposals for a reasonable compromise, between [the Companies] and the United States." With little discussion, the House referred the Companies' proposal to committee. The same day, the memorial was presented to the Senate, which two days later also referred it to committee.[47] The Companies were invited to appear before both committees with proof and arguments, as well as their terms of compromise.

The Companies worked out the requested terms of compromise at Hubley's Tavern in Philadelphia on December 17, 1791. After much discussion, the attending quorum agreed to authorize agents to offer three-fourths of their lands to the United States in exchange for federal recognition of their title to the remaining fourth ("or even one eighth if better terms cannot be obtained").[48] To present the offer and the claim, the Companies designated as agents their four most prominent resident members: James Wilson, associate justice of the new Supreme Court of the United States; Robert Morris, U.S. senator from Pennsylvania; William Smith, until recently provost of the College of Philadelphia; and General John Shee. They were a powerful group, and their timing could not have been better. They made their case before the House committee, and, to the Companies' delight, the House committee agreed to compromise on the Companies' terms.[49]

Every lost cause has a high-water mark, and this would prove the Companies'. The House as a whole was clearly tempted. Acceptance of the compromise terms would provide the United States with an enormous amount of strategically situated real estate free of charge. On the other hand, any sort of deal would infuriate the Virginia delegates. In addition, five months had passed since the military debacle, and the Illinois country had not seen further bloodshed, at least on such a distressing scale. In the end, the House tabled the committee's report.[50]

Meanwhile, the Companies' agents had been far less persuasive before the Senate committee. After deliberating, on March 26, 1792, the Senate committee recommended to the Senate as a whole that it reject the compromise offer on the grounds that the deeds had been "obtained by private persons from the Indians, without any antecedent authority or subsequent confirmation . . . from the government," and that in any event, to recognize the claims would be inconsistent with the "common fund" condition of the Virginia cession.[51]

The Senate committee's report, if adopted by the Senate as a whole, would eliminate any chance of the Companies' winning a compromise during the session. To forestall this dead end, Robert Morris presented to the Senate a new memorial from the Companies, "praying to be heard by counsel." Morris's gambit paid off. The Senate tabled this memorial but agreed not to take up the damning committee report.[52] For the time being, neither house would agree to compromise, but neither would reject the offer outright. Congress was keeping its options open, and the Companies, encouraged by the House committee report, interpreted this as an invitation to persevere.

When Congress reconvened the following fall, it quickly became apparent that circumstances had changed. From their offensive rush in the previous year, the Companies passed to the defensive. Three days into the session news arrived that a peace treaty had been concluded with the Wabash and the Illinois Indians.[53] Despite this setback, the Companies resolved that Morris would continue to attempt to forestall action on the Senate report, while shareholder Congressman Daniel Heister of Pennsylvania would press the House to adopt the recommendations of the House committee.[54] Given the peace treaty, the latter cause was hopeless, and forestalling any action by either house was the best they could hope to achieve. In this, they were successful.[55] The second session also closed with the Companies' claims uncompromised, but unrejected.

For the next five years, neither Congress nor the Companies raised the issue of the Companies' title. Congress had no incentive to do so. The compromise offer remained on the table; Congress might yet find it attractive, depending on the reception with which their purchasing agents met as they moved west across Ohio and into the Illinois country. The Companies awaited some change in circumstances: either an event increasing the cost to the United States of purchasing the Indian title from the Piankashaws and Illinois, which would make the Companies' offer more attractive, or an event within their own ranks compelling renewed petitioning.

In 1797, the Companies were struck by an event within their own ranks. Early in 1796, the Bank of England limited its discounts; credit grew tight, loans were called, and debtors, including many land speculators, were compelled to borrow at exorbitant rates. "Ruin is staring in the face of the land speculators," one Philadelphian wrote. "The day of reckoning is at hand, and no prospect of disposing of their lands."[56] Among those likely to meet with ruin was James Wilson, president of the Companies. Desperate for cash, Wilson convened the shareholders. The attending quorum agreed that despite the odds, the compromise offer should immediately be renewed.

On January 13, 1797, James Ross of Pennsylvania presented the Companies' third memorial to the Senate, which referred it to committee.[57] The House did the same. On February 3, the House and Senate committees jointly recommended that Congress adopt the 1792 Senate committee report recommending rejection of the compromise offer and the claims.[58] Two weeks later, the Senate voted by an undisclosed majority to adopt this report; a motion, likely Ross's, to reconsider "for the purpose of reading a petition on the subject" was summarily defeated. In the House, the Companies barely managed to stave off total defeat; despite its stated intention to call a vote on February 6, the House took no action.[59]

From the Companies' vantage, the record of events in the thirteen years since the Virginia cession, though discouraging, was not so bleak as it might have been. Although the Senate had rejected outright the Companies' offer of compromise, the House had not, and the Senate might be persuaded to change its mind. The active shareholders of the Companies had only grown in public stature during this time. In 1789, James Wilson had been named an associate justice of the Supreme Court of the United States; in 1796, Maryland shareholder Samuel Chase joined him on the Court.[60] Several shareholders, including Daniel Heister, remained seated in Congress. Were more shareholders to attain positions of influence, the Companies might yet persuade Congress to deal.

The fatal flaw in this plan became evident in 1800. All of the most prominent shareholders were members of the governing Federalist Party. In 1800, in what was then termed a "revolution," Thomas Jefferson's Republicans swept the Federalists from both the House of Representatives and the Executive Mansion; two years later, Jefferson's party took control of the Senate. The campaign for control of the government had been extremely acrimonious, and governance of the nation had passed to persons almost certain to be hostile to the thought of enriching the Federalist shareholders of the Illinois and Wabash Land Companies. The Federalists never again dominated the U.S. Congress, and after the election in 1800, it was absolutely clear to the Illinois and Wabash Land Companies that any hope of success in prosecuting their claim would have to rest elsewhere.

In the waning days of the last Federalist administration, President John Adams and the Federalist Congress took steps to ensure that they would not entirely relinquish the country to Jefferson and his party. In February 1801, shortly before the new administration took office, Adams signed a new Judiciary Act, creating sixteen new judgeships, which Adams promptly filled with Federalists.[61] Chief Justice Oliver Ellsworth of the Supreme Court had resigned, and on January 20, 1801, Adams nominated Federalist John Marshall of Virginia to fill his place. Within a few years after taking office, Marshall would claim for the Supreme Court the power to declare acts of Congress and the state legislatures unconstitutional and void, thereby transforming the hitherto weak federal high court into arguably the most powerful political institution in the land. "They have retired into the judiciary as a stronghold," incoming President Jefferson bitterly observed. "There the remains of federalism are to be preserved and fed from the treasury, and from that battery all the works of republicanism are to be beaten down and erased."[62] From that battery might come as well, the Companies hoped, a salvo sufficient to force even a Republican Congress to recognize or compromise their claims. With the election of Thomas Jefferson and the passage of the Judiciary Act of 1801, the Illinois and Wabash Land Companies prepared to go to court.

Jurisdictional Impediments to Judicial Recognition, and Petitions to the Land Commissions

The strategy was straightforward: get a case before the increasingly powerful U.S. Supreme Court, get a decision from the Court upholding the Companies' claims, then negotiate with Congress the sale of the lands to the United States. Execution was more complicated. The suit would be a claim for title to land. In the early nineteenth century such lawsuits were called "ejectment" actions. These were "local" actions that could be tried only before juries composed of residents of the area in which the disputed lands lay. The rationale for this rule was that only neighbors familiar with the property would be sufficiently knowledgeable to understand the interests at stake. Consequently, the actions had to be filed in a court with geographic jurisdiction over the lands. If the lands were located in the Northwest Territory, as the Illinois and Wabash lands were, that meant the lawsuit had to be filed in the Northwest Territorial Court.

The problem was that a decision of the Northwest Territorial Court in favor of the Companies was not likely to persuade a politically hostile Congress to recognize the Companies' claims. Indeed, the Republican-dominated Congress would likely have laughed at the notion of rewarding a group of Federalist land speculators with millions of acres of strategically sited land simply because a territorial judge west of the mountains told them to. Recognition of the Companies' claim by a territorial judge, in short, would be essentially meaningless. To have value the decision would have to be appealed to the Supreme Court of the United States, which would then itself have to decide in the Companies' favor. However, Congress had not yet exercised its power to authorize appeals from territorial court decisions, so there was no way to get a decision from the Northwest Territorial Court before the Supreme Court.[63]

Once the Companies made the decision to look to the Supreme Court for help, they started lobbying Congress to create an appeal route from the territorial courts. They could not be too direct. In March 1802, the Companies presented their fourth memorial, gingerly asking Congress to "devise some speedy and effectual mode for a final investigation and decision of the claims of the memorialists . . . either in the courts of the United

States, or by law commissioners specially to be appointed for that purpose." The Senate rejected this request immediately, and the House declined to answer either way.[64]

The situation got worse the following year. In October 1803, President Jefferson announced to Congress that over the summer recess, he had agreed to purchase the Louisiana territory. This was not all, Jefferson continued: the United States had also purchased the lands of the Kaskaskias, "extending along the Mississippi from the mouth of the Illinois to and up the Ohio."[65] These lands included most of the lower Illinois Company purchase. Ten days later, before Jefferson presented the treaty to the Senate for ratification, the Companies frantically renewed their request that Congress provide them a judicial forum. Both houses tabled the request.[66] On October 31, Jefferson sent the Kaskaskia treaty to the Senate, which promptly ratified it. To the Companies' horror, the following day the Senate ratified a companion treaty with the Piankashaws, by which the United States bought a large section of the Wabash purchase.[67]

In December, the Companies renewed their request for a judicial avenue for recognition of title before the House, which finally referred the Companies' request to committee. In February, the committee recommended, and the House resolved, that the Companies' title claim and request be denied.[68] The committee's stated rationale on the title claim was part contract law and part pragmatism. According to its report, the tribal representatives who signed the deed polls acted without authority, the Companies' purchases were not mentioned in the just ratified treaties, and the United States had just bought the same lands.[69]

Events now moved rapidly against the speculators. In March 1804, Jefferson signed legislation setting out procedures for selling the newly acquired Kaskaskia and Piankashaw lands.[70] Land offices were established at Vincennes and Kaskaskia to handle sales, and persons with claims to any land slotted for sale were given until January 1 to submit them to the land commissioners at these offices for decision. The land commissioners were directed to report their judgments to the secretary of the treasury, who would communicate them to Congress for acceptance or rejection. Disappointed claimants had no appeal to the federal courts.

In August, the United States signed another treaty with the Piankashaws by which they bought even more of the Wabash claim, and the treaty was ratified by the Senate in January.[71] In March 1805, Jefferson signed an act assigning these newly acquired lands to the district of Vincennes and extending the deadline for the filing of claims within the district until November 1.[72]

Having no apparent alternative, the Illinois and Wabash Land Companies prepared to assert their claims before the land commissioners. To represent them before the Vincennes commissioners, the Companies hired Benjamin Parke, attorney general for the Indiana Territory and a close friend of Territorial Governor William Henry Harrison.[73] Nothing Parke could have done would have saved the claim. Jefferson's secretary of the treasury, Albert Gallatin, had forwarded to the land commissioners a copy of the Proclamation of 1763, which forbade unlicensed individual purchases, and this appeared to him "conclusive."[74] In March 1806, the commissioners compliantly reported to Gallatin that it appeared to them that the Wabash purchase had been "a private transaction between the Indians and an Individual, in direct violation of the proclamation . . . and consequently illegal."[75] In January 1807, Gallatin laid this report before Congress.[76] The same fate befell the Companies in Kaskaskia. Because of widespread perjury by other claimants to lands within the Kaskaskia District, the Kaskaskia commissioners were unable to report until December 1809.[77] They, too, found the Companies' claim invalid on the grounds that the underlying purchase from the Illinois had been "illegal and unauthorized."[78]

For thirty years, the Illinois and Wabash speculators had unsuccessfully sought executive and legislative recognition of their title to the lands. The United States had bought a large part of the lands purchased by Murray, and, with the adoption of the land commission reports, the government would begin distribution. Congress had refused to create an appeal route from the territorial court, leaving the speculators no way of presenting a favorable territorial court decision to the Supreme Court and therefore no hope of forcing congressional compromise on the matter. By all rights, the Illinois and Wabash claims should now have expired.

That they did not resulted from the Companies' unexpected rescue, in 1809, by the New England Mississippi Land Company and its enterprising chief counsel, Robert Goodloe Harper. The success of the New England

Mississippi Land Company in winning judicial recognition of its own claims to lands acquired under questionable circumstances would inspire the Illinois and Wabash Companies with renewed hope. The Companies would invite Harper to assume control of the Illinois and Wabash claims, and he would mastermind the litigation that would finally bring them before the Supreme Court, in the process playing accidental midwife to the discovery doctrine.

CHAPTER 2

Harper

While the Illinois and Wabash speculators were exploiting the young nation's instability to further their claims to lands in the Northwest Territory, the New England Mississippi Land Company was attempting the same to appropriate title to lands farther south. Ultimately, the New England Mississippi Land Company's chief counsel, Robert Goodloe Harper, would present both its claims and those of the United Illinois and Wabash Land Companies to the Supreme Court, tying together two of the Court's most important early decisions, *Johnson v. M'Intosh* and *Fletcher v. Peck*, and setting the stage for the judicial conquest of Native America.

The *Fletcher v. Peck* Claim, Robert Goodloe Harper, and a New Course for the Illinois and Wabash Land Companies

In 1795, the predecessor to the New England Mississippi Land Company, the Georgia Mississippi Company, and three other land speculation concerns purchased from the State of Georgia grants of land totaling thirty-five million acres in the Yazoo River region of what became the Mississippi Territory. The act authorizing the sale of these land grants was the product of widespread corruption. When a preliminary sale bill passed in December 1794, only one of the legislators voting for it had not been bribed. An outraged Georgia electorate turned the Yazoo sellers out of office in 1796, and the new legislature repealed the grants, signaling their contempt for their predecessors by ordering all records of the grants excised from the state's public records and the original act of sale publicly burned.[1]

On the very day the act of sale was repealed, the Georgia Mississippi Company sold its eleven million–acre stake in the Yazoo lands to the New England Mississippi Land Company for $1,138,000.[2] A battle over title ensued, Georgia contending that the repeal had invalidated the original sale, the speculators claiming their title was good. In 1802, when Georgia transferred its western land claims to the United States, as Virginia had done in 1784, the dispute carried over to Congress. Opposition to the claims of the Yazoo speculators was focused on the corruption attending the passage of the original act of sale. On the floor of Congress, pro- and anti-Yazooists debated incessantly the legitimacy of the original grants and the validity of the subsequent repeal.

The New England Mississippi Land Company was far more aggressive than the Illinois and Wabash Companies in its campaign for recognition, regularly employing numerous high-ranking agents, including future Supreme Court associate justice Joseph Story, as Capitol Hill lobbyists. But despite its efforts, it had no greater luck at forcing Congress to recognize its claim. Consequently, the New England Mississippi Land Company also set its sights on the Supreme Court. Because the Yazoo lands were within the jurisdiction of the Mississippi Territorial Court, however, the New England Mississippi Land Company faced precisely the same barrier to satisfactory judicial resolution as had the United Illinois and Wabash Land Companies: no hope of Congress's compromising without a Supreme Court decision, and no way of appealing a territorial court decision to the Supreme Court.

With its greater resources, however, and more enterprising counsel, the New England Mississippi Land Company came up with a way to get the question of the validity of its claim before the Supreme Court despite this barrier. Ejectment actions were local actions, requiring local juries, but other actions, including breach of contract actions, were "transitory" actions and could be brought anywhere. The New England Mississippi Land Company lawyers accordingly feigned a breach of contract action and filed it in a regular federal court.[3] In June 1803, New England Mississippi Land Company shareholder Robert Fletcher of New Hampshire filed suit against fellow shareholder John Peck of Massachusetts in the U.S. Circuit Court for the District of Massachusetts for making false warranties, or covenants, in a fabricated deed between the parties purporting to convey 15,000 acres of the New England Mississippi Land Company's Yazoo lands from Peck to Fletcher.[4] According to Fletcher, the supposed purchaser, the deed falsely represented (1) that at the time of the passage of the 1795 act, Georgia owned the land; (2) that the Georgia legislature had a right to sell and dispose of the land; (3) that Georgia had lawful authority to issue a grant to the land by virtue of the act authorizing sale; (4) that all the title that Georgia had in the land had been legally conveyed to Peck; and (5) that the title to this land had been in no way constitutionally or legally impaired by virtue of any subsequent legislation of the Georgia legislature.[5] By consent of the parties, the circuit court continued the case until October 1806, when it was tried before a jury. A year later, the court rendered judgment for Peck, finding that all the covenants were valid. At Fletcher's request, a writ of error was issued by the U.S. Supreme Court directing the circuit court to send it the case so the justices could examine certain alleged errors and either reverse, correct, or affirm the circuit court's judgment. The case was set for argument at the Supreme Court's February 1809 term.

By this clever strategy, the New England Mississippi Land Company circumvented the jurisdictional barrier posed by Congress's refusal to authorize appeals from the territorial courts to the Supreme Court. If the Supreme Court should now find in favor of Peck and uphold the validity of the covenants in the fabricated deed, the Yazoo speculators might force Congress to the table.

The New England Mississippi Land Company lawyers thought victory before the Supreme Court very likely. The Court was presided over by fifty-eight-year-old Chief Justice John Marshall of Virginia. The fourth chief justice, Marshall was a Revolutionary War veteran and former Virginia legislator who had served as President John Adams's secretary of state. He was also a well-known land speculator and a committed Federalist, both of which tendencies, it was thought, would incline him toward the Yazooists. Marshall would not disappoint them. In March 1809, he reversed in part the circuit court's opinion because of technical errors in the papers filed, but intimated from the bench that when the case came properly before the Court, he would rule for Peck.[6] Counsel for the parties stipulated a correction to the errors, and the case was set for final argument at the Court's February 1810 term.

The likelihood that the Court, and subsequently Congress, would recognize the Yazoo claims based on *Fletcher* encouraged the Illinois and Wabash Companies, and they moved to follow suit. The lawyer who had brought *Fletcher* before the Supreme Court, forty-five-year-old Robert Goodloe Harper, happened to be the son-in-law of Illinois and Wabash Companies shareholder Charles Carroll of Carrollton. Before *Fletcher's* reargument, the Companies invited Harper to become a member of their Baltimore committee, representing his father-in-law's shares. Harper would not only join the committee, but would thereafter manage the Companies' campaign for recognition of title.

As well as being a leading Supreme Court advocate, Harper was one of America's most experienced, if not most successful, land speculators. In 1795, he went to Congress as a Republican representative from South Carolina largely to further the interests of the South Carolina Yazoo Company, another Georgia grantee. After arriving in Philadelphia he converted to Federalism, evidently because he thought his personal interests likelier to be enhanced by alliance with the governing party. Jefferson's election in 1800 destroyed this plan, and Harper left Congress for Baltimore, where, with the aid of fellow Federalists Samuel Chase and James McHenry, he commenced a successful legal practice. Harper married Carroll's daughter Catherine in May 1801, partly to secure his father-in-law's assistance in discharging the enormous debts he had built up over the years as a failed land speculator.[7] Carroll was then the wealthiest man in America and Harper would depend on his grudging largesse for the remainder of his life.

Harper enthusiastically assumed the management of the Illinois and Wabash claims. Even before *Fletcher* came back before the Supreme Court, and following the model set by the New England Mississippi Land Company, Harper set about recruiting agents to press the Illinois and Wabash

FIGURE 2

Portrait of Robert Goodloe Harper, c. 1820, by unattributed American (formerly Charles Bird King). Harper, an experienced (if unsuccessful) land speculator himself, joined the United Illinois and Wabash Land Companies as the representative of his father-in-law, Charles Carroll of Carrollton, and as their attorney took the Companies' claim to the Supreme Court. (Courtesy of The Maryland Historical Society, Baltimore, Maryland, 1986.24 Robert Goodloe Harper) claim in Congress. These eventually included former secretary of the navy Benjamin Stoddert; Thomas Turner, former accountant of the navy; and Walter Jones, district attorney in Washington and son of a Virginia congressman.[8] In addition to these Washington agents, Harper thought it worthwhile to attempt to interest "some man of talents, activity and influence, in the country where the lands lye [*sic*]."[9] In January, shortly before the *Fletcher* reargument, Baltimore shareholder Solomon Etting reported that "Governor H[arrison] of the Western Territory will perhaps be with us—one of the Co[mpany]. . . . This between ourselves."[10]

That Harper and Etting thought William Henry Harrison a likely candidate is not surprising. In 1808, to the distress of Treasury Secretary Gallatin, Harrison had joined a company engaged in the purchase and sale of public lands in Indiana.[11] Further, Harrison had a long acquaintance with Harper; they had met in Philadelphia in 1791 when Harrison was a student and Harper the manager of the South Carolina Yazoo Company.[12] In 1798, Harper, then a congressman, had lobbied for Harrison's appointment as secretary of the Northwest Territory.[13] Despite the connection and Harrison's known affinity for speculation, however, the Companies appear not to have issued any shares to him at this time, and it is unlikely he chose then to involve himself in the Companies' fortunes. As it turned out, he would have another opportunity.

Harper was uncertain whether to press the Companies' claim on Congress before the Court had ruled in *Fletcher* or to wait and risk an adverse judgment. There were sound reasons favoring the former strategy. The New England Mississippi Land Company claim was pending before the House Committee of Claims. In December, Congressman Daniel Heister of Pennsylvania, whose father was an Illinois and Wabash Companies shareholder, wrote to shareholder John Hill Brinton that he had "recently discovered a liberal mind in some of the members as to claims. . . . Several of those who were opposed to granting the Yazoo Company five million acres as was at one time nearly concluded on, now regret that the grant had not been made, saying that the claim would now be quieted and the remainder of the land could be disposed of."[14] By the end of January, however, when all of the Companies' agents had at last been hired, Harper felt that Congress's planned May 1 adjournment allowed the Companies insufficient time to make an adequate presentation. Harper decided to postpone the application to Congress until the next session, scheduled to open on December 3, "in order to come then, more strongly fortified with proofs, against the objections which have been opposed to our claim."[15]

In the meantime, Harper and Joseph Story presented their final arguments in *Fletcher v. Peck*. For the plaintiff, Fletcher, attorney Luther Martin offered a weak counterargument, ignoring two of the principal disputed questions: whether bribery nullified the act of sale and whether the repeal of that act was unconstitutional. The impression Martin created was not enhanced by his evident intoxication, which was reportedly so pronounced that Chief Justice Marshall felt compelled to adjourn the Court until he dried out.[16] On March 16, 1810, Marshall handed down the Court's decision affirming the validity of all the covenants—a total victory for the Yazoo speculators.[17] Stunned anti-Yazooists in Congress, their cause derailed, suspended discussion of the merits of the Yazoo claims to allow themselves time to think about the impact of *Fletcher v. Peck*.[18]

Fletcher appeared to have achieved its ends, but, as it happened, its pleading strategy could not be replicated by the Illinois and Wabash Companies. The case had been feigned by the parties as a transitory contract action to defeat the absence of an appeal route from the Mississippi Territorial Court. Not surprisingly, this infuriated anti-Yazooist members of Congress.[19] Moreover, and of greater concern to Harper and the Illinois and Wabash speculators, the Supreme Court itself had expressed reservations about the pleading strategy. In March 1809, when the case first appeared before the Court, Chief Justice Marshall mentioned to Court Reporter William Cranch, as did Justice Brockholst Livingston to Harper's then co-counsel, John Quincy Adams, "the reluctance of the Court to decide the case at all, as it appeared manifestly made up for the purpose of getting the Court's judgment upon all the points. And although they have given some decisions in such cases," noted Adams, recounting these conversations in his diary, "they appear not disposed to do so now."[20] The Court, of course, did hear the case, but Justice William Johnson took care to note in his separate opinion (dissenting in part): "I have been very unwilling to proceed to the decision of this cause at all. It appears to me to bear strong evidence, upon the face of it, of being a mere feigned case. It is our duty to decide on the rights but not on the speculations of parties. My confidence, however, in the respectable gentlemen who have been engaged for the parties, has induced me to abandon my scruples, in the belief that they would never consent to impose a mere feigned case upon this Court."[21] The instruction to Harper, as chief counsel, was crystal clear: *Do not try this again.* Harper might bring the Illinois and Wabash Companies' claim before the Court, but only via a conventional and limited ejectment action.

For a brief moment, it appeared that it might not matter. Fortuitously, the issue of whether appeals should be allowed from territorial courts to the Supreme Court had reappeared in Congress. In March 1810, a bill was pending allowing such appeals in cases between private parties. Harper went avidly to work to secure its passage, instructing Stoddert to "say nothing about" the Companies' claims in Congress for fear of tipping his hand on the appeals bill.[22] Walter Jones, despite the fact that he was "not so sanguine as Mr. Harper, as to the event before a court of Law," lobbied with Harper for the bill's passage. Despite their best efforts, however, the appeals bill went nowhere.[23] Congress would not authorize appeals from territorial courts, and, in the end, as a result of the Court's intimation that it would not accept a feigned breach of contract suit on the Illinois and Wabash claims, Harper and the Companies would have to wait ten years before they could file their claim.

The 1810 Memorial to Congress

No doubt disappointed by the failure of the appeals bill, Harper returned to his earlier plan to press Congress with influential agents and a new memorial. He drafted the memorial during the following summer and fall. When completed, it constituted the most thorough exposition ever prepared of the claims of the Illinois and Wabash Land Companies. More important, as discussed in the following chapter, it provided grist for the document that would form the centerpiece of Harper's litigation strategy once he was ultimately able to bring the case before the federal courts.

The memorial contained two general sections. The first set out the history of the purchases, concluding that they were "fair . . . , for valuable consideration, [and] from the original owners of the land, whom no law did or could forbid to sell their property," then traced the procedural history of the claims through the adverse Vincennes Land Commission report of 1806.[24] The second listed and addressed every ground on which the "successive rejections" of the claim had been based: that the tribes that had sold the lands had not in fact owned them, as the lands really belonged to the Six Nations of the Iroquois Confederacy; that the tribal representatives who signed the deeds had not been authorized by their tribes to do so; that the lands had been bought "by private individuals, without any public treaty, or other act of notoriety; without any public authority or previous liberty from the government, or its subsequent confirmation; and therefore contrary to the common and known usage in such cases, and to the express prohibitions contained in the King's proclamation of October 7th, 1763"; that one of the tracts in the Illinois deed was described in such a way as to make it impossible to locate; that the United States had not received contemporaneous notice of the Wabash purchase; that the lands had been sold to the United States; and that, according to the terms of the 1784 Virginia cession, the proceeds of all sales of lands in the West belonging to the United States were to be used to discharge the public debt. Each of these objections Harper addressed and, he thought, demolished in turn.

In light of subsequent events, the most important objection turned out to be the third: that the lands had been bought "by private individuals, without any public treaty, or other act of notoriety; without any public authority or previous liberty from the government, or its subsequent confirmation; and therefore contrary to the common and known usage in such cases, and to the express prohibitions contained in the King's proclamation of October 7th, 1763." Harper declared that this objection, "first brought into view, though very imperfectly," by the 1781 Continental Congress committee report, then "unnoticed in all the subsequent reports, till it was brought forward" again in 1806 by the Vincennes land commissioners, reduced to a charge that the purchases were invalid because they had been made without government approval.[25] Harper admitted that the Crown had not authorized the purchases, but argued that this was irrelevant because Crown approval was not required. According to Harper, neither the charters creating the colonies nor the Proclamation of 1763 deprived the Indians of the power to sell their land to individuals. Indeed, the former notion "never entered the head of any man in England": the charters merely conferred powers of government over colonies of British subjects and defined the boundaries within which those powers might be exercised. As for the proclamation, it could only have deprived the tribes of their power to sell their lands if issued subsequent to conquest, and Great Britain never conquered the Piankashaw and Illinois Nations. Nor, under the unwritten British constitution, did the Crown have the power to restrict the right of British subjects to buy land. Should any doubt remain on this point, Harper concluded, one need only look to the Camden-Yorke opinion, which he disingenuously stated had been rendered "on the 1st of August, 1772," that is, after the Proclamation of 1763 and before the 1773 and 1775 Illinois and Wabash purchases. The Camden-Yorke opinion, he urged, "not only supports the validity of Indian sales to individuals, made after the proclamation; but shews the true use and operation of the Royal Charters: which was not to transfer the right of soil, or even the preemptive right; but to establish Governments, and extend to the settlements the privileges of British subjects, and the protection of the British Crown." The opinion "clearly proves that the proclamation of October 7th, 1763, was not considered in England as restraining the power of the Indians to sell, or the right of British subjects to buy."[26]

Harper closed the memorial by offering to compromise. The Companies would yield their claim in exchange for either confirmation of the eastern half of the lower Wabash tract, or issuance of transferable interest-bearing debt certificates in an amount equal to the number of acres in the eastern half of this tract times $2, payable after the lands were resold by the United States.[27]

As of December 10, 1810, the date of the memorial, Congress had not yet agreed to compensate the Yazoo claimants, victorious in *Fletcher v. Peck*. Indeed, opposition continued to be fierce. On December 17, Congressman George Troup of Georgia suggested from the House floor that armed force might be employed to remove Yazoo claimants from the lands awarded them by the *Fletcher* opinion.[28] Four days later, Archibald Van Horn presented the Illinois and Wabash Companies' memorial to the House of Representatives,[29] which referred it to committee. In January, the committee recommended that the claim be rejected, principally on the ground that the purchases were barred by the Proclamation of 1763.[30] The committee having recommended denial, the memorial was immediately referred to the House sitting as a Committee of the Whole.[31] Hoping to stave off adoption of the committee report and recommendation rejecting their claim, the Companies lobbied to defer consideration until the next session, expected to be held that summer, so that they might "appear by Counsel at the Bar of the house . . . to be heard at large."[32] In this effort, at least, they were successful.

Harper believed that he had the better of the committee on the question of the constitutional validity of the proclamation's proscription on sales or purchases, but he worried that the claims might fail on various factual grounds. To bolster his case, in mid-February, he met with John Rice Jones,[33] former attorney general of the Indiana Territory, who was in Washington to testify against Territorial Governor William Henry Harrison. Jones, a lawyer, had moved to Indiana from Pennsylvania in 1786. Originally a Harrison supporter, he had a falling out with the governor's party before 1808 and participated in a bitter newspaper war with the administration.[34] Jones's 1811 trip to Washington was sponsored by a group of Harrison administration opponents determined to induce the president to remove Harrison as governor. Among the chief architects of this project was William M'Intosh. Because it was a local dispute, Harper almost certainly knew none of this.

Jones welcomed the opportunity to be of service to the Illinois and Wabash Companies. He agreed to obtain depositions establishing that the Piankashaws and Illinois Nations really had owned the lands; that the witnesses to the deeds were, with one exception, dead; that the payment of consideration for the lands could be proven "at least as satisfactorily as facts of such remote dates are susceptible of"; that the principal argument used by the United States to induce the Piankashaws to cede their lands in 1805 was that the government sought only a part of what the Piankashaws had already given to the inhabitants of Vincennes by a reservation contained in the deed to the Wabash Company; and that the United States paid the Piankashaws nothing for this land.[35] Harper was eager for Jones to return to Indiana so that he might have these depositions prior to the commencement of Congress's anticipated summer session. In early April, however, Jones was in Philadelphia, and Harper learned that he planned to spend the spring and summer in the east. With that news, Harper dismissed him, immediately contracting a new agency with three Harrison supporters: George Wallace; General Washington Johnston, member of the Territorial House of Representatives and postmaster at Vincennes; and Henry Hurst, clerk of the Indiana General Court.[36] Harrison's aid was also enlisted, although it appears he was not issued any shares; Harper wrote to him on several occasions "detailing the testimony we wish to obtain" and identifying first Jones and then Wallace as the Companies' agents.[37]

On March 10, 1811, shareholder Jacob Gratz wrote his brother Joseph in Europe: "Mr. Harper is as sanguine as a reasonable person can probably be—God grant success—I then hope we will touch the cash."[38] God, and the American electorate, had other plans. The anticipated extra session was not held. Over the summer, relations with Great Britain rapidly deteriorated, so much so that "as the autumn advanced, the Republican newspapers broke into a general cry for war."[39] Congress reconvened on November 4 with seventy new members in attendance, the position of speaker of the House of Representatives passing to the thirty-four-year-old representative from Kentucky, Henry Clay. Talk of war quickly turned to action, the first great clash of arms occurring, somewhat ironically, less than a week after the session started on the banks of the Wabash at Tippecanoe, at the center of the northernmost of the Companies' Wabash tracts. The majority of New England Federalists opposed the War of 1812, and their opposition, which in the end would rise to the level of threatened secession, so tainted the party that it would never again be politically viable. Harper's opportunity had clearly passed. This new Congress would crush the memorial, if only for the Federalist credentials of its best-known shareholders, including Harper himself. Consequently, the memorial, on which so much hope rested, was quietly withdrawn.

The 1816 Memorial to Congress and the Opening
of a Judicial Avenue

Three years passed before further prosecution of the claims would be possible. Then, in the space of eleven months, two events occurred that sent the Illinois and Wabash Companies back to Congress for the presentation of their final memorial. In March 1814, Congress finally implemented a plan for providing compensation to shareholders of the New England Mississippi Land Company, who had won in *Fletcher v. Peck*.[40] On February 16, 1815, the Senate ratified the Treaty of Ghent, ending the War of 1812.

On December 19, 1815, John Hill Brinton wrote Harper: "It is the opinion of some gentlemen, that this is a favorable time to make application to Congress, for that when the Yazoo claim was recognized by them & several millions of Dollars appropriated to satisfy it, many of the members acknowledged they w[oul]d now have to settle the claim of the Illinois & Ouabache companies."[41] Harper and Etting not only agreed, but had already begun to act. Benjamin Stoddert, former secretary of the navy, whom Harper had hired to lobby the 1810 memorial in Congress, had died on December 23, 1813.[42] In October 1815, Etting hired a replacement, John Law.[43] Then, most impressively, Harper engineered his own reentry into national politics. Harper had left the House of Representatives in 1800. On January 27, 1816, he persuaded the Maryland legislature to elect him that state's new U.S. senator for a term to run through March 1821.[44] He took his seat on February 5, 1816, alongside fellow Maryland shareholder Robert Goldsborough.[45]

With Law as his nominal chief lobbyist, Harper directed the final congressional campaign. Law's principal contribution appears to have been to suggest, somewhat impolitically, the garnering of more legal muscle. Lacking Harper's faith in Harper's forensic abilities, Law urged that "the opinions of our first civilians & Lawyers should be obtained on the operation of the Proclamation of 1763 & on the general validity of Indian titles. . . . The words of the Proclamation of 1763 are such that nothing but indefatigable exertions can ensure success to the claim."[46] Harper, no doubt piqued, "d[id] not think that mere opinions of counsel would be of much avail," but conceded that "those . . . of Rawle, Ingersol Senior, Emmett, Wirt of Richmond, & Tazewell of Norfolk, if favorable, and attainable in time, might do good."[47]

There was no time. The Philadelphia shareholders were anxious not to miss the present opportunity, and Harper and Etting accommodated them by simply instructing their Baltimore publisher to reprint the 1810 memorial, appending a 1775 opinion by a London lawyer recognizing the validity of individual purchases of Indian lands together with endorsements of the opinion by London lawyer John Glynn, Philadelphia patriot Benjamin Franklin, and Virginia revolutionary firebrand Patrick Henry.[48] The 1816 memorial closed with an extract from the Companies' 1797 memorial, "presented," it was noted, "by [Supreme Court] Judge [James] Wilson," affirming the validity of an unlicensed seventeenth-century transfer of Mohegan Indian lands in Connecticut to Major John Mason. One other change was made, presumably to avoid the appearance of any conflict of interest: Harper's name, which had appeared prominently at the close of the 1810 memorial, was deleted from the 1816 version.

The First Session of the Fourteenth Congress convened on December 4, 1815. On January 25, 1816, Jeremiah Morrow of Ohio presented the memorial to the Senate; the memorial was read and referred to committee.[49] Two days later, as noted, Maryland elected Harper a senator. When he arrived at the Capitol on February 5, Harper immediately went to work on his new colleagues. As the month progressed, his efforts appeared to be bearing fruit; on February 28, Brinton, Simon Gratz, and Callender Irvine wrote from Philadelphia that they had been "most gratified by the latest accounts from Washington" stating "that there is a greater disposition prevailing to do justice to the claims of the Illinois and Wabash Companies than heretofore and that there is every reason to believe we shall have a favorable Report in the Senate."[50]

Only eight weeks remained in the session, however. The Companies began fearing that "the business w[ould] not be taken up" before Congress recessed for the summer, "owing to the press of business of a public nature." Congress, they knew, was always "disinclined . . . towards the conclusion [of a session] to enter on matters that they take little Interest in."[51] In the end, despite the best efforts of Harper and his agents, this is precisely what happened. Congress adjourned on April 30 with no action having been taken by the Senate committee.[52]

Ironically, however, the same Congress did finally break the logjam on an appeal route to the Supreme Court. On January 2, 1816, three weeks before the Illinois and Wabash memorial was presented to the Senate, President Madison communicated to that body a memorial of the Indiana Legislative Council and House of Representatives, stating that their population entitled them to admission to statehood and praying that a convention be authorized to determine on its expediency.[53] Fourteen weeks later, the Senate passed a bill "to enable the people of the Indiana Territory to form a constitution and State government, and for the admission of such State into the Union on an equal footing with the original States." The House concurred in an amended version of the Senate bill on April 15, and the bill was subsequently signed into law.[54] Over the summer, the Indiana Constitutional Convention met and approved a constitution for the state. After that, from the perspective of the Illinois and Wabash Companies, it was only a matter of time. Indiana would become a state and, more important, a federal judicial district, from which appeals could be taken to the highest federal court. After almost forty years of petitioning, the Illinois and Wabash Companies would finally have "the opportunity so very desired of presenting [their] claim" before the Supreme Court of the United States.[55]

The Companies consequently abandoned the memorial in favor of pressing their claim before the Court. On December 1, 1816, the day before Congress reconvened, with the appeal route secured, Harper resigned his Senate seat; according to his nineteenth-century biographer, he had determined that "a conscientious discharge of public duties would rob him wholly of time for his private concerns."[56] Ten days later, Indiana was admitted to the Union. On March 3, 1817, President Monroe signed into law a bill creating a federal district court in the new state, to be presided over by one district judge.[57] The district included within its bounds half of the Wabash lands purchased by Murray from the Piankashaws.

The district judge himself was appointed on March 6, 1817, three days after the court was established. Although there is no evidence that the Companies or their agents had anything to do with his selection, the shareholders can hardly have been displeased with the choice: the Companies' former local counsel in Vincennes, Benjamin Parke.[58]

The question of the validity of the Illinois and Wabash land purchases would now finally become a judicial question. This circumstance allowed for enormous manipulation by both litigants and court. Shortcomings in the judicial structure, tolerance for collusion and misstatement of fact, conflicts between states and between states and the federal government, and the enthusiastic willingness of the chief justice of the United States to use one case to resolve another would all play their role in the action that followed. The result was the judicial conquest of Native America.

CHAPTER 3

———◆———

Before the Court

Thirty years after the ratification of the Constitution, the United Illinois and Wabash Land Companies finally had a route by which to bring their claim before the Supreme Court of the United States. No further petitions would be submitted to Congress, at least until the Companies had received a favorable decision from the high court. All of the Companies' resources, and all of Robert Goodloe Harper's creative energies, would be devoted to crafting and prosecuting a suit to win such a decision.

The Judicial System and the Parties, Local Counsel, and Judge

To appreciate the ingenuity brought to bear on this task, it is essential to understand the structure—and deficiencies—of the judicial system in which Harper operated, as well as the various procedural devices available to him. In the federal court system in the early twenty-first century, most cases heard by the Supreme Court are first tried in a federal district court, then reviewed by the federal circuit court of appeals with jurisdiction over the district, and finally reach the Supreme Court by writ of certiorari. In 1817, by contrast, the federal circuit courts acted as trial courts for civil suits in which more than $500 was in dispute. Moreover, unlike present-day circuit courts, which are staffed by circuit court judges assigned exclusively to those courts, the circuit courts of the early nineteenth century were made up of the district court judge for the district in which the circuit court happened to be sitting and the Supreme Court justice assigned to that circuit. The circuit courts changed their composition as the court moved from district to district within the circuit. For example, in 1817, the federal circuit court for the third circuit, which included the districts of Pennsylvania and New Jersey, commenced its sessions in Philadelphia as the U.S. Circuit Court for the District of Pennsylvania consisting of the associate Supreme Court justice assigned to that circuit and the federal district judge for the district of Pennsylvania. Once that court's docket was finished, the associate Supreme Court justice moved on to Trenton, New Jersey, where, with the federal district judge for the district of New Jersey by his side, he convened the U.S. Circuit Court for the District of New Jersey.

Because the Supreme Court justices experienced great hardship in "riding circuit" from district to district, Congress, which was empowered under the Constitution to set the rules on such matters, agreed not to impose the burden of traveling to districts far from the seat of government. Under the 1789 Judiciary Act, for example, Kentucky was not included in a circuit. Instead, the district court in Kentucky was authorized to act as a circuit court for the purpose of conducting trials. Appeals from the district court in Kentucky were reviewable directly by the U.S. Supreme Court.[1] Review was obtained in most instances by the issuance by a Supreme Court justice of a writ of error, which directed the lower court to send the case to the Court, where the justices would examine it and either reverse, correct, or affirm the lower court's judgment.

This was the judicial structure to which the district of Indiana was added in 1817. The first apparent deficiency of this structure was the noted absence of circuit courts in certain parts of the country. Because Indiana was relatively remote, like Kentucky in 1789, it too was not assigned to a circuit, and its new district court was authorized to exercise "the same jurisdiction and powers which were, by law, given to the judge of the Kentucky district" in the Judiciary Act of 1789. Consequently, the Indiana district court would function as a circuit court for the purpose of conducting trials, and disappointed litigants could appeal directly to the Supreme Court.[2]

The court in which Harper planned to file his lawsuit was thus specially constituted. The case would not be filed in a circuit court presided over by two judges, one a justice of the Supreme Court, but in a district court acting as a circuit court and presided over by a lone district court judge. Moreover, Judge Parke had formerly been a paid agent of the Illinois and Wabash Land Companies. This scenario promised Harper great control over the course of the trial and the preparation of the record ultimately to be presented to the Supreme Court.

With the Indiana federal court established, Harper set about constructing the suit. His first consideration was the choice of parties to the suit, the plaintiff and the defendant. The federal courts were empowered to hear cases between citizens of different states. The Supreme Court had jurisdiction to review such cases, however, only if the amount in controversy equaled or exceeded $2,000. Consequently, Harper needed a shareholder plaintiff and a defendant from a different state claiming title to land in the claim area valued at $2,000 or more.

As plaintiff, Harper selected original Wabash Company shareholder Thomas Johnson Jr. Then eighty-five years old and living in retirement with his daughter near Frederick, Maryland, Johnson was, with the possible exception of Harper's father-in-law Carroll, the most venerable of the living shareholders. Johnson had been Maryland's governor during the Confederation. He was also closely associated with George Washington: as a member of the Continental Congress, Johnson had nominated Washington as commander in chief of the Continental Army; as president, in 1791 Washington appointed Johnson an associate justice of the U.S. Supreme Court and in 1795 offered him the position of secretary of state. Harper knew that Johnson would command the respect of Chief Justice John Marshall, whose father had been among Washington's close companions and who was himself a Washington protégé. Johnson also had ties to the current presidential administration: his niece, Louisa Catherine Johnson, was married to Secretary of State John Quincy Adams. Finally, Johnson was an original party to the Wabash deed (which conveyed all the Companies' lands in Indiana), thus obviating the need to demonstrate any

FIGURE 3
Portrait of Chief Justice John Marshall, 1824, by Edward F. Peticolas. Marshall
used *Johnson v. M'Intosh* as a vehicle for shoring up the claims of Virginia militia
veterans to lands in western Kentucky, then nine years later reversed the core of
the opinion in *Worcester v. Georgia*. (Courtesy of Kirby Collection of Historical
Paintings, Lafayette College, Easton, Pennsylvania)

subsequent transfer of shares to him or the Companies' organizational documents.

To defend the action, Harper needed a non-Marylander claiming lands in the Wabash purchase valued at $2,000 or more. He also needed local counsel to oversee the case before Judge Parke. As it happened, shareholder Benjamin Gratz planned to journey to Kentucky in the fall of 1818 to settle various family accounts there.[3] To Gratz fell the task of locating a suitable defendant and local counsel; Harper, whose personal presence would not be required given the planned simplicity of the trial, would then manage the case from Baltimore.

Gratz left Philadelphia in October 1818; floating down the Ohio from Pittsburgh, then disembarking at Maysville, he reached Lexington, Kentucky, before December 15. Seven weeks later, in Louisville, he located a pair of likely defendants: Thomas and Cuthbert Bullitt, "large land holders in the upper Wabash grant," who had "laid out a town, called Terre Haute," the value of which, Gratz believed, would "far exceed the amount required to give the Supreme Court jurisdiction."[4] By February 23, Gratz had also retained local counsel: Charles Dewey, a thirty-four-year-old attorney practicing in Paoli, Indiana.[5] Dewey, a Massachusetts native and graduate of Williams College, was relatively new to Indiana, having located there in 1816. In two years, however, he had acquired a local reputation for advocacy sufficient to inspire comparisons to Daniel Webster and a practice covering much of southwestern Indiana.[6]

By late February Gratz had contacted Judge Benjamin Parke, the former Companies counsel presiding over the new court, to communicate the Companies' intention to file an action to confirm the validity of the Wabash deed. Parke had long known the Gratz family and was likely not surprised when Benjamin Gratz appeared and announced his purpose. However, concerned about his prior representation of the Companies, Parke did not welcome the news. The Companies' claim would force him into a corner. Federal law provided that in any federal district court action in which the judge had been of counsel to either party, the judge must, on application of either party, send the case to the circuit court for the district, which would then oversee the trial as if it had been originally filed there.[7] The district judge (sitting as a circuit judge) would still hear the matter, but, in most cases, any perception of potential bias would be checked by the presence at the circuit court trial of the Supreme Court justice assigned to that circuit. There was no Supreme Court justice assigned to Indiana, however. For trial purposes, the Indiana federal district court acted as its own circuit court. Parke, in other words, would presumably have been asked to send the case from the district court, over which he alone presided, to the district court acting as a circuit court, over which he alone presided. This would hardly solve the problem of potential bias. If Parke recused himself, there was no one left to hear the case. The structure Congress had created was flawed, and Parke was likely the first to see this.

Unsympathetic to Parke's plight, Companies' shareholder and Philadelphia Committee Secretary Edward Ingersoll urged that "nothing is left for us but to go on as if he had no scruples and insist on his trying the cause; I do not see how he can refuse without a dereliction of duty and if he dares refuse he must be impeached, I suppose, but probably when it comes to the point he will not." In the end, Ingersoll may have been right, and the case may well have gone forward without complication. Referral to a circuit court was mandated only where one party objected to the conflicted judge's hearing the case. On March 20, 1819, to tempt the defendants to participate in the litigation, Gratz was authorized to offer to pay all the expenses they might incur in the suit.[8] He might, as a condition, have required that they raise no objection to Parke's resolving the case, and Parke's problem would have disappeared. Although bringing the suit in Indiana in May 1819 would not have changed the ultimate verdict, it would almost certainly have resulted in a significantly different opinion from the Supreme Court, as the delay allowed for the occurrence of other events that would materially influence the decision.

Robert Goodloe Harper opted not to force the matter. By the time Parke's reticence became known, the Companies thought they could afford to spare him the discomfort by accessing a newly formed, and apparently friendly, district court in Illinois.[9] Six months earlier, in December 1818, Illinois had been admitted to the Union. The following March, a federal district court for the new district of Illinois was established,[10] with terms to commence the first Mondays in May and December. Significantly, as in Indiana, the Illinois court would function as a circuit court, with appeals and writs of error directly to the Supreme Court.[11] Before the end of the month, President James Monroe appointed former Illinois representative Nathaniel Pope the district's first judge.[12] Within his court's territorial jurisdiction were the remainder of the lands purchased from the Piankashaws and all of the lands purchased from the Illinois.

Like Parke, Pope was a known commodity; his brother, John Pope, a former U.S. senator from Kentucky, had married plaintiff Thomas Johnson's niece.[13] At Harper's direction, in the face of Parke's reticence, Gratz and Dewey shifted their attention across the Wabash River to the district of Illinois. With this move, Harper needed a new defendant, someone with a competing claim to lands in Illinois. With Dewey's assistance, however, Gratz had no difficulty in locating a replacement: John Rice Jones's former confederate, William M'Intosh, then living in semiretirement in Illinois at the Grand Rapids of the Wabash River, twelve miles south of Vincennes.

William M'Intosh was a sexagenarian Scottish immigrant who had fought for the British during the Revolutionary War. After the war, he operated in the Illinois country as an agent for a fur trading concern based in Detroit. Settling in Vincennes, he applied his knowledge of French and his enterprising nature to the representation of French land claimants. According to a later detractor, he took these cases on a contingent fee basis, thereby amassing a fortune: "By magnifying the difficulty of obtaining confirmations, and other vile deceptions upon those illiterate and credulous people, he succeeded frequently in obtaining two hundred out of four hundred acres for barely presenting the claim."[14] He also claimed to own 11,560 acres within the lower Wabash purchase, which would provide a sufficient base for the ejectment action.[15]

M'Intosh was financially ambitious, and this certainly played a role in his decision to collude with the Illinois and Wabash Companies. But he was also likely motivated in part by his desire to embarrass William Henry Harrison and to get back at the wealthier citizens of Vincennes. Harrison had been governor of the Indiana territory and the chief U.S. negotiator in its treaties to acquire the lands of the territory's Indian tribes, including those tribes that had previously sold their lands to the Illinois and Wabash Companies. He and M'Intosh had once been friends. Indeed, in 1800, when Harrison arrived to assume the post of territorial governor, he and M'Intosh immediately entered into land speculation together, and in 1801, his friendship with the governor led to M'Intosh's appointment as treasurer for the Indiana territory.

M'Intosh's relationship with Governor Harrison soured, however, in the summer of 1804, evidently as a result of M'Intosh's opposition to Indiana's advancing to the second grade of territorial status. The federal territories passed through a series of grades on their way to statehood. With each new grade, territorial government became larger and more complex. As a large landowner, M'Intosh feared that the growth in government would lead to the imposition of hefty real property taxes.[16] When Harrison persisted in pressing for the advancement, M'Intosh commenced a newspaper war designed to force the governor's removal. Harrison's new chief adjutant, Benjamin Parke, who would later become Indiana's federal district judge, pleaded Harrison's cause, publicly pronouncing M'Intosh "an arrant knave, a profligate villain, a dastardly cheat, a perfidious rascal, an impertinent puppy, an absolute liar and a mean cowardly person," with M'Intosh responding in kind.[17]

Indiana did advance to the second grade, and M'Intosh thereafter positioned himself as one of the principal opponents of the Harrison government. In January 1808, when that government was implicated in former vice president Aaron Burr's quixotic conspiracy to lead the western states into rebellion against the United States, M'Intosh drafted a series of resolutions defending the citizens of the territory against charges that they had supported Burr but denouncing the territorial legislature for electing as its clerk indicted Burr conspirator Davis Floyd. Anti-Harrison articles, penned by M'Intosh, former land commissioner Elijah Backus, and John Rice Jones, whom Harper would later hire as an agent, contemporaneously appeared in the Frankfort, Kentucky *Western World* over the signatures "Philo Tristram" and "Tristram."[18] "Anti Tristram"—possibly Benjamin Parke again—responded, declaring M'Intosh, Backus, and Jones "a triumvirate worthy of each other and the vile cause of slander and detraction in which they are engaged" and suggesting that M'Intosh was a British agent.[19]

In 1810, M'Intosh and Jones orchestrated the unsuccessful attack on Harrison that culminated in Jones's trip to Washington, where he met and was, for a brief time, retained by Harper and the Illinois and Wabash Companies. This time, M'Intosh challenged the fairness of Harrison's 1809 Fort Wayne treaty with the Delawares, Potawatomies, Miamis, and Eel River Miamis, by which the tribes conveyed to the United States an enormous tract and received in exchange permanent annuities of $500, $500, $500, and $200, respectively.[20] According to witnesses, M'Intosh openly asserted that Harrison "had cheated the Indians" at Fort Wayne. In response, Harrison sued for slander. A Vincennes jury awarded Harrison $4,000, and the execution of this judgment forced the sale of a large amount of M'Intosh's lands.[21]

Harrison's slander suit, and more particularly the heavy damages assessed, silenced M'Intosh's opposition to the territorial administration. Thereafter, he attempted to keep out of the public eye. His personal situation, however, quickly made this impossible. Soon after the slander trial, M'Intosh took as his common law wife a former slave, Lydia, who, based on the existing court record, was every bit as independent as M'Intosh.[22] In 1815, after repeated indignities at the hands of the citizens of Vincennes, M'Intosh and his wife abandoned the city to settle in relative isolation on lands he had purchased with Harrison at the Grand Rapids of the Wabash. He would remain there, alone with his family, for the rest of his life.

What Gratz and Dewey now offered M'Intosh was a chance to participate in a lawsuit that, if properly managed, would undermine Harrison's Indian treaties and the land titles of many, if not all, of the wealthier citizens of Vincennes. Given the scope of his collusion, they almost certainly also offered him a share in the Companies as well. In the end, the offer proved irresistible.

Drafting the Pleadings and Presenting the Case to the District Court

With the parties in place and local counsel and a forum secured, Robert Goodloe Harper turned his attention to the preparation of the pleadings, the documents Dewey had to file to start the suit. It is at this stage that the susceptibility of the system to manipulation becomes most starkly apparent. The plaintiffs would file two documents with Judge Nathaniel Pope of the U.S. District Court for the District of Illinois. First was the actual plea in ejectment, which constituted Johnson's formal complaint against M'Intosh. Pleas in ejectment were formulaic, literally copied from form books, and it is likely Harper left the plea's drafting in Dewey's hands to guarantee the submission of a form familiar to Judge Pope. Ejectment pleadings were formulaic because they were built on legal fictions: after the lands had been described, the plaintiff established jurisdiction by alleging that his tenant, who in fact did not exist, had been driven by force of arms ("vi et armis") from the disputed lands by the defendant's tenant, the "casual ejector," who also did not exist.[23] Counsel had only to add to the formula the names of the parties and a description of the land.

To supplement the plea, Harper would file an agreed statement of facts, a statement from both parties listing all material facts not in dispute. Agreed statements served an important end, narrowing the issues to be decided at trial and saving the time otherwise necessarily expended proving undisputed facts. Of greater importance, from Harper's perspective, facts established by agreement between the parties were not susceptible to jury or court review. The integrity of the judicial process was theoretically assured by the natural unwillingness of adversarial parties to agree to facts detrimental to their cause. This integrity, of course, was undermined when the defendant stood to gain by his own defeat.

The agreed statement was the key to Harper's litigation strategy. In drafting the 1810 memorial, Harper had become aware of the various grounds of objection raised against the claims by the only bodies that had ever explicitly ruled on them: the congressional committees and the Vincennes land commission. Some of these grounds were factual, including the objection that the Companies had failed to satisfy the basic legal requirements for valid deeds—most crucial, that the Piankashaws, and not the Iroquois, had owned the lands and had power to sell. The plaintiffs would bear the burden of proof on these issues at trial, so if there were any question about what the facts were, the plaintiffs would lose.

The goal of the ejectment action was to win from the Supreme Court a decision destroying the previously identified factual and legal objections to the greatest extent possible. This, of course, had been the goal in *Fletcher*. The problem Harper faced in *Johnson* that he had not faced in *Fletcher* was that, owing to the age of the claims, the burden of proof on the factual grounds of objection—proving, for example, that the Piankashaws had owned the land—would be almost impossible to meet: only one of the witnesses to the Wabash deed, John Rice Jones had informed him, was alive in 1810, and Harper had no reason to believe that even he had survived to testify nine years later. Were the district court to demand proof on the various factual objections, Harper could offer no more than the deed itself and forty-five years of company representations. If the case failed before the district court on factual grounds, it would fail before the Supreme Court: Section 22 of the Judiciary Act of 1789, which was still the law in 1819, denied the Supreme Court the authority to reverse lower court judgments for errors in fact.

An agreed statement of facts, in which the plaintiff and defendant agreed to the truth of the Companies' factual representations, would solve this problem. In addition, an agreed statement could shape the issues to be decided at trial and on appeal. With these thoughts in mind and the 1810 memorial before him, Harper went to work.[24] In twenty-four paragraphs, Harper set forth the chain of title of each of the parties.[25] He first traced Virginia's charter claim to the area containing the lands at issue (paragraphs 1 through 4 and 6) and outlined the silencing of French claims to the area at the conclusion of the Seven Years' War (paragraph 5). He then traced the vendor Indians' title to the lands at issue (paragraphs 7 through 9 and 11) and described the circumstances of the 1773 and 1775 purchases (paragraphs 13 through 16). In paragraphs 17 through 19, he described Virginia's cession of its claims to the United States. In paragraphs 20 and 21, he related the transfer by the United States to M'Intosh and stipulated that M'Intosh's claimed lands lay within those claimed by the plaintiffs under the 1775 Wabash deed. Last, he stipulated that the plaintiffs inherited their claim from Thomas Johnson (paragraph 22),[26] that the specific jurisdictional requirements were satisfied (paragraph 23), and that the plaintiffs and their predecessors in interest had been prevented from obtaining possession by the Revolution and had submitted numerous memorials to Congress for confirmation of title (paragraph 24). In paragraph 10, Harper incorporated into the record the Proclamation of 1763.

In these paragraphs, Harper eliminated all of the factual objections ever raised against the claim by Congress, congressional committee, or land commission: the Piankashaws did own the lands, their signers did have the authority to sign, the purchasers had paid a fair price, and so on.[27] One legal objection, however, he did not stipulate away because he wished it to serve as both the basis for M'Intosh's defense and the sole issue on appeal. This was the ground for which the land commissions had found the purchases invalid, and it formed the heart, as Harper saw it, of the third objection he had identified in the 1810 memorial: that the purchases were barred by the Proclamation of 1763. This objection had dogged the Companies since the purchases were first made, and it was time to deal with it. The agreed statement not only left the objection unanswered (i.e., there was no paragraph stating that the proclamation was not a bar): in paragraph 10, as noted, Harper incorporated the proclamation into the record so that the document would be admitted into evidence for the parties to address.

By means of the agreed statement, Harper had made *Johnson v. M'Intosh* a case exclusively about the effect of the Royal Proclamation of 1763 on a pre–Revolutionary War land purchase. He had, he thought, demolished this ground for denial in the 1810 memorial by arguing that, although Parliament might have barred such a purchase, under the British constitution the Crown could not. He had since discovered further judicial authority in support of this argument.[28] Accordingly, Harper would leave the collaborating defendant M'Intosh with a single, weak issue on appeal. With the Supreme Court's judgment that the proclamation was not a bar, he might force a compromise with Congress.

One procedural matter remained. The party in control of the case before the Supreme Court—the party requesting the writ of error and, more important, the party arguing first and last—would be the party who lost before the district court. For this reason, it was decided that, before the district court, M'Intosh should win. Harper did not, however, want Judge Pope to issue a lengthy opinion in M'Intosh's favor listing reasons why the Proclamation of 1763 defeated the Companies' claims; such an opinion would merely place another hurdle in the Companies' path when Harper appeared before the bar of the Supreme Court. Instead, Harper would invite the district court to rule for M'Intosh pro forma, that is, without an articulated opinion and solely for the purpose of facilitating an appeal.

Plans to file the suit at the December 1819 term of the district court at Vandalia, Illinois, were dashed when, on October 26, 1819, plaintiff Thomas

Johnson died. Rather than select a new plaintiff, and perhaps eager to preserve the advantage of the family connection with Illinois's new federal judge, Harper elected simply to substitute for Johnson his two principal heirs, Johnson's son, Joshua Johnson, and twenty-five-year-old grandson, Thomas Jennings Grahame, both of whom had undoubtedly long since been apprised of the suit and were prepared to lend their names to its prosecution.[29] Neither could stand as plaintiff, however, until Johnson's estate, including his Illinois and Wabash interest, was distributed, a process requiring the approval of the Maryland State Court. On December 28, Johnson's will was submitted to probate,[30] where it remained until the court approved a final accounting. Thereafter, the court transferred title to the Illinois-Wabash shares to his heirs, Johnson and Grahame, and the Illinois action went forward.

On December 4, 1820, Charles Dewey filed a plea in ejectment in the U.S. District Court for the District of Illinois in Vandalia. According to the plea, "Thomas Troublesome [the fictional casual ejector], late of Illinois District, a citizen of the State of Illinois, . . . was attached to answer unto Simeon Peaceable [the fictional tenant], a citizen of the State of Maryland, . . . in a plea whereof with force and arms &c at Illinois District aforesaid, he the said Thomas entered into" Johnson and Grahame's share of the lower Wabash tract and "eject[ed]" Peaceable and committed "other wrongs . . . to the great damage of the said Simeon, and against the peace government and dignity of the . . . United States."

In the court's record of the case, the fictional Troublesome thereupon executed a notice "to Mr. William M'Intosh in possession of the premises or some part thereof," advising him that, because Troublesome had "no claim or interest in the said premises," M'Intosh should "appear in the District Court of the United States to be held at Vandalia on the first Monday of December next by some attorney of that court, and there by rule of said court . . . cause yourself to be made defendant in my stead, otherwise I shall suffer judgment to be entered against me, and you will be turned out of possession." M'Intosh accordingly appeared by his counsel, Henry Starr, agreed to stand for Troublesome, and pleaded "Not Guilty." On December 6, the court empaneled a jury, then, the parties having agreed to all material facts, discharged it.[31] The court then formally granted the parties leave to submit the agreed statement, which was entered into the record. Thereafter, as Harper desired and presumably at both parties' request, Judge Pope issued a pro forma decision in favor of M'Intosh:

> Upon the facts so stated and agreed, it is the opinion of the Court, that the said William M'Intosh is not guilty of the trespass and ejectment in the said Plaintiffs declaration against him alledged [*sic*].
>
> It is therefore considered by the Court that the said plaintiff Simeon Peaceable take nothing by his plaint aforesaid, and that the said William M'Intosh go hence without d[el]ay; and have and recover of the said lessors of the said plaintiff his costs and charges by him in his defense in this behalf expended—And the said lessors in mercy &c.[32]

Pope then granted Dewey leave to appeal, after which the court entered an agreement on the record whereby M'Intosh, further evidencing collusion, consented to waive the posting by Johnson of an appeal bond and the otherwise required citation for M'Intosh to appear before the Supreme Court at Washington. When the Supreme Court's February 1821 term convened, Chief Justice Marshall, at Harper's request, executed a writ of error, and the case was set for argument.[33]

The magnitude of Harper's accomplishment, and the facility with which he achieved it, can hardly be overstated. By taking advantage of the existing federal judicial structure (in particular, the fact that the lone judge of the federal district court for the district of Illinois was authorized to act as a circuit court judge, thereby removing one justice of the Supreme Court as a potential obstacle to the entry on the record of the agreed statement and the issuance of the pro forma decision) and accepted procedural devices (the agreed statement and the pro forma decision), Harper brought before the Supreme Court a claim uncomplicated by factual problems and confined to an issue he felt sure he could win based on his argument in the 1810 memorial. It was as if Harper had delivered to the Supreme Court a copy of the Companies' 1810 memorial, denied it the power to find against the Companies based on any of the material facts, and requested its opinion on the Proclamation of 1763 issue without the benefit of a counterargument on this issue from either M'Intosh's trial lawyer or the district court.

In effect, by means of the agreed statement, Congress's failure to provide for an Illinois circuit court, and Judge Pope's willingness to issue a pro forma decision, Harper had used the lower federal court system Congress had created to engineer a trial of the case on the agreed statement before the highest court in the land.

Harper's use of the existing jurisdictional and constitutional structure to place the Illinois and Wabash claims within one stroke of recognition demonstrates the way this structure was exploitable for private gain. The tension, both political and institutional, that existed between the federal legislature and the judiciary offered parties the chance to try to use one against the other. Resolution of disputes brought before the Court had balance of power consequences. In the case of large land claims, such resolution also had potential economic consequences, even if the decision resulted in a cash payment by Congress and not the ouster of existing settlers. Finally, and in ways more profound than now widely appreciated, such resolution commonly affected (and was influenced by) the relationship between the states and the federal government and relationships among the states themselves. This "federalism" calculus played a key role in *Johnson v. M'Intosh*. To appreciate just how key it was, one must first understand the circumstances under which the case was presented to the Supreme Court.

Selecting Counsel and Preparing for Argument before the Supreme Court

The writ of error signed by Chief Justice Marshall in February 1821 directed the parties to present the case for argument "on the first Monday in February next," that is, at the commencement of the Supreme Court's February 1822 term.[34] Harper wasted no time in beginning to prepare. As his practice had been to appear before the Court with co-counsel, and the participation of otherwise disinterested co-counsel would in any event make the case appear less personal to Harper, he first set about retaining a partner. His initial choice fell on fifty-seven-year-old William Pinkney, former attorney general and current U.S. senator from Maryland, a fellow Baltimore attorney and at the time the most renowned member of the Supreme Court bar. Pinkney accepted the Companies' cash retainer in the spring of 1821.

When the February 1822 term commenced, it was crowded, and many cases preceded *Johnson v. M'Intosh* on the docket. The illness of U.S. Attorney General William Wirt temporarily moved the case forward, as Wirt's cases were postponed, but by the third week in February, Wirt had recovered, and *Johnson v. M'Intosh* was again moved lower down the docket. Then, on February 25, Pinkney died. Pinkney had not been especially attentive to the case. By subsequent account, Harper, despite his best efforts, "never could induce him to give it a moment's thought," and even before his death, Harper had tentatively set about finding suitable replacement counsel. Nevertheless, Companies' secretary Edward Ingersoll, in Washington to observe the argument, viewed Pinkney's death as "disastrous . . . for the present opportunity of doing business," and Harper and Ingersoll convened during the brief adjournment called by the Court in Pinkney's honor to discuss the case's prosecution before the term's conclusion. According to Ingersoll, Harper was less concerned about Pinkney's absence than about the case's docket position. The session was fast advancing, and Harper believed "it would be bad policy to argue [the case] so near the close of the term." Harper feared that a late-term argument would delay the issuance of an opinion until the following February term. This prospect was "attended with considerable danger and disadvantage," because "if the Court separate before they decide and then make up their minds singly & at home there will be much more room for the bias which we fear. They will forget some of the arguments, hear it argued again in conversation. The advantage of *concluding* the argument will be lost to us and our chance of a favorable decision very much diminished." On the other hand, Harper considered, "an argument early in the Session would be followed by a decision at the same session made up in consultation only among the judges themselves and while the effect of the concluding counsel's argument would be fresh on their minds." An additional reason counseled delay. Harper was "not *quite* ready to argue the case,"[35] because he had just learned of a potential legal objection to the purchase of which he had been previously unaware: that the purchases had been voided by the Virginia Declaratory Act of 1779, in which the Virginia legislature had declared that

FIGURE 4

Portrait of Daniel Webster, 1827, by Sarah Goodridge. Webster joined Harper as attorney for the United Illinois and Wabash Land Companies after Harper's first co-counsel, William Pinkney, died. Webster not only had by then earned a reputation as the leading Supreme Court advocate, he also had an extensive knowledge of New England land titles, including those derived from Indian purchases. (Courtesy of Massachusetts Historical Society, Boston, Massachusetts) all unlicensed Indian land purchases that had ever been made in Virginia were invalid. The act had not been cited in any congressional committee report, and it is unclear from whom Harper learned of its existence. He was persuaded, however, that a lack of resolution of the point would possibly jam up the Companies' settlement drive in Congress once a favorable verdict on the proclamation had been won, and accordingly he wanted time to obtain a copy and to prepare a response.

Harper had decided to offer Pinkney's position as co-counsel to forty-year-old Daniel Webster, who by common assent had assumed Pinkney's mantle as the leading advocate before the Supreme Court. Webster, an 1801 graduate of Dartmouth College, began the practice of law in New Hampshire in 1805. He was elected to Congress in 1812 and 1814 as a Federalist, but declined to run for reelection in 1816, preferring to devote full time to his increasingly successful law practice. National fame as a Supreme Court advocate came after 1818, when he successfully represented his alma mater in *Dartmouth College v. Woodward*, an important constitutional law case, decided in 1819. Harper believed that Webster "would be a very powerful adjunct" in *Johnson v. M'Intosh* owing to "his thorough knowledge of Indian titles in New England, his great industry and distinguished abilities." Ingersoll, who favored John Sergeant, was prepared to concede after Pinkney's death that "the general opinion is that Webster is *now* the most powerful advocate of all that attend the Supreme Court."[36] Before the 1822 term ended, with the Companies' authorization Ingersoll would accordingly retain Webster on the same terms the Companies had offered Pinkney.[37]

One other matter was discussed between Harper and Ingersoll in the brief period of adjournment following Pinkney's death. Harper had determined that "the case must be, for effect, thoroughly argued and well argued for the Defendant." With this in mind, he had written to M'Intosh, who, at his prompting, had offered the case to two of Harper's Maryland colleagues, William Henry Winder of Baltimore and Henry Maynadier Murray of Annapolis.[38] Harper now directed that the Companies pay their fees, which he set at $300–$500. Ingersoll, troubled more by the proposed amount of compensation than its source, agreed to "talk with Mr. Murray and Gen. Winder (it seems they know where their fee is to come from)," and "to tell them frankly how poor we are and ask them to name the lowest

FIGURE 5

Portrait of William Winder, from Benson J. Lossing, *Pictorial Fieldbook of War of 1812* (New York: Harper & Brothers, 1868). Winder, a Baltimore attorney, represented William M'Intosh before the Supreme Court "for effect" and in the pay of the United Illinois and Wabash Land Companies.

sum for which they will engage."[39] When Ingersoll subsequently executed this task, both Winder and Murray agreed to take the case. They would argue against Harper and Webster "for effect," and they would do so in the employ of the Illinois and Wabash Land Companies.

Having made these key arrangements, Harper settled back to await the commencement of the Supreme Court's February 1823 term. He had prepared a winnable brief, confined to a single, winnable issue: the effect of the Proclamation of 1763 on pre–Revolutionary War Indian land sales. He had retained as co-counsel the best advocate then appearing before the Supreme Court, and together they would face opposing counsel who were not only less qualified but also in the pay of his clients. The odds had never looked better.

Congress Changes the Odds

Congress, however, was already in the process of changing the odds, via its review of a decades-old petition unrelated to the Illinois and Wabash claims. In 1806, a New England cleric, the Reverend Samuel Peters, had presented to the House a claim to lands in the present states of Wisconsin and Minnesota allegedly deeded to British Captain Jonathan Carver by two representatives of the Sioux in 1767.[40] The House committee to which the claim was then referred never reported on it, but its members did express their disinclination to recognize it, primarily, according to Peters, because the circumstances of the conveyance were shaky. Speculation in "Carver Grant" shares evidently picked up after 1818, when Peters returned from the west with further evidence supporting his claim of a valid conveyance. On January 29, 1822, less than a month before Pinkney's death, Congressman Reuben H. Walworth of New York, stating that "frauds [were being] committed, and innocent purchasers drawn in by persons pretending to a title to these lands," successfully moved Congress to request copies of Executive Department reports on the claim.[41] Three months later, President James Monroe forwarded to the House Committee on Public Lands a report from the General Land Office finding the claim invalid as in direct violation of the Proclamation of 1763.[42] Soon after, Congress adjourned.

On December 27, 1822, one month after Congress reconvened and five weeks before the Supreme Court was scheduled to commence its February 1823 term, the Carver Grant claim reappeared before the Senate when James Lanman of Connecticut presented a new petition from Samuel Peters. This petition as well as the original 1806 petition were referred to the Senate Committee on Public Lands. On January 23, Nicholas Van Dyke of Delaware reported the Committee's opinion that the claim was invalid because the deed violated the express terms of the Proclamation of 1763.[43] On Wednesday, January 29, five days before the opening of the Supreme Court's February 1823 term, the Senate voted to deny the claim.[44]

The message thus sent to the justices of the Supreme Court, about to convene in the basement of the Capitol, was unmistakable: in the view of the Senate, the Proclamation of 1763 barred Indian land sales west of the proclamation line made subsequent to that date. A decision to the contrary by the Court would contravene not merely successive congressional committee reports, but the sense of a majority of the sitting Senate.

The Senate's rejection of the Carver petitions doomed the claims of the Illinois and Wabash Land Companies. Immediately prior to the Peters petition's presentation in the Senate, Webster evidently attempted to withdraw from the case.[45] In the end, he did not leave, but his continued participation alone could not assuage Harper's growing sense of foreboding. On January 23, the Companies attempted to strengthen Harper's resolve by issuing him an additional share "as a further compensation for the services to be performed by him in the present suit depending [sic] in the Supreme Court of the United States, in any future controversy that may result from a successful issue of the present suit and in any application to [C]ongress that may become necessary."[46] At the same time, the Companies began selling shares at the best price obtainable.[47]

The Supreme Court Convenes

On Monday, February 3, the Supreme Court convened its February 1823 term. Ingersoll arrived in Washington in the late afternoon on Monday, February 10, "after a fatiguing ride" from Philadelphia.[48] By Thursday,

February 13, the case was "not yet reached"; according to Ingersoll, he, Harper, and Webster were "growing stronger every day. I have found a good deal in the libraries here. Among other matters an Act of Parliament passed in 1774 [the Quebec Act] which neither Mr. Harper nor Mr. Webster knew anything about, declaring the operation of the Proclamation of 1763 to have been limited to the newly ceded territories—and rescinding it from the 1st May 1775 as to all the lands between the Ohio & Mississippi—uniting the territory however to the Govt of Quebec, except which belonged to other colonies. There is no difficulty in fixing these lands within the bounds of Virginia."[49] Ingersoll's discovery of new, potentially important legislation on the eve of argument was not a good sign. When Webster made a last-minute request that Ingersoll locate a copy of "'Chalmer's Collection of opinions of counsel relative to the colonies'—or a book with a title resembling that," Ingersoll fretfully wrote his colleagues in Philadelphia, "I suppose our counsel will make good arguments, but I do not believe they are so fully prepared as they might be and rather hope the case may not be reached for a week yet."[50] They would have two days.

M'Intosh's Lawyers Prepare for Argument

Winder and Murray, meanwhile, finished preparations in their argument for M'Intosh. Harper had provided them with a copy of both the agreed statement and the Companies' 1816 memorial. It is likely, given the history of the case, that Harper explicitly instructed Winder and Murray to center their argument on the second part of the third objection discussed in the memorial, which covered the Proclamation of 1763, and to say something about the effect of the Virginia Declaratory Act of 1779. Beyond this, however—perhaps because of a miscommunication, perhaps only "for effect," perhaps because, despite their retainer, they felt some obligation to make hard argument for M'Intosh—they also prepared argument on an issue Harper had intended to moot in the agreed statement of facts: the first part of the third objection, that the Indians "were divested of their right to sell their lands, by the acts of the British Government, in establishing colonies whose nominal limits included those lands." Harper had argued in his response to this objection that "surely to state so extravagant a proposition is to refute it," and it may have been this dismissive attitude that persuaded Winder and Murray, who had no incentive to win, that any argument they might make on this point Harper could easily destroy. This would prove a tragic miscalculation.

It was likely in this spirit, too, that they chose to build their argument on this point on an argument made by Harper and John Quincy Adams in *Fletcher v. Peck. Fletcher*, as noted, had arisen from a grant by the Georgia legislature to the predecessor in interest to the New England Mississippi Land Company. Among the many hurdles that the claimants had to overcome was the fact that, at the time of the grants, some of the lands conveyed had been occupied by Indian nations. The Georgia legislature had addressed this problem by simply proclaiming the lands "vacant" and assuming dominion. The adoption of the "purchase" policy by the federal government had made this declaration suspect, however, and accordingly, among the covenants on which *Fletcher* had been tried was one providing "that the State of Georgia . . . was, at the time of the passing of the [1795] act of [sale of the Yazoo lands], . . . legally seised in fee of [i.e., legally owned the title to] the soil thereof, subject only to the extinguishment [i.e., nullification, by purchase or conquest] of part of the Indian title thereon." The argument pirated by Winder and Murray was presented when the case came before the Supreme Court in February 1809. The "Indian title," Harper and Adams had urged, "is a mere occupancy for the purpose of hunting. It is not like our tenures; they have no idea of a title to the soil itself. It is overrun by them, rather than inhabited. It is not a true and legal possession." This objection had never been raised against the Illinois and Wabash purchases, and Harper had not thought to say anything about it in the 1810/1816 memorial. When *Fletcher* was decided in 1810, the argument had received at best a lukewarm reception from the Supreme Court. Justice Johnson found it simply wrong. "Innumerable treaties with [the Indians] acknowledge them to be an independent people," he wrote, "and the uniform practice of acknowledging their right of soil, by purchasing from them, and restraining all persons from encroaching upon their territory, makes it unnecessary to insist upon their right of soil." For the Yazoo speculators to win in *Fletcher*, however, Chief Justice Marshall needed to find that the state had a significant property interest enough to justify his holding that the state had entered into an enforceable contract, the repeal of which had violated the Constitution's Article I, Section 10 prohibition on states' passing laws "impairing the obligation of contracts." Yet he could garner a majority only in support of a statement "that the nature of Indian title, which is certainly to be respected by all courts, until it be legitimately extinguished, is not such as to be absolutely repugnant to seisin in fee on the part of the state."[51] From Winder and Murray's perspective, the argument thus would not likely prove fatal in *Johnson v. M'Intosh*. The central issue, as planned, would still be the effect of the Companies' perennial bane, the Proclamation of 1763.

Before the Court

On Friday, February 14, 1823, Harper and Murray dined at the White House, where Murray, as noted earlier, boasted of being in Washington to argue a case in which "seven[ty] millions of acres of land are in controversy." On Saturday, February 15, the case of *Johnson v. M'Intosh* was called for argument before the Supreme Court of the United States. The day was cold—twenty-six degrees—but even so the argument attracted spectators.[52] The order of presentation was determined by the relative positions of the parties. Harper and Webster, representing the plaintiff in error, would lead; Winder and Murray would then present M'Intosh's case; and Harper and Webster would close with their reply.

Supreme Court reporter Henry Wheaton's summary is the fullest surviving record of the arguments presented before the Court during the three days in February that Harper, Webster, Winder, and Murray held the floor.[53] Though terse, it nevertheless conveys something of the sense of impending doom that descended over plaintiff's counsel as the argument progressed.

Webster Opens for Johnson

Webster opened for Johnson and Grahame by attacking Winder's forthcoming argument on the first part of the third objection, including the argument from *Fletcher*. No objection, Webster observed, could properly be

FIGURE 6

Old Supreme Court chamber. In this courtroom directly below the Old Senate Chamber in the Capitol the U.S. Supreme Court heard argument in *Johnson v. M'Intosh*. (Courtesy of Architect of the U.S. Capitol)

raised as to either the interest held by or power to alienate of the vendor Piankashaws. The agreed statement had taken care of both questions: "Upon the facts stated in the case, the Piankashaw Indians were the owners of the lands in dispute, at the time of executing the deed of October 10th, 1775, and had power to sell." Even had the parties not stipulated as to these facts, M'Intosh, as a purchaser from the United States, could hardly so object: his vendor "had purchased the same lands of the same Indians. . . . Both parties," in other words, "claim from the same source."[54]

For this reason, Webster concluded, "it would seem . . . to be unnecessary, and merely speculative, to discuss" the *Fletcher* question, that is, "the question respecting the sort of title or ownership, which may be thought to belong to savage tribes, in the lands on which they live." Nevertheless, Webster would settle the question at the outset. "Probably," he began, "their title by occupancy is to be respected, as much as that of an individual, obtained by the same right, in a civilized state." Because the tribes had lived on these lands for so long, the lands were theirs: they owned them. It did not matter that the tribes held the lands collectively.[55] Grotius had said as much: "Any places that have been taken possession of in the name of a sovereign, or of a whole people, though not portioned out amongst individuals, are not to be considered as waste lands, but as the property of the first occupier, whether it be the King, or a whole people."[56] British policy, moreover, had long recognized the Indians' right of soil, as had the U.S. Supreme Court and the Supreme Court of New York.[57] In *Fletcher v. Peck*, Marshall had indeed affirmed that the Indian title, whatever it was, was "to be respected by all courts."[58] In *Jackson v. Wood*, decided in 1810, Chief Justice Kent for the Supreme Court of New York ruled that "it is a fact too notorious to admit of discussion or to require proof, that the Oneida Indians still reside within this state, as a distinct and independent tribe, and upon lands which they have never alienated, but hold and enjoy as the original proprietors of the soil."[59]

Although Wheaton did not record the fact, Webster likely followed with a listing of recognized Indian purchases; he had been hired, after all, in part because of his expertise in the matter of New England land titles. He concluded that "all, or nearly all, the lands in the United States, is holden under purchases from the Indian nations; and the only question in this case must be, whether it be competent to individuals to make such purchases, or whether that be the exclusive prerogative of government."[60]

Having dispensed with the Indian title matter, Webster next advanced his argument on the Proclamation of 1763, which mirrored Harper's 1810 argument. The proclamation could not affect the Indians' right to sell their lands "because they were not British subjects, nor in any manner bound by the authority of the British government, legislative or executive." Even if they had been subjects, the British *executive* had no power constitutionally to divest them of their right to sell land.[61] Nor could the proclamation restrain Johnson from purchasing. As the Court of King's Bench had stated in *Campbell v. Hall*, while the Crown had power to proscribe land purchasing in newly conquered territories under military occupation, "the establishment of a government establishes a system of laws, and excludes the power of legislating by proclamation."[62] These lands lay within the boundaries of the colony of Virginia, and the Crown might by proclamation no more effectually bar their purchase than it might by proclamation bar the purchase of land in England or Canada.[63] Were there any doubt remaining, Webster argued, it must be laid to rest by the Camden-Yorke opinion, the relevant language of which he subsequently provided the Court.

Next, Webster turned to the Virginia 1779 Declaratory Act, which purported retroactively to invalidate unlicensed Indian land purchases. The act was invalid, Webster argued, because "on general principles, and by the constitution of Virginia, the legislature was not competent to take away private, vested rights, or appropriate private property to public use, under the circumstances of this case." In any event, the act must "be considered as repealed," because it was left out of the 1794 Virginia Code revision, and "the repeal reinstates all rights that might have been affected by the act," despite the fact that Virginia's western land claims had been previously ceded to the United States. Apart from the Declaratory Act, there was no conceivable statutory bar.[64]

Having thus demonstrated that the purchases were not invalid under the Proclamation of 1763, the 1779 Declaratory Act, or any other executive or legislative act, Webster finally turned to "the general inquiry, whether individuals, in Virginia, at the time of this purchase, could legally obtain Indian titles." It had likely not been his original intention to close this way, but his reception impelled him to reiterate the recognized validity of colonial Indian grants not prohibited by statute. "In New-England, titles have certainly been obtained in this mode," he reaffirmed. The Indian grants to John Whelewright, Major Mason, and William Penn, discussed by Harper in the 1810 memorial, soundly evidenced the historical public recognition of the Indians' right of soil. He may well have advanced other examples. At the end, according to Wheaton, Webster reiterated—rather weakly—his principal point: that such purchases could only be proscribed by legislative act. "Whatever may be said on the more general question, and in reference to other colonies or States, the fact being, that in Virginia there was no statute existing at the time against such purchases, mere general considerations would not apply."[65]

Webster thus closed the opening argument in *Johnson v. M'Intosh*. It had not gone entirely as planned. The Court, as the opinion would show, had been less interested in Webster's argument on the proclamation and

Declaratory Act than in his comments on the "general considerations" surrounding the question of Indian title. "In the S. Court today," spectator
George Brydges Rodney noted in his diary, "Mr. Webster argued a cause
upon a land trial to determine the validity of Indian deeds. It is a doctrine
which has not been recognized by the government, and which if adopted,
would perhaps result in much inconvenience. Webster argued for the right
of the Indians to dispose of the soil . . . [to] individuals and contended
for the validity of the deed. He went into a discussion upon the origin of
property and managed it skillfully for a bad cause."[66]

Winder and Murray Offer M'Intosh's Reply

Sunday, the Court was in recess, and on Monday, February 17, Winder and
Murray held the floor.[67] As expected, they opened with their argument on
the nature of Indian title. The topic had by this time seized center stage,
and Harper must have winced as he watched the justices' response to their
presentation of arguments he himself had developed thirteen years earlier.

"The uniform understanding and practice of European nations, and
the settled law, as laid down by the tribunals of civilized states," Winder and
Murray began, echoing Harper and Adams, "denied the right of the Indians to be considered as independent communities, having a permanent
property in the soil, capable of alienation to private individuals." What is
more, "the whole theory of their titles to lands in America, rests upon
this hypothesis, that the Indians had no right of soil as sovereign, independent states."[68] Stated differently, the hypothesis was a necessary corol-
lary to the political reality. Discovery vested in the discoverer's ownership
of the discovered lands. And if the discoverer owned these lands, the Indians did not.

Having introduced Harper's *Fletcher* argument, Winder and Murray
next advanced an alternative argument derived from an appendix to the
1816 memorial.[69] In it, the argument had been made that the exercise by a
tribe of its sovereign power to sell lands "admits a capacity in the grantee,
to take under the deed *according to their [i.e., the tribe's] laws or usage,* and
there is no law I ever heard of, that restrains the subjects of the crown of
England from purchasing in foreign dominions."[70] Winder and Murray

attempted—rather awkwardly—to take this argument one step further: "If it be admitted that [the Piankashaws] are now independent and foreign states," they suggested, "the title of the plaintiffs would still be invalid: as grantees from the *Indians*, they must take according to *their* laws of property, and as Indian subjects." The Indians did not recognize individual property; they recognized only collective property. Therefore, Thomas Johnson Jr., who had left his share in the Illinois and Wabash Companies to the plaintiffs, could not have purchased land from them as an individual. The purchase was invalid.[71]

Winder and Murray now returned to *Fletcher*. Because the Indians resided within the territorial bounds of the United States, they were subject to our laws. Because they were "an inferior race of people, without the privileges of citizens," their rights were less expansive than ours. The law recognized them as a distinct class: "perpetual inhabitants with diminutive rights."[72] It followed, Winder and Murray argued, that their title to the soil was "a mere right of usufruct and habitation, without power of alienation. By the law of nature, they had not acquired a fixed property capable of being transferred."[73]

Winder and Murray closed by finally turning to the effect of the Proclamation of 1763. There were two possibilities, they contended: "If the Indians are to be regarded as independent sovereign states, then, by the treaty of peace, they became subject to the prerogative legislation of the crown, as a conquered people, in a territory acquired, jure belli [i.e., by the right or law of war], and ceded at the peace. If, on the contrary, this country be regarded as a royal colony, then the crown had a direct power of legislation; or at least the power of prescribing the limits within which grants of land and settlements should be made within the colony."[74] In either case, the Proclamation of 1763 was a valid bar.

Harper Closes as Hope Fades

At least one of the Justices had heard enough. On Tuesday, Justice Story, who had served after Adams as Harper's co-counsel in *Fletcher*, "absented himself" from the courtroom, "whether from indisposition or ill will," Ingersoll, who noted the fact, could not say.[75] That day and the following,

Harper held the floor in reply. When he finished, it was clear that he had failed to carry the Court. George Brydges Rodney noted in his diary, "Several arguments have been made in the S. Court, and a very long one on the subject of the Indian deed granting a large tract of Illinois to certain individuals. The validity of the deed was maintained by Webster and Harper and opposed by Winder and Murray of Ann[a]p[oli]s. The court would not give their opinion but it will doubtless be against the grant."[76]

Many of the Illinois and Wabash shareholders agreed with Rodney's forecast. Ingersoll, eager to realize at least some profit from his investment, pleaded with the Philadelphia committee promptly to issue him an additional share, to which he had expressed his feeling of entitlement for some time, that he might "sell it immediately without waiting for the rise in value, which in truth I never expect to see."[77] The following day he was more desperate still. "The shares are lottery-tickets of a certain marketable value," he wrote. A 1/4 share he had received previously, "worth $125, when given to me, [was] now worth perhaps $300—*no* it is not because I cant [*sic*] sell it having no deed for it. But I don't want to take the risk, I wish to sell for present profits, [as] I calculate on an unfavorable decision."[78] It was too late.

Harper also knew the cause was lost. Before he finished his closing argument on Wednesday, Attorney General Wirt, Treasury Secretary William Crawford, and Secretary of State John Quincy Adams—the latter two of whom were leading presidential contenders—had all pronounced the agreed statement to be "collusive and to agree to facts that could not be proved by evidence."[79] For the Supreme Court to find for Johnson now would be to defy not merely the Senate but three members of the Cabinet. Further, the *Fletcher* taint of suspicious pleading had completely infected *Johnson v. M'Intosh*. A decision in favor of the speculators would revive against the Supreme Court all those allegations of bias and misuse of power to which they had been subjected in 1810.

Under the circumstances, Harper's only hope lay in a continuance. After he finished on Wednesday, Harper "intimated to some of the Judges [his] wish to have a further argument, by which [he] ha[d] no doubt that the case would be strengthened." Three days later, he was at least guardedly optimistic that the Court might go along with this request, reporting to

Philadelphia that the case might "very probably be withheld for further deliberation, till next term, and perhaps for further argument."[80] It was a forlorn hope.

The Court Issues Its Opinion and Undoes Harper's Well-Made Plan

On Thursday, February 27, merely eight days after Harper closed his argument, Marshall delivered the Court's opinion in the case of *Johnson v. M'Intosh*.[81] Harper and Ingersoll can hardly have been surprised at the judgment: the decision of the district court was affirmed. The Proclamation of 1763, the Court wrote, "has been considered, and, we think, with reason, as constituting an . . . objection to the title of the plaintiffs. By that proclamation, the crown . . . strictly forbade all British subjects from making any purchases or settlements whatever, or taking possession of the reserved lands." The present claims were therefore barred. As for the 1779 Virginia Declaratory Act, the Court found it to be "an unequivocal affirmance, on the part of Virginia, of the broad principle which had always been maintained, that the exclusive right to purchase from the Indians resided in the government."[82] Harper had lost on his two principal contentions, and with that, the Illinois and Wabash Land Companies disappeared into history.[83]

Had this been all the Court decided, the case of *Johnson v. M'Intosh* would long since have been forgotten. In addition to finding the claims barred by the proclamation and the Declaratory Act, however, Marshall identified an additional ground for decision: that upon discovery by Europeans, the Indians lost to the discovering sovereign title to the lands they occupied; all that remained to them was an occupancy right, which only the sovereign might acquire. In the Court's words:

> In the establishment of the relationship between [the discoverer and the discovered], the rights of the original inhabitants were, in no instance, entirely disregarded; but were necessarily, to a considerable extent, impaired. They were admitted to be the rightful occupants of the soil, with a legal as well as just claim to retain possession of it, and to use it according to their own discretion; but their rights to

complete sovereignty, as independent nations, were necessarily diminished, and their power to dispose of the soil at their own will, to whomsoever they pleased, was denied by the original fundamental principle, that discovery gave exclusive title to those who made it.[84]

It was this ground—the discovery doctrine—that proved *Johnson*'s most important legacy. In ways the Court did not then appreciate, it would serve to justify the dispossession of indigenous title to lands across the globe. Ironically, it would also play a central role in the greatest crisis ever faced by the Marshall Court.

Where did the discovery doctrine come from? The Court clearly drew on Winder and Murray's *Fletcher*-derived first argument, that "Indians had no right of soil," but this argument, as Webster noted, should have failed because the parties had agreed to Piankashaw ownership and power to sell in the agreed statement of facts. Given that the Senate would have been satisfied with the Court's finding the purchase barred by the Proclamation of 1763, why did Marshall include the discovery doctrine in the *Johnson* opinion? To whom was it directed? What problem was it intended to solve? The answers to these questions are essential to an understanding of the meaning of *Johnson v. M'Intosh*.

CHAPTER 4

Virginia, Kentucky, and the Complex Politics of Early Republican Federalism

Chief Justice Marshall himself anticipated that questions might arise as to why he ventured so far beyond the minimum rationale necessary to support the Court's finding that the Illinois and Wabash purchases were invalid. To forestall such inquiry, he attributed the "degree of attention" that he "bestow[ed] upon this subject" to "the magnitude of the interest in litigation, and the able and elaborate arguments" advanced by Harper, Webster, Winder, and Murray.[1] The true explanation is somewhat more complicated. Marshall's motives were mixed. Like others of his generation, his interests were not entirely divorced from his politics. His decision in *Johnson* reflected his institutional concern for the power of the Supreme Court and his personal concern to secure land grants to Revolutionary War soldiers.

After twenty years of increasing Supreme Court power, John Marshall faced not only a backlash from the states, but also some very real disputes involving Virginia and Kentucky. Related disputes involving unfulfilled promises to Virginia's Revolutionary War veterans threatened to victimize a politically significant and personally (to Marshall) important group. In drafting *Johnson*, he attempted to resolve these problems as well as the Illinois and Wabash claims. His method was the strategic incorporation of obiter dicta: language that sounds authoritative and might be followed as persuasive but that technically has no precedential value.

The Supreme Court Under Fire

Marshall's institutional concern was most immediately grounded in recent state challenges to the Supreme Court's constitutional authority. During the two years that *Johnson v. M'Intosh* sat on the Supreme Court's docket, the Court had become embroiled in a struggle with Virginia over the scope of this authority, a struggle that at times seemed likely to result in the effective elimination of the independence of the federal judiciary. Conflict intensified when a potentially similar dispute arose with Kentucky at the same time.

In the Court's 1803 opinion in *Marbury v. Madison*, Marshall had claimed the power to review acts of Congress and invalidate them as unconstitutional.[2] In 1810, in *Fletcher v. Peck*, by invalidating the Georgia legislature's repeal of the Yazoo grants, Marshall had claimed and exercised the power to do the same to acts of the state legislatures. The exercise of this "judicial review" power was not clearly provided for in the U.S. Constitution, and many believed it to be a dangerous usurpation of power.

Opposition to perceived Supreme Court overreaching became especially heated after 1820. John Marshall had never been popular with Virginia Republicans, and in 1821 the state's simmering antipathy exploded when the Court granted a writ of error in the case of *Cohens v. Virginia*. The *Cohens* case created a dangerous political rift between the Court and powerful Virginians that the *Johnson* opinion would help to close.

Cohens v. Virginia: Virginia against the Court

Cohens involved a challenge to the constitutionality of Virginia's imposition of a fine.[3] In June 1820, six months before Judge Pope issued his pro forma decision in *Johnson v. M'Intosh*, Philip and Mendes Cohen were charged by a Norfolk, Virginia, grand jury with having sold tickets to a national lottery in violation of Virginia law. In September 1820, the Cohens pleaded not guilty. They admitted selling a ticket but argued that they could not be prosecuted under the Virginia act because the sale had been authorized by federal law. The Norfolk borough court found the Cohens guilty and fined them $100 plus costs. The Cohens tried to appeal to the Norfolk County Superior Court but were refused on the ground that "cases of this sort are not subject to revision by any other court of the Commonwealth."[4] Consequently, in October, the Cohens appealed to the Supreme Court of the United States.

The threshold question was whether the Supreme Court had jurisdiction. The Cohens argued that the Court could hear the appeal under Section 25 of the Judiciary Act of 1789, which authorized the Court to review "final judgments" by "the highest [state] court[s]" whenever the state courts determined that an allegedly unconstitutional state statute did not violate the U.S. Constitution.[5] According to the Cohens, the Virginia lottery law was unconstitutional. Because they could not appeal from the Norfolk borough court, they argued, the borough court was effectively the "highest court" in Virginia for the purposes of Section 25 review. The Supreme Court issued a writ of error, and Virginia was ordered to appear.

For the first time, a state had been summoned before the Supreme Court to defend a state criminal law decision rendered by a state trial court. Virginia was outraged. The General Assembly passed two resolutions: the first declared that the Supreme Court "had no rightful authority under the Constitution" to hear the case; the second announced that the state's lawyers would confine their argument "to the question of jurisdiction; and if the jurisdiction of the Court should be sustained, . . . they will consider their duties at an end."[6] If the justices disagreed with Virginia on the question of jurisdiction, in other words, Virginia would refuse to accede to their decision. In February 1821, Philip Barbour and Alexander Smyth appeared before the Court for Virginia and moved to dismiss the writ of error for lack of jurisdiction. In arguing that the Court had no business interfering with Virginia's trial courts, Smyth warned ominously, "The confidence of the people constitutes the real strength of this government. Nothing can so much endanger it as exciting the hostility of the State governments. With them it is to determine how long this government shall endure."[7] Sentiments such as this would eventually, of course, lead Virginia and other states to secede. Chief Justice Marshall rather boldly opted not to be intimidated and denied the motion to dismiss the case for lack of jurisdiction.

With that, the Virginia lawyers withdrew from the case. Rather than have the Commonwealth go unrepresented, the Court drafted Daniel Webster to argue in favor of the state lottery statute. Ultimately, the Court upheld the statute's constitutionality, but this was hardly a sufficient salve. Virginians, feeling the Court had overreached itself, reacted angrily against *Cohens* and the increasing "consolidation" of power in federal hands. *Cohens* was excoriated in the Richmond and Washington press. In June 1821, Marshall wrote that the Court had been "attacked with a virulence superior even to that which was employed" after the Court interpreted the Constitution to allow Congress wide powers in *McCulloch v. Maryland*.[8] Seven months later, Justice Story despaired that "if . . . the Judiciary is to be destroyed, I should be glad to have the decisive blow now struck, while I am young, and can return to the profession and earn an honest livelihood."[9]

Green v. Biddle: Kentucky against the Court

Virginia was not the only state railing against the Court. Two days after Marshall delivered the Court's decision in *Cohens*, Justice Story read its opinion in the case of *Green v. Biddle*, which invalidated a series of "occupying claimant" laws passed by Kentucky between 1797 and 1820 to protect the interests of Kentuckians occupying lands claimed by non-Kentuckians under grants from Virginia, which had governed Kentucky as a county prior to Kentucky's admission to the union in 1792. The 1821 opinion in *Green* was likely intended in part to mollify Virginia after *Cohens*, but at the cost of infuriating Kentucky. In the face of Kentucky's outraged protests, the Court agreed to withdraw the opinion and allow counsel the opportunity to argue *Green* anew the following year.

As it happens, in its second incarnation, *Green* would play an integral role in shaping the Court's opinion in *Johnson v. M'Intosh*. In fact, *Green v. Biddle* was *Johnson*'s companion case, its underlying politics holding the key to understanding the origins of the discovery doctrine. In combination,

Virginia and Kentucky might well have forced a constitutional crisis in 1823. John Marshall would deftly defuse this possibility by employing *Green* and *Johnson* to convert the two potential allies into adversaries. Understanding the *Green* litigation is essential to understanding *Johnson*.

Green v. Biddle arose when the heirs of absentee owner John Green challenged the validity of the occupying claimant laws via an ejectment action filed against an occupant, Richard Biddle, in the Federal Circuit Court for the District of Kentucky. The circuit court's decision was appealed to the Supreme Court. In his opinion for the Court, Justice Story found the occupying claimant laws invalid under the 1789 Virginia-Kentucky compact, which set forth the terms under which Virginia consented to Kentucky's separation from Virginia.[10] Article 3 of the compact provided that "all private rights and interests in lands . . . derived from the laws of Virginia prior to such separation, shall remain valid and secure . . . and shall be determined by the laws" then in force in Virginia. Story found that the challenged Kentucky laws violated this provision.[11]

The *Green* decision threatened to unravel Kentucky's entire land title scheme. Because "the rights of numerous occupants of land in Kentucky . . . would be irrevocably determined by this decision" and counsel had not appeared for Biddle, the Court agreed to grant a rehearing for the February 1822 term.[12]

Kentucky Maneuvers out of Court

To prevail at the case's second appearance before the Court, Kentucky's chief Supreme Court advocate, Henry Clay, determined to obtain in the interim Virginia's assent to the proposition that Justice Story's construction of Article 3 of the Virginia-Kentucky compact was simply wrong. Should Virginia not assent, Clay would urge the establishment of a commission to construe the article. Article 8 of the Virginia-Kentucky compact had provided for the establishment of just such a commission whenever disputes should arise over the meaning of compact terms and provisions. The convening of a commission on the authority of the compact, Clay calculated, would likely appeal to Virginians smarting under the Supreme Court's exercise of jurisdiction in *Cohens*.

In July 1821, the Kentucky General Assembly formally dispatched Clay and George Bibb to Richmond to garner Virginia's support for Kentucky's construction of Article 3 or, in the alternative, for an Article 8 commission to decide the same question. In February 1822, Clay and Bibb appeared before the Virginia legislature and urged the delegates to agree that the occupying claimant laws did not violate the Virginia-Kentucky compact. They were asking a lot: if Virginia supported Kentucky and the Supreme Court upheld the occupying claimant laws, many Virginians would lose their Kentucky investments. Short of this, Clay and Bibb urged a more politically realistic alternative: that the General Assembly agree to establish an Article 8 board of commissioners to decide on the validity of the occupying claimant laws. Playing on the reaction to *Cohens*, Bibb "asked the House whether they would turn [Kentucky] over to the supreme court, for some of whose decisions Kentucky had as little penchant as Virginia could have—and whether it did not become the magnanimity of Virginia to interpose and save them from the host of evils which one decision of the court might bring upon Kentucky."[13] The Supreme Court, it was true, had in *Green* preliminarily ruled against the occupying claimant laws, and this worked to the advantage of many Virginians. But Clay urged that the legislature adhere to principle and disprove sentiment he had heard expressed by "persons who did not know the character of Virginia" that the state would "talk against the decisions of the Supreme Court, when they were against her," but make use of them "when they operated against her sister states." In short, Clay urged, "would it not be better to settle this family quarrel, between parent and child, by the aid of a family tribunal which they had marked out for that purpose, than to leave it to strangers to settle?"[14]

Virginia was not prepared to concede the rights of its absentee land claimants and rejected Kentucky's proposed construction of Article 3. Nevertheless, the legislature was willing to submit the question to an Article 8 commission, signaling to the Supreme Court Virginia's continuing position that important disputes were best kept out of the overreaching federal high court. However, it would do this only on one condition: that the commission be empowered to settle as well an additional question in dispute between the states, involving title to Revolutionary War military bounty lands in the southwestern corner of Kentucky west of the Tennessee

River.[15] It is this dispute that provides the key to *Johnson v. M'Intosh*. In the end, John Marshall would help resolve it in favor of Virginia's Revolutionary War veterans by dispossessing Native America of its title claim to a continent.

The Virginia Militia Bounty Lands Problem

In May 1779, the Virginia legislature had established a land office for the distribution of its "waste and unappropriated" lands, excepting, inter alia, the lands between the Green and Tennessee Rivers, which were reserved as bounty lands for the officers and soldiers of the Virginia line serving in the Continental Army.[16] Two years later, when Virginia's boundary line with North Carolina was run west of the Appalachian Mountains, the legislature discovered that "a considerable part" of the lands intended to be so reserved was in fact in North Carolina and enacted that the lands west of the Tennessee should be substituted for those lands lost by virtue of the survey. At the same time, the benefits of the bounty lands statute were extended to officers serving in state militia units. By agreement between the militia and continental beneficiaries, the lands west of the Tennessee would go to the former, and those east of the Tennessee would go to the latter.[17]

Bounty lands were to be distributed according to a set procedure. First, Virginia would issue the beneficiary a "warrant" indicating the number of acres to which he was entitled based on his rank and term of military service. For example, a noncommissioned militia officer serving a three-year enlistment was entitled to two hundred acres. Armed with the warrant, the beneficiary would then attempt to "locate" lands within the appropriate bounty lands area in an amount equaling the warranted acreage. Once he had identified the lands, the beneficiary would have a description of the lands "entered" on the books of an approved surveyor. This description would be in narrative form and cite prominent local landmarks as boundary indicators. The surveyor would then survey the entered lands. After the survey was complete, the entry and survey would be delivered to the state land office and a "patent" evidencing title issued to the beneficiary. At this point the land would be his.

In October 1783, as the Revolutionary War wound down, the Virginia General Assembly provided that specified officers should appoint two principal surveyors and superintendents for the state and continental lines for the purpose of regulating surveying.[18] In the spring of 1784, the superintendents repaired to Kentucky to inspect the lands reserved for the military. There they found the lands west of the Tennessee, which had been reserved to the militia, in full possession of the Chickasaw Nation. Attempts to rally Kentucky troops to force the Chickasaws to permit access failed, and in January 1785, fearing war with the Chickasaws, Governor Patrick Henry suspended the surveying and taking possession of these lands. The following January, U.S. commissioners made surveying and taking possession impossible when they negotiated a treaty at Hopewell guaranteeing to the Chickasaws their rights to the lands west of the Tennessee.[19]

When the Virginia-Kentucky compact was drafted, the drafting committee attempted to safeguard the interests of the frustrated militia veterans in Article 6, which provided that the "unlocated lands" in Kentucky "appropriated" by Virginia "for military or other services shall be exempt from [Kentucky's] disposition, and . . . subject to be disposed of by [Virginia], according to such appropriation," until May 1, 1792, after which they would be subject to disposition by Kentucky. Prior to May 1, 1792, Virginia issued warrants for services on state establishment for more than a million acres, approximately 10 percent of which were unlocated as of this date.[20] In Virginia's view, a property right in these unlocated lands had passed to its veterans upon the issuance of warrants. Unlocated lands required entry and surveying before patents could be issued; the effect of Article 6 was to require that, after May 1, 1792, militia claimants enter their lands on the books of surveyors licensed by Kentucky. Kentucky viewed the matter differently: the issuance of warrants vested no property right in the grantees, and all lands unlocated after May 1, 1792 were Kentucky's to grant to whomever it chose.

The Treaty of Hopewell's explicit guarantee of the Chickasaws' land rights delayed resolution of this difference in interpretation beyond 1792. Even though Kentucky wanted to distribute and settle lands west of the Tennessee, its citizens could not cross the river as long as the federal government fixed the river as the Chickasaw Nation's eastern boundary. Periodic petitioning of the federal government on behalf of the citizens of the state proved futile. Finally, under threat of expulsion, in October 1818 at Old Town in Mississippi, the Chickasaw Nation signed a treaty with Andrew Jackson and former Kentucky governor Isaac Shelby relinquishing their title to the lands west of the Tennessee.[21] The question of who owned these lands now became live.

To forestall an expected land rush by Kentucky claimants, two months after the Old Town treaty was signed the Kentucky legislature passed an act prohibiting any entry or survey from being made on any of the newly ceded lands.[22] In February 1820, the legislature authorized the appointment of a public superintendent to survey the lands west of the Tennessee,[23] and William T. Henderson, who was named to this post, proceeded to lay out townships and sections to facilitate location. In December 1820, Virginia's designated surveyor, William Croghan, was permitted to survey "without delay" those military entries that had been made prior to May 1, 1792, and directed to show "where and how" they interfered with Henderson's townships and sections. The Kentucky legislature allotted eleven months to the completion of this task and informed claimants that if they failed to file a certificate of survey with the Kentucky land office by January 1, 1823, they would forfeit their lands to the state.[24] In December 1821, the Kentucky legislature extended the period for the completion of the Virginia surveys by one year, until December 1, 1822.[25] Two days later, the governor approved a law directing the register of the land office to commence sales of the lands west of the Tennessee in September 1822; military lands entered prior to May 1, 1792, were to be excluded only if claimants served on the register entries or surveys for those lands.[26] On February 6, Henry Clay and George Bibb arrived in Richmond.

A select committee appointed by the Virginia legislature in the wake of Clay's address to evaluate the impact of these various Kentucky laws and the validity of the Virginia militia claims determined that two potential impediments lay in the militia claimants' path. The claimants' case against Kentucky depended on findings that (1) a property right had vested in the veterans when the warrants were issued, and (2) Article 6 did not extinguish this right but merely shifted to Kentucky surveyors the responsibility for entering and surveying. The first requirement occasioned extensive discussion in the committee report. Kentucky had made two principal arguments. First, Kentucky contended that real property rights vested not when warrants were issued, but when descriptions were entered on the surveyor's books. The committee dismissed this argument as based on a misunderstanding of Virginia's land grant procedures. Second, Kentucky argued that, in any event, Virginia could convey to its grantees no interest in Indian lands because these lands were not Virginia's to grant. The committee dismissed this argument by declaring that "the anomalous relation" between the tribes and the "government, within whose limits they abide, has never been regarded as presenting any other than a temporary impediment, to the execution of the contracts between the government and its citizens, for the lands, which they inhabit" and that "locations within the Indian boundary, if authorised, by the government, have been held to give inchoate rights, to be perfected, when the Indian title should be extinguished."[27] Stated differently, where the state had, in the past, granted Indian lands to its citizens, the grants had always been enforced once the Indians were gone.

Marshall's Interest in the Plight of the Militia Veterans

John Marshall undoubtedly followed these proceedings with great interest. He was no stranger, of course, to the issues raised by the occupying claimant laws, which had been before the Court in *Green v. Biddle*. Nor was he a stranger to the issues raised by Kentucky's assertion of authority over the militia lands. Marshall had served as an officer in the continental line, and as such, was a beneficiary of the Virginia legislature's grant of lands in the military district north of the Ohio and between the Green and Tennessee Rivers. He was well acquainted with the plight of the militia warrant holders, including the rather dismal hand they had been dealt by error at the time of the 1784 Virginia cession: Virginia had originally intended that enough lands be reserved from the cession of its western lands to Congress to satisfy the claims of Virginia soldiers in state and continental service left unsatisfied by the lands in Kentucky; when the cession was communicated to Congress, however, the militia claimants were erroneously omitted from the reservation. Marshall was openly sympathetic. In March 1822, the day the *Richmond Enquirer* published the last installment of the select committee's report, Marshall delivered the Supreme Court's opinion in *Hoofnagle v. Anderson* upholding the right of the transferee of a Virginia state militia warrant grantee to Ohio lands for which the grantee had erroneously received an 1804 patent.[28]

Marshall had other reasons for familiarity. Thomas Marshall, John Marshall's father, had served as superintendent of the militia claims and led the aborted surveying expedition to the Chickasaw country in 1784. In 1792, John Marshall's brother, James Marshall, was a leading member of the Kentucky convention elected to consider the proposed terms of separation from Virginia.[29] In 1789, John Marshall himself, then a member of the Virginia House of Delegates, was a member of the committee assigned to prepare these terms; they ultimately became the Virginia-Kentucky compact. He almost certainly played the major role in drafting that document, including Article 6, which was intended to safeguard the interests of the militia.[30] He can hardly have been disinterested in the dispute between Virginia and Kentucky over how that article should now be interpreted.

John Marshall was also well acquainted with the question of the impact on the militia claims of Virginia's failure to extinguish the Chickasaw title prior to issuing warrants. The federal government had consistently denied the validity of such claims, perhaps the strongest expression of this position having been articulated by Marshall's cousin, Thomas Jefferson, when serving as secretary of state in 1791: "The Indians have a right to the occupation of their Lands independent of the States within whose chartered lines they happen to be," Jefferson wrote, and "until they cede them by Treaty or other transaction equivalent to the Treaty, no act of a State can give a right to such Lands."[31] Moreover, the very question of the effect of the Chickasaw claim on the militia grants had been considered by the Virginia Court of Appeals that same year, 1791, in a case brought by Thomas Marshall on behalf of the militia, and the court had offered only a modest variation on Jefferson's rule. In 1780, a year before the lands west of the Tennessee were appropriated to the military district, George Rogers Clark made several entries in the area on warrants issued for "waste and unappropriated land" pursuant to Virginia's 1779 Land Office Act. In June 1784, two surveys were made for Clark on the authority of these warrants, each for approximately 37,000 acres. In January 1786, after Clark's claim became known, the superintendents of the Virginia line challenged his title. Litigation ensued in the Supreme Court for the District of Kentucky, then still a part of Virginia. The Kentucky court being "in doubt" on various questions arising from the case and the judges having an interest in its outcome, the case was sent to the Virginia Court of Appeals, which decided it in November 1791.

Seven questions were presented to the Virginia court in *Marshall v. Clark*. In the second, the court was asked to determine whether, if Indians still held title to the lands west of the Tennessee, the lands could be considered "waste and unappropriated" under the Land Office Act and therefore open to claim by warrant. Edmund Pendleton, writing for the court, decided that whether the tribes still held title "is of no consequence in this dispute between citizens claiming under the commonwealth." The "title of the Indian tribes" was "to be extinguished by government, either by purchase or conquest; and when that was done, it enured to the benefit of the citizen, who had previously acquired a title from the crown."[32] The warrant recipient had a claim enforceable against the entity granting the warrant, in this case Virginia, which after all had granted the warrant knowing that the lands were Indian lands. By extension, the warrant recipient had a claim good against later Virginia grantees. Clark's title was upheld.

The select committee plainly relied on *Marshall v. Clark* in averring that "locations within the Indian boundary, if authorised, by the government, have been held to give inchoate [i.e., imperfectly formed] rights, to be perfected, when the Indian title should be extinguished." As Marshall no doubt realized on reading the committee's report, however, this reliance was problematic. In *Marshall v. Clark*, both parties claimed their lands under the same source: Virginia. Competing claimants to lands west of the Tennessee would claim under grants from different states. The right protected in *Marshall v. Clark* was a contract right, enforceable against Virginia and other Virginia grantees. Nothing in *Marshall v. Clark*—or in the select committee's report—provided a legal basis for holding that the issuance of the military warrants had vested a *property* right in the veterans enforceable against *Kentucky grantees*. Stated differently, if Kentucky distributed the lands west of the Tennessee, a frustrated Virginia warrant holder might sue

Virginia for breach of contract but would have no legal basis for enforcing a land claim against Kentucky or its grantees.

Nor had the U.S. Supreme Court definitively resolved this question. The Court had considered the interest conveyed by a state's grant of Indian lands only once, in *Fletcher v. Peck*, but the Court's brief conclusion—that Indian title was not "absolutely repugnant to" ownership of the underlying title to the land on the part of the state or its grantee—had been unaccompanied by any discussion and had provoked dissent from Justice Johnson, who opined that the state's interest in Indian lands "amounted to nothing more than a mere possibility." Moreover, Congress had refused to interpret *Fletcher* as establishing a state's ownership of Indian lands.[33]

Had it not been for the militia claims question, Virginia would almost certainly have abandoned its principles and left the fate of the occupying claimant laws to the Supreme Court, which had already rejected them and was unlikely to reverse its judgment on the strength of Clay's forthcoming reargument. The militia claims, however, complicated matters, primarily because it was not clear, for the foregoing reasons, that they would survive judicial challenge.

Following Clay's presentation, the Virginia legislature resolved that "under the provisions of the compact," it was "incumbent on Kentucky to make provision by law for the satisfaction of" the militia claims.[34] On March 2, the legislature dispatched Benjamin Watkins Leigh to Frankfort to ask the Kentucky legislature to do just that. Should the Kentucky General Assembly refuse to pass laws to protect the militia claimants, Leigh was to negotiate the organization of an Article 8 board of commissioners with authority to decide the question.[35]

The Virginia-Kentucky Commission Debates

Clay and Bibb, having failed in their immediate object, traveled to Washington and appeared before the Supreme Court to reargue *Green v. Biddle*. Following reargument, the Court announced it would withhold its opinion until the following term.[36] The occupying claimants issue was thus left open, and Leigh left Richmond for Kentucky.

Leigh arrived in Frankfort the first week of May, and on May 17 appeared before Kentucky's General Assembly, governor, executive officers, and judges of the state and federal courts. He spoke, a "very ingenious, impressive, and argumentative speech," for three hours and fifteen minutes.[37] The Kentucky legislature was no more prepared to yield on the militia lands question than Virginia had been on the question of the validity of the occupying claimant laws. Clay was tasked to arrange with Leigh the organization of an Article 8 board of commissioners. On June 5, they agreed that a board of six commissioners—two appointed by each state, two by the commissioners themselves—should meet in Washington on the fourth Monday in January 1823, or as soon thereafter as possible, to resolve the occupying claimants and militia claims issues before the Supreme Court ruled in *Green v. Biddle*. In addition, Leigh agreed that if the commissioners found in favor of Kentucky on the militia lands question, Virginia would guarantee that the warrant holders would "submit to and abide by the decision" and indemnify Kentucky against any judicial claims the warrant holders might subsequently assert.[38] The Kentucky General Assembly approved these terms, and in November, the legislature elected Hugh Lawson White of Tennessee and Judge Jacob Burnett of Ohio its commissioners and Clay and Judge John Rowan counsel for the state to appear before the board.[39]

Leigh, meanwhile, returned to Richmond to present the plan for the board to the Virginia General Assembly. He arrived to find the capital angry at Kentucky's refusal to recognize the militia claimants' rights. "A Revolutionary Soldier," writing in the October 22, 1822, *Richmond Enquirer*, urged that given the fact that it was "a highly benefitted part of Virginia when" the militia grants were made, Kentucky "ought to be the last to endeavour to benefit and enrich itself by those revolutionary claims, through the ignorance or the neglect of the soldier, much less the want of the extinguishment of the Indian title."[40] Despite the popular resentment, in December the Virginia House of Delegates ratified the convention agreement.[41] When the ratification bill reached the Senate, however, it faced serious opposition. The prime sticking point was Leigh's guarantee that the warrant holders would submit to the commission's decision and that Virginia would indemnify Kentucky if they did not. On January 1, with the House in attendance, Leigh addressed the Senate for two and a half hours. The debate over the guarantee became caught up in the ongoing battle over the supremacy of the federal judiciary. Leigh argued that the legislature might as well agree to the guarantee because if the commission decided against the militia claimants, their only legal recourse would be in the Kentucky courts, and there they were sure to lose.[42] A narrow majority, led by Henry St. George Tucker, disagreed: the federal courts could hear these claims, and despite Virginia's hostility to these courts, they were preferable to "some ephemeral tribunal."[43] Tucker carried the day, and the Senate returned the bill to the House with the guarantee removed.[44]

Two weeks later, the House sent it back with the guarantee restored.[45] On January 20, the Senate again rejected the guarantee.[46] "The Kentucky compromise is all blown," Francis Walker Gilmer wrote. "Tucker has overthrown . . . Leigh horse, foot & dragoon: not by superior abilities, but because L's guaranty was a hooker."[47] In an unsuccessful attempt to break the impasse, the House and Senate referred the bill to a conference committee.[48] This failed, too. On January 28 the House again declared its commitment to the guarantee.[49] Two days later the Senate voted to stick to its own position.[50] On February 7, the House voted one last time in favor of the guarantee, and the convention bill was dead.[51]

The Failure of the Virginia-Kentucky Compromise Invites Judicial Resolution Via *Green* and *Johnson*

Henry Clay had arrived in Washington on January 26, Judge Burnett two days later.[52] The Supreme Court opened its February 1823 term on February 3, and on February 6, Clay, hoping to gain whatever advantage yet remained, "communicated to the Court the Convention between Virginia and Kentucky respecting the Occupying Claimant Law of the latter State."[53] The convention bill died the following day, and on February 27, Justice Washington delivered the Court's opinion in *Green v. Biddle*, again expressly declaring the Kentucky occupying claimant laws to be invalid. Clay's colleague John Rowan was livid, noting that the "opinion was delivered towards the end of the term and about the same time it was ascertained that Virginia would not affirm the arrangements which she had, by her authorised agent, made with Kentucky, for the final adjustment of those interesting topics, by a tribunal of the compact. Whether Virginia found a motive for the strange and unprecedented capriciousness of her conduct in this particular, in the anticipation of what would be the opinion of the court," Rowan added, was "not for [him] to conjecture."[54]

One day after the Court issued the *Green* opinion, Chief Justice Marshall delivered the Court's opinion in *Johnson v. M'Intosh*, settling once and for all, by way of the Indian title discussion, the question of the rights of state grantees in lands conveyed before the extinguishment of the Indian title. Under the discovery doctrine, the discovering sovereign acquired title to all discovered lands, and Virginia had inherited this title to pass on to its militia veterans despite the Chickasaw occupation. In effect, via *Green* and *Johnson*, the circle had been closed on three-quarters of the Virginia-Kentucky controversy: the occupying claimant laws were invalid, and the militia claims could not be denied based on the conflicting tribal claim. All that remained in dispute between the states was the meaning of the protective language in Article 6 of the Virginia-Kentucky compact, which authorized Kentucky to "dispose of" unlocated militia lands after May 1, 1792, and the Court's open siding with Virginia in *Green* and *Johnson* left little doubt how Kentucky would fare in litigation on that issue. Kentucky was forced to the wall.

John Marshall intended *Johnson v. M'Intosh* concurrently to settle both the Illinois and Wabash Companies' claim and the problem created by Virginia's grant of military bounties to lands still in possession of the Chickasaws. To reach both controversies, Marshall had to convert *Johnson* from a case about the effect of the Proclamation of 1763 on pre–Revolutionary War Indian land purchases into a case covering as well the validity of Revolutionary War–era state land grants. Conversion of this sort typified his approach to adjudication, or at least so his enemies claimed. Three months after the chief justice delivered the *Johnson* opinion, Thomas Jefferson complained to Justice William Johnson, "This practice of Judge Marshall, of travelling out of his case to prescribe what the law would be in a moot case not before the court, is very irregular and very censurable." The problem, as Jefferson saw it, was that Marshall's "travelling" was so subtle as to blur the line between holding and obiter dicta, between that which must be followed as precedential and that which might be followed as persuasive. The constitutional discussion in *Marbury v. Madison*, for example, Jefferson reminded Johnson, was "merely an *obiter* dissertation of the Chief Justice," yet the case was "continually cited by bench and bar, as if it were settled law."[55]

Johnson v. M'Intosh well illustrates the process by which John Marshall integrated holding and obiter dicta to make palatable his use of one case to resolve another. At the same time, the opinion reveals the weakness in the method. When the Court sought to resolve matters not directly before it, it proceeded without benefit of argument. Given their own limited time and resources, the justices could not possibly hope to understand relevant law and the potential consequences of various decisions as well as they might had counsel developed these themes in litigation. Without such understanding, the Court's resolution might well be materially deficient. To understand how this played out in *Johnson*, one must turn to the text of the opinion itself.

CHAPTER 5

The Opinion

John Marshall's goal in drafting *Johnson* was to deny the Illinois and Wabash claims and lay the groundwork for the successful resolution of the claims of the Virginia militia grantees and their transferees. His judgment on the Proclamation of 1763 challenge would take care of the former but do nothing to help resolve the latter. Protecting the Virginia militia grantees required establishing that by its grants Virginia had actually conveyed a property right that would oblige Kentucky to recognize the grantees' claims to land. This required first establishing that Virginia itself possessed a right that it could convey. It may be recalled that the British Crown had claimed a "preemption" right to lands west of the Proclamation of 1763 line: an exclusive right to purchase those lands, whenever the Indians were willing to sell. Virginia's right had to be something more. If Virginia had conveyed to the militia grantees an exclusive right to purchase lands and Kentucky had chosen to ignore the preemption right and distribute the lands itself, the militia grantees would have had no legal remedy against Kentucky. A state-granted preemption right was enforceable only against other claimants within the state. Marshall's challenge was to establish that Virginia had actually owned the Chickasaw lands.

Under the English common law of real property (i.e., land), the most complete form of ownership was ownership "in fee simple." Owners of land in fee simple held their land until they or their heirs chose to relinquish it. The land was freely alienable (meaning it could be sold or given away) and inheritable. Fee simple ownership ordinarily included the right to possess and use the land, however, and this would prove the complication in the Chickasaw case. If he were somehow to assign Virginia fee simple ownership of the Chickasaw lands, how could he reconcile that with the fact that the Chickasaws continued to live there long after Virginia issued the militia warrants, particularly with their land rights having been recognized by the national government in the Treaty of Hopewell? Moreover, Marshall could not simply assert that Virginia had such an ownership right; he would have to provide some authority for it. In the end, he opted to recognize Virginia's fee right and ground that right in history. However, the history he chose was of dubious reliability and relevance. Under close scrutiny, in the light of the real history of land grants by states and the United States, the shortcomings of the fee title portion of the discovery doctrine are starkly apparent.

Marshall Expands the Question Presented and Adds a Title Component to Preemption

"When conversing with Marshall," Jefferson reportedly said, "I never admit anything. So sure as you admit any position to be good, no matter how remote from the conclusion he seeks to establish, you are gone."[1] This was the method by which Marshall brought *Johnson v. M'Intosh* around to a resolution of the Virginia militia claims. From the first, the opinion was an exercise in expansion, often by omission and implication, from apparently harmless initial premises.

The key expansion Marshall worked at the outset was to convert the case from one about pre–Revolutionary War Indian land transactions to one about post–Revolutionary War Indian land transactions. This was essential, because a decision that the Illinois and Wabash purchases were invalid under late colonial English law would not have established the legitimacy of the claims of veterans receiving grants from Virginia after independence was won and new laws came into play. He did this in the following way. "The plaintiffs in this cause claim the land, in their declaration mentioned," Marshall began, "under two grants, purporting to be made, the first in 1773, and the last in 1775, by the chiefs of certain Indian tribes, constituting the Illinois and Piankeshaw nations; and the question is," he declared, "whether this title can be recognised in the Courts of the United States?" By admitting the relevance of the Illinois grant, the Court quietly announced that its holding would not be confined in its application to the Wabash purchase, a circumstance that would not have disappointed Robert Goodloe Harper. Marshall's framing of the question presented was a different matter. The question pleaded had been, in essence, whether the Companies' title would have been recognized in the courts of Great Britain at the time of transacting, and, if so, whether the courts of the United States were obliged to recognize it in 1823. The shorter formulation employed by Marshall, though not necessarily incompatible with this, effectively worked an abandonment of the first analytical clause in favor of the second. The case would not necessarily be about British law in 1775, but would necessarily consider U.S. law since the Revolution. Having thus stated the question, Marshall next acknowledged the agreed statement of facts, then accorded it its intended effect—to narrow the Court's focus—but in a way unintended by Harper. "The facts," Marshall wrote, "as stated in the case agreed, show the authority of the chiefs who executed this conveyance, so far as it could be given by their own people; and likewise show, that the particular tribes for whom these chiefs acted were in rightful possession of the land they sold." As discussed above, the parties' stipulated facts provided that the tribes were not merely "in rightful possession" but the absolute owners of the lands. Thus, again, although Marshall's formulation was not necessarily incompatible with the agreed statement, by omission he steered the opinion away from the case as pleaded. Then he restated the question: "The inquiry, therefore, is, in great measure, confined to the power of Indians to give, and of private individuals to receive, a title which can be sustained in the Courts of this country."[2]

This second formulation of the question pleaded reiterated the Court's intent to disregard the legal question of whether the purchase was valid when made, and then, by use of the present tense, expanded the relevant time period. As initially stated by the Court, the question was whether the titles conveyed in 1773 and 1775 (the relevant time period) could be recognized by the courts (the legal question) in 1823. As now reformulated, the question was whether in 1823 Indians could give, and individuals receive, a title that could then be so recognized. By means of this second framing, Marshall converted *Johnson* into a case about the validity of *post–Revolutionary War* Indian land transactions.

There was a risk to expanding the opinion to cover contemporaneous transactions. The perceived unjust treatment accorded the Indians increasingly distressed many persons, particularly in the New England states. To distance himself from this debate, Marshall paused after his reformulation of the question to announce that his decision would depend in part on positive law, thus laying the groundwork for a wholesale transfer of the blame for any new perceived injustice to the legislative and executive branches. In Marshall's words:

> As the right of society, to prescribe those rules by which property may be acquired and preserved is not, and cannot be drawn into question; as the title to lands, especially, is and must be admitted to depend entirely on the law of the nation in which they lie; it will be necessary, in pursuing this inquiry, to examine, not singly those principles of abstract justice, which the Creator of all things has impressed on the mind of his creature man, and which are admitted to regulate, in a great degree, the rights of civilized nations, whose perfect independence is acknowledged; but *those principles also which our own government has adopted in the particular case, and given us as the rule for our decision.*[3]

Having thus suggested the source of the rule, Marshall next stated and applied it. First, he posited that the preemption right, which Congress asserted in the Trade and Intercourse Act, had vested in the various European sovereigns upon their discovery of the continent:

> On the discovery of this immense continent, the great nations of Europe were eager to appropriate to themselves so much of it as they could respectively acquire. Its vast extent offered an ample field

to the ambition and enterprise of all; and the character and religion of its inhabitants afforded an apology for considering them as a people over whom the superior genius of Europe might claim an ascendancy. The potentates of the old world found no difficulty in convincing themselves that they made ample compensation to the inhabitants of the new, by bestowing on them civilization and Christianity, in exchange for unlimited independence.

But, as they were all in pursuit of nearly the same object, it was necessary, in order to avoid conflicting settlements, and consequent war with each other, to establish a principle, which all should acknowledge as the law by which the right of acquisition, which they all asserted, should be regulated as between themselves. This principle was, that discovery gave title to the government by whose subjects, or by whose authority, it was made, against all other European governments, which title might be consummated by possession.[4]

Preemption historically had meant no more than the exclusive right to engage in a particular purchase transaction. The preemption right had not carried with it title to the land to which the right was claimed. Marshall's language—"that discovery gave *title* to the government by whose subjects . . . it was made, . . . which title might be consummated by possession," thus worked a significant, if subtle, expansion, in the same way that his restatement of the question presented had drawn the discussion forward temporally.

Next, having fashioned a title component to the preemption right, Marshall underscored that the right was exclusive. "The exclusion of all other Europeans," he wrote, "necessarily gave to the nation making the discovery the sole right of acquiring the soil from the natives, and establishing settlements upon it. It was a right with which no Europeans could interfere. It was a right which all asserted for themselves, and to the assertion of which, by others, all assented." Relations "between the discoverer and the natives, were to be regulated by themselves. The rights thus acquired being exclusive, no other power could interpose between them."[5]

Exclusivity necessarily resulted in the impairment of Indian real property rights. The Indians "were admitted to be the rightful *occupants* of the soil, with a legal as well as just claim to retain *possession* of it, and to *use* it according to their own discretion; but their rights to complete sovereignty, as independent nations, were necessarily diminished, and their power to dispose of the soil at their own will, to whomsoever they pleased, was denied by the original fundamental principle, that discovery gave exclusive *title* to those who made it."[6] Having determined that the positive law of the discovering sovereign fixed the property rights of the Indians in the lands discovered, Marshall thus determined that under this law, the Indians were admitted to be "the rightful occupants of the soil," with a legal claim to possession and use, but that their right to dispose of the soil was diminished by the principle that discovery gave exclusive title to the discoverer. That numerous colonial statutes had "diminished" their right to dispose of the soil by requiring that purchasers of Indian lands be licensed had never been disputed, and Marshall might simply have accorded this restriction on sale a common law status and thereby decided the case without reference to the locus of title. The discussion of the preemption right enabled Marshall to advance his views on the property interest held by Indians subsequent to discovery.

The rule thus declared—that Indians had merely occupancy rights—led the Court to within two steps of resolution of the militia claims question. The first of these steps was to establish that Great Britain had claimed the right to grant Indian lands; the second was to show that Virginia had inherited this right.

Marshall Decides That Great Britain Claimed the Right to Grant Fee Title to Indian Lands

The first step was hardly uncontroversial. "While the different nations of Europe respected the right of the natives, as occupants," Marshall wrote, "they asserted the ultimate dominion to be in themselves; and *claimed and exercised, as a consequence of this ultimate dominion, a power to grant the soil, while yet in possession of the natives. These grants have been understood by all, to convey a title to the grantees, subject only to the Indian right of occupancy.*"[7] These propositions were not nearly so generally conceded as Marshall's language suggested.[8] Jefferson had expressed doubts as to the British Crown's purported exercise of the power to grant Indian lands in his *Notes on the State of Virginia*. "That the lands of this country were taken from [the Indians] by conquest," he wrote, "is not so general a truth as is supposed. I find in our historians and records, repeated proofs of purchase, which cover a considerable part of the lower country; and many more would doubtless be found on further search."[9] St. George Tucker echoed this perception in his edition of Blackstone's *Commentaries*, first published in 1803. "How the lands thus granted by the authority of the government of England were acquired [by the Crown], no authentic documents, that the editor has had access to, ascertain," he wrote, but Jefferson intimates they were not claimed by conquest. Moreover, Tucker observed, even "in the earliest times of our settlement," the assembly passed title to Indian lands only "*if the lands prayed for were already cleared of the Indian title.*"[10] Many in Congress shared this view. For example, in 1795, in urging rejection of a claim to Indian lands in western North Carolina based on an alleged state grant, Elias Boudinot of New Jersey commented, "The Crown of Britain had never pretended to any right of this kind, nor ever thought it had a title to lands till they were first purchased from the Indians," and a majority of his colleagues in both houses agreed.[11]

Certainly aware of this alternative history, Marshall felt compelled to defend his assertion. In the next twelve paragraphs of the opinion, he recited his own history of the colonization of North America, focusing on events and acts reinforcing his contention that the European discoverers considered themselves empowered to grant lands still in possession of the Indians. It may seem remarkable that Marshall was able to compose such a history in the eight days he had between the close of argument and the issuance of the opinion. A review of the information presented in these twelve paragraphs leaves the impression that in preparing them Marshall engaged in exhaustive research. In fact, he borrowed almost all of his history from an eight-hundred-page tome that had been panned by critics when it was first published in Philadelphia in 1804: volume 1 in an eventual five-volume series entitled *The Life of George Washington*, by John Marshall.[12] Marshall had taken on the Washington biography, his only literary work, at the urging of Washington's nephew, Associate Justice Bushrod

Washington. He now imported whole paragraphs from the introductory volume in the series to form this portion of the *Johnson* opinion, linked by sentences reiterating his conclusion that such grants were valid.[13] "The history of America, from its discovery to the present day, proves, we think, the universal recognition of these principles," the section began. Subsequent reiterative conjunctions included: "No one of the powers of Europe gave its full assent to this principle, more unequivocally than England"; "Thus asserting a right to take possession, notwithstanding the occupancy of the natives"; "Thus has our whole country been granted by the crown, while in the occupation of the Indians."[14]

For authority, Marshall pulled from the first volume in his Washington biography the terms and his interpretation of the legal significance of various European charters. The charter quotations themselves are unobjectionable, as a review of any standard charter compilation makes clear. Less clear is the reliability of his interpretation of the contemporaneous legal import of these documents. To understand why there is cause for concern, one need look no further than Marshall's sources.

Marshall had been moved, he wrote, to devote volume 1 of *The Life of George Washington* to the colonial period by a desire to acquaint readers "with the genius, character, and resources of the people about to engage in" the Revolutionary War, a subject that would occupy volumes 2 through 4. The dedication of an entire volume to the colonial era "appeared the more necessary," Marshall informed his readers, "as that period is but little known to ourselves."[15]

Despite his seemingly good intentions, Marshall was not up to the task of shedding much light on the colonial era. The problem was that primary source materials for "the complete execution of such a work" were "not to be found in America." Even if they had been, he lamented, "neither the impatience of the public, nor the situation of the author," would allow him to undertake the research needed to find them. Consequently, Marshall's history was a patchwork compilation of passages imported from secondary materials.[16] For Massachusetts and New Hampshire, Marshall relied on Jeremy Belknap's *The History of New-Hampshire* (1784–92), Thomas Hutchinson's *The History of the Colony of Massachusetts Bay* (1760–68), George Richard Minot's *Continuation of the History of the Province of Massachusetts Bay, from the Year 1748* (1798–1803), and William Robertson's *History of America* (1777). For New York, he looked to William Smith's *The History of the Province of New-York* (1757). For Virginia, he borrowed from William Robertson, William Stith's *The History of the First Discovery and Settlement of Virginia* (1747) and Robert Beverley's *The History of the Present State of Virginia* (1705). For the most southern colonies, Marshall relied on Alexander Hewatt's *An Historical Account of the Rise and Progress of the Colonies of South Carolina and Georgia* (1779). For the colonies as a whole, at least to the reign of William and Mary, Marshall relied on George Chalmers's *Political Annals of the Present United Colonies* (1780). Although these authors, unlike Marshall, made use of primary materials, only one, Chalmers, had had access to British colonial records. And Chalmers had made no effort either to identify or trace the legal consequences of discovery. Thus, the reliability of these authors as guides to the explication of these consequences is questionable.

It bears repeating that, as evidenced by his preface to volume 1, John Marshall knew that these sources were methodologically deficient at the time he issued the opinion. Moreover, he clearly knew that alternative histories, including Jefferson's *Notes on the State of Virginia*, were available. Ultimately, these two factors would facilitate his effectively repudiating his own historical account a decade later in *Worcester v. Georgia*. For the present, Marshall had no interest in considering alternatives to his history. His aim was to present evidence in support of his principal conclusions, which were that "all the nations of Europe, who have acquired territory on this continent, have asserted in themselves, and have recognized in others, the exclusive right of the discoverer to appropriate the lands occupied by Indians," and that the sovereigns of Europe had granted lands still in possession of Indians.[17]

Marshall Decides That Virginia Inherited Great Britain's Right to Grant Fee Title to Indian Lands

After reciting his history of British colonial policy, Marshall brought the question squarely to the militia claims dispute: "Have *the American states* rejected or adopted this principle?"[18] Again, the terminology illuminates the underlying purpose: the "American states" included not merely the United States, but Virginia in its individual capacity. Of course, whether the American states had rejected or adopted the principle was irrelevant to the questions of whether the pre-independence Wabash purchase was valid when made and whether the Court, if it was, had any obligation to recognize it.

Four paragraphs followed in which Marshall set forth episodes of the post-independence history of these states designed to demonstrate that they had indeed considered themselves empowered to grant Indian lands by virtue of title acquired through discovery. The first resolved the militia claims question, the second and third reinforced this resolution, and the fourth attempted to justify it by placing it in an international context. In the first, and most important, of these paragraphs, Marshall wrote that, since the Treaty of Paris, "*it has never been doubted, that either the United States, or the several states, had a clear title to all the lands described within the boundary lines described in the treaty*, subject only to the Indian right of occupancy, and that the exclusive right to extinguish that right, was vested in that government which might constitutionally exercise it."[19] This proposition depended on the British having claimed that right, and, as discussed above, this was questionable at best.

Even more questionable was whether, assuming the British had claimed title to Indian lands in 1783, the United States had done so then and in the years following. This was the weakest link in the chain connecting *Johnson* to the Virginia militia claims. Understanding why requires some digression.

First, it is important to understand that the question of the nature of the U.S. interest in Indian lands became academic soon after independence was won because the national government adopted a policy of purchasing tribal lands rather than asserting a claim to title and then enforcing it without compensation. The Continental Congress made two abortive attempts to claim Indian lands by right of conquest. At Fort Stanwix in October 1784, federal treaty commissioner Richard Butler asserted title to many of the lands of the Six Nations, pursuant to the theory, as explained to the latter, that "the King of Great Britain ceded to the United States *the whole*, [and] by the right of conquest they might *claim the whole*."[20] In the same spirit, at Fort McIntosh on the Ohio, on January 21, 1785, commissioners Butler,

Arthur Lee, and George Rogers Clark, in "allotting" land to the Wyandots and Delawares, told them: "We claim the country by conquest; and are to give not to receive."[21] Soon faced with growing tribal disaffection, however, on May 17, 1786, Congress disbanded the treaty commissions and on August 7 established northern and southern districts with a superintendent in each responsible for carrying out congressional instructions relative to the Indians and answerable to Congress through the secretary of war.

In February 1787, the Continental Congress issued instructions to the superintendents informing them that "the United States are fixed in their determination that justice and public faith shall be the basis of all their transactions with the Indians."[22] In practice, this meant that Indian lands would henceforth be acquired only by purchase. Congress so fully repudiated the conquest theory that it ordered new treaties executed to provide compensation for lands already seized. On January 9, 1789, two such treaties were signed, the first by the Wyandots and other western tribes accepting consideration for the lands ceded at Fort McIntosh, the second by the representatives of the Six Nations (except the Mohawks) doing the same for the lands ceded at Fort Stanwix.[23] In 1790, the first federal Trade and Intercourse Act expressly made the preemption right exclusive of both the states and unauthorized individuals: only the United States might purchase Indian lands. In consequence of this history, no question was ever raised concerning either the title the United States had acquired by virtue of discovery, the right of the United States to grant lands to which the Indian title had not been purchased, or the title that might thereby have passed.

As far as the several states were concerned, the matter was somewhat more complicated. After the Treaty of Paris but before the adoption of the Constitution and passage of the first Trade and Intercourse Act, several states claimed and exercised a right to grant Indian lands to individuals. The theory behind the assertion of this right varied from state to state. In Virginia and Georgia, for example, the legislature declared the Indian lands vacant and therefore subject to public distribution; in North Carolina, the legislature declared the lands conquered. When the title conveyed by these grants came into question in state court actions, the deciding state courts reached essentially the same conclusion: that the grants had created contract rights enforceable against other grantees from the same state. The Virginia court, as noted, found such grants valid in a claim by one commonwealth grantee against another, but went no further. The Tennessee court, which had jurisdiction over the lands conveyed by North Carolina, similarly held that "citizens of, and claiming lands under the same government, are estopped to" deny that government's right to grant Indian lands.[24]

Problems arose, however, when states granted Indian lands to individuals and the federal government subsequently guaranteed the same lands to the tribes by treaty. When the state grantees in these cases petitioned Congress for compensation, the House and Senate repeatedly denied their claims. The North Carolina grants provoked the greatest discussion. On May 17, 1783, North Carolina had passed a law extending its western boundary to the Mississippi, declaring the Indian title to lands within this boundary conquered and thereby forfeit to the state and opening a land office for entering and surveying all ungranted lands, excepting certain lands expressly reserved to the Indians and a military district. On November 28, 1785, federal treaty commissioners executed at Hopewell a treaty reserving to the Indians many of the lands entered and surveyed under the 1783 North Carolina act, as well as a part of the military district established by that act. In the face of a North Carolina Senate resolution expressing "utmost horror" at this arrangement, Congress unsuccessfully attempted to negotiate a more favorable tribal cession. On November 21, 1789, the same day North Carolina ratified the Constitution and joined the Union, Congress ratified the Treaty of Hopewell.[25] The following month, on December 22, 1789, North Carolina, which had continued to guarantee to its otherwise abandoned grantees title to their lands, ceded its western lands to the United States, on condition that all entries and grants made "agreeable to law" within the ceded lands "should have the same force and effect as if such cession had not been made; and that all" occupancy and preemption rights of existing settlers "shall continue to be in full force, in the same manner as if the cession had not been made, and as conditions upon which the said lands are ceded to the United States."[26] Congress accepted the cession on these terms on April 2, 1790.

One of the affected grantees was North Carolina legislator Thomas Person, who had opposed the North Carolina cession. In 1794, North Carolina submitted to Congress the claims of Person and others "to certain lands lying on the frontier of the state of North Carolina, and ceded by the Commissioners of the United States to the Indians." In the House, defenders of North Carolina's right to grant the Indian lands, all of them from the South, argued that the Indians had no right to these lands and that North Carolina had merely followed the practice of the British Crown. Virginian John Nicholas, for example, contended that "the Indians never had been fit to occupy these lands. It could never have been the design of nature that these people should be termed the possessors of land which they were incapable to enjoy." North Carolina's Thomas Blount, himself a claimant, similarly "denied that the Indians ever occupied the lands in question, or were fit to occupy them, in any proper sense of the word. To walk across a country, and to shoot in it, was different from an occupation." William Smith of South Carolina argued that when North Carolina became a sovereign state in 1776, "she conceived herself as succeeding to the right of the British Crown, and as having a right to bestow grants in the same way as the Kings of Great Britain had done." The Crown had long considered itself entitled to "bestow grants," he averred, and the state similarly "did not intend merely to sell the right of pre-emption from the Indians, but the absolute title to the lands." Blount's compatriot Nathaniel Macon stated, "The Crown of Britain . . . transferred the absolute property of lands, without inquiring for permission from the Indians. This evidence [goes] strongly to prove that North Carolina held the same title." Georgia's Thomas P. Carnes, whose state was even then finalizing the disposition of its own Indian-occupied western lands, contended "that the fee simple of all the soil within the chartered limits belonged to the State," and the grants were therefore proper and enforceable.[27]

Opponents in the House challenged both the history and the policy endorsed by the foregoing. Elias Boudinot of New Jersey, for example, angrily declared, "This claim of North Carolina to sell the lands [is] wrong, and this doctrine ha[s] been the cause of all the disputes [with the Indians] in which the Federal Government has been engaged. The Crown of Britain . . . never pretended to any right of this kind, nor ever thought it had a title to lands till they were first purchased from the Indians. . . . The State of North Carolina only had a right to sell the privilege of pre-emption. This was the only right which the purchasers obtained, and this they still possess."[28]

William Vans Murray of Maryland similarly professed that the purchasers "were never possessed of any right but that which North Carolina could give them—the pre-emption right; that right they now possessed as fully as they did at the time of the cession to the United States."[29] On January 30, 1795, at the conclusion of debate, the House soundly rejected four proposed resolutions offering the claimants recognition or compensation.[30]

The following year, North Carolina forwarded to the U.S. Senate a materially identical petition submitted by James Glasgow, together with supporting memorials from the North Carolina and Tennessee legislatures. On March 1, 1797, the committee assigned to consider the petition reported that "whatever right the claimants have, can be no other than a pre-emptive right to said land, and only such of them as, by conforming to the laws of the State of North Carolina, so as to have secured to themselves a title under such laws,"[31] and the Senate subsequently declined to find the petitioner entitled to compensation.

A year later, the House of Representatives denied the petitions of two Virginia militia grantees, John Nelson and Charles Russell. Nelson and Russell sought compensation for alleged deprivation of property occasioned by the 1786 Hopewell treaty with the Chickasaws. The House, with the Person petition under its belt, emphatically resolved "that the United States are not bound to satisfy the claims of the petitioners, *or any others of the like kind.*"[32]

The poor reception accorded the Person petition failed to deter Georgia from attempting a grant even more extravagant than North Carolina's. Georgia laid the groundwork for distribution in 1787, when, by "an Act for Suppressing the Violences of the Indians," the legislature declared that "all lands without the limits [of the respective counties of the state were] . . . vacant."[33] Then, again by statute, the state asserted its fee ownership, and sales began. In 1789, Governor George Walton signed land warrants for up to 50,000 acres per person. Five years later, Governor George Matthews conveyed 1,500,000 acres to a single speculator.[34] In 1791, as noted above, then secretary of state Thomas Jefferson derided the state's efforts, urging that the "Government should firmly maintain this ground, that the Indians have a right to the occupation of their Lands independent of the States within whose chartered lines they happen to be; that *until they cede them by*

Treaty or other transaction equivalent to a Treaty, no act of a State can give a right to such Lands."[35] Conflict between the state and federal governments was avoided when the purchasers failed to make required specie payments and Georgia voided the grants. While the Person petition was pending, however, the Georgia legislature determined to make one more attempt. On January 7, 1795, the legislature, asserting that the state had never ceded to the United States its "right of soil or pre-emption, in any part of the vacant territory within the limits" of the state and "that the State of Georgia is in full possession, and in the full exercise of the jurisdictional and territorial right, and the fee simple thereof," proceeded to convey title to 35 million acres of land, two-thirds of Georgia's territory west of the Chattahoochee, to four land companies, including the predecessor in interest to the New England Mississippi Land Company.[36] As discussed above, this was too much for the citizens of Georgia. In February 1796, a new legislature passed a repeal act, thereby giving birth to the Yazoo controversy. In April 1802 the lands, and the problem of title, were ceded by Georgia to the United States.

On February 16, 1803, a three-person commission appointed by Congress to negotiate the terms of the Georgia cession recommended that the United States compromise the claims of the Yazoo speculators on "equitable" grounds.[37] Opposition to the recommendation was immediate and intense. The debate over the interest possessed by the speculators—which almost immediately became wound up in the threshold question of whether the repeal had effectively killed the grants, an affirmative answer to which would moot any question of the interest conveyed—was essentially settled by the Supreme Court in 1810, but, as noted above, the Court's brief conclusion, that the Indian title was "not absolutely repugnant to seisin in fee on the part of the state," was unaccompanied by any discussion and had inspired dissent from Justice Johnson, who contended that the state's interest in the Indian lands was "nothing more than what was assumed at the first settlement of this country, to wit, a right of conquest or of purchase, exclusively of all competitors within certain defined limits."[38] In this spirit, Congress itself refused to admit to any fee right, or right to grant title, in the granting state, insisting long after the decision on referring to the claim of the successful Yazoo speculators as "equitable."

In sum, since the adoption of the Constitution the United States had legislatively asserted the right of preemption, and no more; state courts had held grants by states to have conveyed an interest enforceable against other state grantees, but no more; and Congress had declared that such grants did not convey any property right enforceable against the United States. It is against this background that one must evaluate the *Johnson* opinion, in particular the four successive paragraphs in which Marshall professed to demonstrate that the "American states" were empowered to grant Indian lands by virtue of title acquired through discovery. In the first of these paragraphs, as noted, Marshall asserted that "it has never been doubted, that either the United States, or the several states, had a clear title to" these lands. This assertion was clearly wrong. Doubt had infused federal policy from the beginning, and to the extent that the question of the sovereign's interest in the lands had been resolved, it had been resolved in favor of limiting the relevant sovereign's right to a right of preemption. The Court's failure to consider the history of this policy resulted in part, of course, from Marshall's venturing beyond the limitations of the case as pleaded. Because Harper had designed the case so as to limit material argument to the effect of the Proclamation of 1763, counsel offered no evidence of the history of public resolution of claims to Indian lands granted by states. Had this history been presented, Marshall would have had at least to reckon with it. Expressing his conclusions in obiter dicta obviated this need.

In the second of these four paragraphs intended to prove state title, Marshall first construed the Virginia Declaratory Act of 1779, to which counsel had devoted no little argument, as "an unequivocal affirmance, on the part of Virginia, of the broad principle which had always been maintained, that the exclusive right to purchase from the Indians resided in the government." The Declaratory Act segued neatly into the Virginia Land Office Act, which at once demonstrated state title and tied the decision more closely to the militia grants. "In pursuance of the same idea," Marshall noted, "Virginia proceeded, at the same session, to open her land-office, for the sale of that country which now constitutes Kentucky, a country, every acre of which was then claimed and possessed by Indians, who maintained their title with as much persevering courage as was ever manifested by any people."[39] By clear implication, Marshall affirmed that in his view this assertion of the right to grant Indian lands was legally correct.

In the third paragraph, Marshall recited the terms of Virginia's 1784 cession of its western land claims to the United States and concluded by asserting, "The ceded territory was occupied by numerous and warlike tribes of Indians; but the exclusive right of the United States to extinguish their title, and to grant the soil, has never, we believe, been doubted."[40] The exclusive right of the United States to extinguish the Indian title should have ceased to be doubted with the passage of the first Trade and Intercourse Act in 1790 (although, as Marshall undoubtedly knew, certain parties, including the State of New York, had ignored the act and its assertion of an exclusive federal right and engaged in their own purchases of Indian lands). Nor had the exclusive right of the United States to grant these lands been doubted, provided, of course, according to the federal government's own policy, that the Indian title had first been purchased. It had been doubted, however, as noted above, whether the Crown had possessed the exclusive right to purchase Indian lands in 1773 and 1775 and whether the states had possessed the right to transfer title to these lands after the Revolution.

In the fourth and last paragraph, Marshall moved briefly beyond Virginia to note, first, that after the Revolution, Spain had ceded to the United States lands occupied by Indians and, second, that the Louisiana purchase from France was "of a country almost entirely occupied by numerous tribes of Indians, who are in fact independent," but that nevertheless "any attempt of others to intrude into that country, would be considered as an aggression which would justify war."[41] These propositions were unobjectionable but failed to warrant a finding that the American states had adopted the principle that discovery gave them *title to* the Indian lands.

Following these four paragraphs, Marshall concluded, again somewhat disingenuously, that

the United States . . . have *unequivocally* acceded to that great and broad rule by which its civilized inhabitants now hold this country. They hold, and assert in themselves, the title by which it was acquired. They maintain, as all others have maintained, that discovery gave an exclusive right to extinguish the Indian title of occupancy, either by purchase or by conquest; and gave also a right to such a degree of sovereignty, as the circumstances of the people would allow them to exercise. *The power now possessed by the government of the United States to grant lands, resided, while we were colonies, in the crown or its grantees. The validity of the titles given by either has never been questioned in our courts. It has been exercised uniformly over territory in possession of the Indians.* The existence of this power must negative the existence of any right which may conflict with and control it. An absolute title to lands cannot exist, at the same time, in different persons, or in different governments. An absolute, must be an exclusive title, or at least a title which excludes all others not compatible with it. All our institutions recognise the absolute title of the crown, subject only to the Indian right of occupancy, and recognise the absolute title of the crown to extinguish that right. This is incompatible with an absolute and complete title in the Indians.[42]

Marshall was correct that the validity of grants of Indian lands by the United States had not been judicially challenged. *There were no such grants*: since the adoption of the Northwest Ordinance in 1784, Congress had granted no lands without previously having purchased title from the Indians. But he carefully omitted reference to a related class of cases well-known to him: those in which state grants of Indian lands had been challenged. And, it bears repeating, in each of those cases, both parties had claimed under the same source.

Marshall Justifies His Decision

Having reiterated his original conclusion, Marshall once again moved to absolve himself of responsibility for any perceived injustice. "We will not," he wrote, "enter into the controversy, whether agriculturists, merchants and manufacturers, have a right, on abstract principles, to expel hunters from the territory they possess, or to contract their limits." The Court was powerless to deny the adopted policy: "Conquest gives a title which the courts of the conqueror cannot deny, whatever the private and speculative opinions of individuals may be, respecting the original justice of the claim which has been successfully asserted." According to Marshall, we were the victims of our colonial inheritance:

> The British government, which was then our government, and whose rights have passed to the United States, asserted a title to all the lands occupied by Indians, within the chartered limits of the British colonies. It asserted also a limited sovereignty over them, and the exclusive right of extinguishing the titles which occupancy gave to them. These claims have been maintained and established as far west as the river Mississippi, by the sword. The title to a vast portion of the lands we now hold, originates in them. It is not for the courts of this country to question the validity of this title, or to sustain one which is incompatible with it.

Despite his avowed reticence, in the three paragraphs that followed, Marshall engaged in a justification of this policy, grounded principally in the "savage" nature of the Indians and the impossibility of assimilation. In the third, he reiterated the point made above and brought the discussion back to *Johnson*:

> However extravagant the pretension of converting the discovery of an inhabited country into conquest may appear; if the principle has been asserted in the first instance, and afterwards sustained; if a country has been acquired and held under it; if the property of the great mass of the community originates in it, it becomes the law of the land, and cannot be questioned. So too, with respect to the concomitant principle, that the Indian inhabitants are to be considered merely as occupants, to be protected, indeed, while in peace, in the possession of their lands, but to be deemed incapable of transferring the absolute title to others. However this restriction may be opposed to natural right, and to the usages of civilized nations, yet, if it be indispensable to that system under which the country has been settled, and be adapted to the actual condition of the two people, it may, perhaps, be supported by reason, and certainly cannot be rejected by courts of justice.[43]

Marshall Briefly Addresses the Remaining Issues

Having resolved both the Indian title component of the militia claims question and *Johnson v. M'Intosh*, Marshall next reminded his readers of *Fletcher v. Peck*, not to cite the latter opinion as precedent, but to note that it "conforms precisely" to the rule he has just announced, that "the absolute ultimate title has been considered as acquired by discovery, subject only to the Indian title of occupancy, which title the discoverers possessed the exclusive right of acquiring." Then, in a nod to Justice Johnson, who had expressed concern in *Fletcher* that the Yazoo speculators might commence a series of ejectment actions against the Indians in the wake of that decision, Marshall noted, "Such [an occupancy] right is no more incompatible with a seisin in fee, than a lease for years, and might as effectually bar an ejectment."[44]

All that remained was to address specific arguments made by counsel. Marshall turned first to M'Intosh attorneys Winder and Murray's argument derived from John Glynn's concurrence to Dagge's opinion on the validity of the Indiana grant appended to the Companies' 1816 memorial. Winder and Murray had argued that "if it be admitted that [the Piankashaws] are now independent and foreign states, the title of the plaintiffs would still be invalid: as grantees from the Indians, they must take according to their laws of property, and . . . the Indians never had any idea of individual property in lands." Marshall was unpersuaded by this argument, but did find a variation compelling. If an individual might purchase the Indian title, Marshall considered, he "incorporate[d] himself with them" and held his title "subject to their laws. . . . If they annul the grant, we know of no tribunal which can revise and set aside the proceeding." The cession to the United States had been made without any reservation of the land allegedly granted to Johnson, thus affording "a fair presumption that the [Piankashaws] considered" the earlier grant "as of no validity."[45] If Johnson wished to protest the Piankashaws' actions, he had best complain to the Piankashaws.

Next, Marshall turned, finally, to the Proclamation of 1763 and used it too to justify his fee title ruling. Harper had argued that under *Campbell v. Hall* the proclamation violated the British constitution. Marshall found that according to the theory of the British constitution, all vacant lands are vested in the crown, as representing the nation; and the exclusive power to grant them is admitted to reside in the crown, as a branch of the royal prerogative. . . . In addition to the proof of this principle, furnished by the immense grants, already mentioned, of lands lying within the chartered limits of Virginia, the continuing right of the crown to grant lands lying within that colony was always admitted. . . . In Virginia, . . . as elsewhere in the British dominions, the complete title of the crown to vacant lands was acknowledged. So far as respected the authority of the crown, no distinction was taken between vacant lands and lands occupied by the Indians. The title, subject only to the right of occupancy by the Indians, was admitted to be in the king, as was his right to grant that title. The lands, then, to which this proclamation referred, were lands which the king had a right to grant, or to reserve for the Indians.

In *Campbell v. Hall*, the court declared unconstitutional "that part of the proclamation . . . which imposed a tax on a conquered province, after a government had been bestowed on it." *Campbell* was, therefore, inapposite. In any event, the power to impose taxes by proclamation had long been denied to be within the royal prerogative, whereas the power to "restrain the encroachments of whites" was "never, we believe, denied by the colonies to the crown."[46] Thus, the Court held, the Proclamation of 1763 barred the Illinois and Wabash purchases.

Last, Marshall devoted thirteen paragraphs to distinguishing from the claims at bar the various opinions and Indian land purchases cited by Webster and Harper as evidencing the validity of the practice and, therefore, their own purchases. The Indian titles held by Massachusetts settlers adverse to the claims of Mason and Gorges "were sanctioned by length of possession," the Court found, "but there is no case, so far as we are informed, of a judicial decision in their favor." The controversy between the Mohegans and Connecticut likewise involved no "assertion of the principle, that individuals might obtain a complete and valid title from the Indians." The Rhode Island charter sanctioned previous unauthorized purchases from the Indians and thus constituted, not an admission that the purchases would have been valid absent such confirmation, but an assertion of the Crown's title. The cited colonial statutes prohibiting unauthorized purchases, the Court found, did not unequivocally evidence that Indian purchases would have been valid without such prohibitions, but instead offered "strong evidence of the general opinion, that such purchases are opposed by the soundest principles of wisdom and national policy."[47]

As a final irony, Marshall unmasked the Camden-Yorke opinion, writing that he and his colleagues "were not a little surprised when [Camden-Yorke] was read, at the doctrine it seemed to advance." During deliberations, however, the Court had come by a copy of *Plain Facts*, written by Samuel Wharton in support of the Indiana Company. Wharton candidly admitted that the opinion related to purchases in the East Indies, and relying on this admission, Marshall found Camden-Yorke "entirely inapplicable to purchases made in America."[48] The opinion that had fired the Illinois-Wabash purchases thus now escorted the Companies into oblivion.

John Marshall had two implicit objectives in mind when he drafted the opinion in *Johnson v. M'Intosh*: to facilitate a favorable settlement of the claims of the Virginia militia warrant holders and to soften Virginia's opposition to the court. To accomplish these ends, he recast the question pleaded by the *Johnson* parties and engaged in questionable historical exposition to resolve it. He may perhaps be excused this exercise by his likely conviction that the decision would be of limited effect. As noted, by 1823 the United States had successfully claimed for itself the exclusive right to acquire Indian lands and long practiced a policy of purchase. The problem caused by the Virginia grants—the granting by states of lands still claimed by Indians—was a constitutional accident that would never recur. The question of title to the Indian lands granted by Georgia and North Carolina had already been compromised by Congress or otherwise settled. From Marshall's vantage, all *Johnson* effected was a resolution of one component of the militia claims.

Was the opinion a success? Did John Marshall succeed in realizing his limited ends? By what process—and at what cost—was *Johnson v. M'Intosh* transformed into a landmark? To answer these questions, one must look to the decision's aftermath.

CHAPTER 6

Legacies

In their immediate objectives, both *Johnson v. M'Intosh* and *Green v. Biddle* were only partly successful. Virginia's opposition to the Court did diminish in the wake of these decisions, but at the cost of Kentucky's increased hostility. The invalidation of the occupying claimant laws, which ought to have benefited Virginia landholders, failed to deliver as expected because Kentucky's legislature and courts refused to follow the *Green* decision.[1] The Virginia militia lands question, which ought to have been helped toward favorable resolution by *Johnson*'s elimination of the Indian title objection as a conceivable bar, was put on hold for a year while Kentucky attempted yet again to garner Virginia's support in protesting the Court's usurpation of power in *Green*.[2] When this was not forthcoming, Kentucky simply opted to ignore Virginia's interests and started distributing the lands west of the Tennessee.

Kentucky's refusal to yield on both fronts eventually redounded to its advantage. The claims of the Virginia militia warrant holders were finally settled in May 1830 by the First Session of the Twenty-First Congress of the United States, which voted, on a request from the Virginia legislature, to allow unsatisfied holders of militia bounty warrants for lands west of the Tennessee to exchange them for scrip good for federal public lands in the states of Ohio, Indiana, and Illinois.[3] Ten months after President Andrew Jackson signed this bill into law, the Supreme Court dramatically qualified *Green* and upheld the most important of the Kentucky occupying claimant laws in the case of *Barney v. Hawkins' Lessee*.[4]

The controversies that had spawned both the aborted Virginia-Kentucky Convention of 1823 and the decisions in *Green* and *Johnson* thus ended roughly contemporaneously eight years after they had begun. Given the limited intent of the decision in *Johnson* and the absence of other lands to which the discovery portion of the opinion might be applied, the opinion ought then to have settled into the enveloping mists of history. Why did it not? Why—and how—did *Johnson* become a landmark? To answer these questions, one must examine the decision's reception within a geographically broadened field.

Georgia Pushes for Indian Removal

While the Kentucky General Assembly wrestled with the questions of how best to respond to the Supreme Court's invalidation of the occupying claimant laws and how to resolve the Virginia militia claims, the State of Georgia seized on *Johnson*'s formulation of the discovery doctrine to support the state's legal claim of the right to coerce the removal of the Cherokee Indians from their lands within Georgia's charter limits. Ironically, the chain of events begun by this seizure also inspired action by the First Session of the Twenty-First Congress: the passage of the Indian Removal Act of 1830. The history of Indian removal contains the answers to the questions of both the how and the why of *Johnson*'s apotheosis.

Indian removal had been a goal of many non-Indian Americans since the Revolution. The idea was to exchange western lands for eastern tribal lands, which would then be opened to non-Indian settlement. The Louisiana Purchase in 1803 made potentially available huge amounts of western lands for exchange. Many supporters of removal saw themselves as pro-Indian. They reasoned that the tribes' only hope of salvation lay in distancing themselves from the expanding non-Indian population. More simply wanted access to eastern tribal lands. Removal had always been at least theoretically voluntary: if the tribes did not want to exchange or sell their lands, the United States would not force them to do so. That changed in the 1820s, when Georgia began aggressively to engineer the ouster of the Cherokees.[5]

When Georgia ceded its western land claims to the United States in 1802, the state secured the federal government's promise that it would extinguish the Indian title to these lands "as early as the same [could] be peaceably obtained on reasonable terms."[6] Twenty years later this promise was unfulfilled, and the United States appeared to be backing away from it. The situation came to a head in February 1824, when, in response to federal solicitation, the Cherokees delivered to the president their "unqualified refusal" ever to sell their lands or to exchange them for lands west of the Mississippi.[7] President Monroe considered force, the only remaining option, beyond the power of the executive. The Cherokees "had a right to the territory," he reluctantly informed Congress, and there was nothing the United States could do about it.[8] To Georgians, this effectively constituted a breach of the compact, "an absolute denial of [Georgia's] rights and the destruction of [its] claims either upon the U. States or upon the Indians now and forever."[9] Faced with federal and Cherokee intransigence and unwilling to leave the Cherokees in possession of the northwestern corner of the state, the Georgians determined that some alternative means of coercion must be devised. In *Johnson*, Marshall offered a solution.

In *Fletcher v. Peck*, the Supreme Court had already declared that Indian title was "not incompatible with seisin in fee on the part of the state." *Johnson* had reinforced this declaration, provided historical justification for it, and offered the state something more. According to *Johnson*, discovery resulted in the transfer of fee ownership of discovered lands to the discovering sovereign. The British Crown had thus, by discovering them, acquired title to the lands of the Cherokee Nation. When Georgia declared independence, it claimed this title for itself. It had not ceded this title to the United States when it ceded its western land claims in 1802. In Georgia's view, Georgia thus still owned the lands of the Cherokee Nation. The Cherokees were Georgia's tenants. If the United States would not force the Cherokees to leave, then, in theory, Georgia might either evict them or coerce their removal by exercising the state's rights as a landlord and subjecting them to Georgia law.

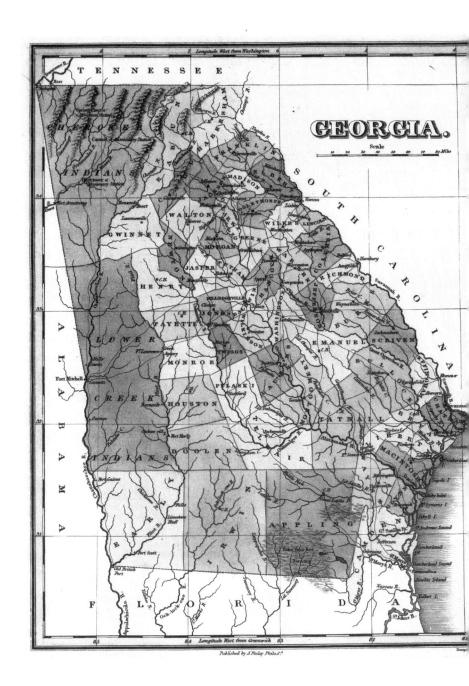

GEORGIA.

Young & Delleker, "Georgia" (1829). In 1829, in hopes of coercing their departure, Georgia attempted to legislate the Cherokee Nation out of existence. Georgians were eager to acquire the Cherokee lands to their northwest. This map is a reissue of an earlier map: by 1829, the Creek Nation had ceded all its Georgia lands. (Georgia, Neg. 3807; Courtesy of Hargrett Rare Book & Manuscript Library/University of Georgia Libraries)

Chief instigator of the new policy was Georgia governor George Troup. Born in 1780 at McIntosh Bluff on the Tombigbee River north of Mobile, Troup was a cousin of William McIntosh, a leader of the Lower Creeks who had allied with Andrew Jackson during the 1813–14 Red Stick War. Troup was elected to the U.S. House of Representatives in 1807 as an anti-Yazooist and, it may be recalled, loudly protested the Court's decision in *Fletcher v. Peck*, even urging the use of federal troops to prevent occupation by the successful speculators. He left the House in 1815 and a year later was elected to the U.S. Senate, where he served from 1816 to 1818. In 1819 and 1821, Troup made two unsuccessful runs for the Georgia governorship. In 1823 he tried again, this time successfully.

Despite his connection to the Lower Creeks, Troup was committed to Creek and Cherokee removal. He laid the legal predicate in his annual address to the Georgia legislature in November 1824, reciting the twin claims to ownership and sovereignty elucidated in *Johnson*: the sovereign, in this case Georgia, had "in theory and practice, uniformly . . . reserved to" itself title to the land, he claimed, "with which is essentially connected jurisdiction and sovereignty."[10] Three months later, under extreme pressure from the Georgians, Troup's cousin William McIntosh and his supporters ceded the Creek Nation's Georgia lands.[11] The cession won Troup a second term as governor, despite the fact that challenges to the cession treaty occupied him, the Creek Nation, and President John Quincy Adams's administration for most of the following year. Ultimately, in January 1826, the 1825 treaty was superseded by the Treaty of Washington. Apparently by oversight, the new treaty left the Creeks a sliver of Georgia land; this land was finally ceded at Fort Mitchell in January 1827, and the Creek Nation severed its last ties with Georgia and Governor Troup.

While the Fort Mitchell discussions were ongoing, the Cherokee National Council made it clear that it would follow a different course. In October 1826, the Council voted to call a constitutional convention to meet the following July 4. The convention produced a document, adopted in 1827, that was patterned after the U.S. Constitution and included as its first article a description of the Nation's territorial boundaries and a statement that they "shall forever hereafter remain unalterably the same."[12] The Cherokee Nation was not going anywhere.

FIGURE 7

Portrait of George Troup by John Maier. Georgia governor George Troup urged using the ownership of Indian lands recognized in *Johnson v. M'Intosh* as justification for imposing Georgia laws on the Cherokee Nation. (Courtesy of Georgia Capitol Museum, Office of Secretary of State)

Troup was furious. In November, in a speech to the Georgia legislature, he let the federal government know that the state's patience was almost exhausted. Paraphrasing and even expanding on *Johnson*, he declared that the state held the Indian land by the same tenure as that by which the legislators held their own lands, that the state had jurisdiction over this land, that "the right of occupancy follow[ed] the *right* of soil and jurisdiction," and that the state held "the same right of occupancy now as ever, unlimited and unrestrained." The Adams administration had proved ineffectual in persuading the Cherokees to remove. It was time, Troup urged, to begin considering the measures the state itself might take "most expedient for the acquisition of [the lands] of the Cherokees within the [state's charter] limits."[13] With that, he left office, yielding the governorship to forty-seven-year-old congressman John Forsyth; a year later, Troup would be elected to the U.S. Senate, where he would serve on the Indian Affairs Committee throughout the debate over Indian removal. His parting message bore fruit. The Georgia legislature in short order approved eight resolutions, communicating his message to the world. The third asserted the state's claim to title and jurisdiction: "That all the lands appropriated and unappropriated which lie within the conventional limits of Georgia, belong to her absolutely; that the title is in her; that the Indians are tenants at her will, and that she may at any time she pleases, determine that tenancy, by taking possession of the premises. And that Georgia has the right to extend her authority and laws over her whole territory, and to coerce obedience to them from all description of people, be they white, red or black, who reside within her limits." The sixth urged the United States for the last time to negotiate with the Indians for the extinguishment of their title. The seventh recommended that should a treaty be attempted, the treaty negotiators impress on the Cherokees "the nature and extent of the Georgia title to the lands in controversy, and the probable consequences which will result from a continued refusal" to sell. "The lands in question *belong* to Georgia," the drafting committee concluded. "She *must* and she *will* have them."[14]

Despite their tone, the Georgia resolutions of 1827 did not lead to the federal government's obtaining an agreement from the Cherokees to cede their lands and remove from the state. The Adams administration, like its predecessor, was unprepared to use force, and the Cherokees persisted in their unwillingness to sell. Dislodgment, as Troup had anticipated, required something more: that Georgia move to enforce its claim to jurisdiction based on its ownership of the Cherokee Nation's lands. This was a risky move, given that the federal government had treaty relations with the Cherokees guaranteeing their national borders, but the election of pro-removal General Andrew Jackson to the White House in 1828 gave Georgians the resolve to attempt it.

Jackson, Georgia, and *Johnson*

Andrew Jackson had been a supporter of the removal of the eastern tribes to lands west of the Mississippi since at least 1814, purportedly on grounds of national security. In August 1814, he negotiated what was then the largest land cession ever negotiated with a southeastern tribe, the Creeks, at the conclusion of the Red Stick War. As U.S. agent, Jackson subsequently negotiated land cession treaties with the Cherokees (1817), Choctaws (1820), and, as noted above, Chickasaws (1816 and 1818). In 1823, Jackson was elected to the U.S. Senate from Tennessee. The following year he ran unsuccessfully for president. John Quincy Adams won that race, allegedly after making a "corrupt bargain" with another candidate, Henry Clay, who, according to rumor, threw his support behind Adams after Adams promised to name him secretary of state. Jackson easily rode the popular resentment at this deal into office four years later. Based on his record, Georgians were confident of his support.

In December 1828, the Georgia legislature enacted a bill to "add the territory within the limits of this State, and occupied by the Cherokee Indians," to five named Georgia counties, "and extend the laws of this State over the same." According to the act, which Troup's successor, John Forsyth, signed on December 20, the annexation and assertion of jurisdiction were to take effect immediately, with the exception that individual Cherokees would not be subject to state laws until after June 1, 1830. In addition, after that date, "all laws, usages, and customs made, established and in force" in the Cherokee Nation were to be null and void.[15] Following Georgia's lead, Alabama enacted similar legislation extending its jurisdiction over the Creeks.[16]

On March 4, 1829, Andrew Jackson was sworn into office as the seventh president of the United States. On December 8, 1829, in his first annual message, he proved the Georgians' confidence in his support well placed, urging Congress to adopt legislation to complement Georgia's and Alabama's extension of jurisdiction over the Cherokees and Creeks, to be predicated on the legal theory espoused in the Georgia resolutions of December 1827. The Cherokees and Creeks had "attempted to erect an independent government within the limits of Georgia and Alabama," he averred. Under the Constitution, the United States could not countenance the creation of new states within the bounds of existing states, and these governments could not stand. The Indians must submit to the states or leave. To facilitate the latter, the United States should "set apart an ample district West of the Mississippi, and without the limits of any State or Territory now formed," to which the Indians might remove in exchange for their lands in Alabama and Georgia. Emigration to this district "should be voluntary," Jackson counseled, but the Indians "should be distinctly informed," as Georgia had urged, "that, if they remain within the limits of the States, they must be subject to their laws." If they refused to remove, the tribes would also be dispossessed of the major portion of their vast communally held lands. To think otherwise, Jackson made clear, was "visionary."[17]

George Troup, in attendance, was of course delighted, as was John Forsyth, who the previous month had left the Georgia governorship to accept appointment to the Senate. The week following publication of the president's address, Georgia's new governor, George Gilmer, another Troup ally, informed the Georgia legislature, "I confidently rely upon the personal knowledge of the President of the United States as to the extent of the limits of the country claimed by the Creeks and Cherokees (as well as his disposition to do us justice)."[18] In Mississippi, the legislature responded to Jackson's address by passing its own law extending state jurisdiction over the Chickasaws and Choctaws.[19]

In Congress, the removal question was referred to the House and Senate Indian Affairs Committees, both chaired by Jackson supporters from Tennessee: Senator Hugh Lawson White and Congressman John Bell. On February 22, 1830, White's committee, which included Troup, reported a bill providing for the exchange of federal lands west of the Mississippi for Indian lands in the east.[20]

When the Senate took up the bill as a Committee of the Whole on April 6, it met with strong opposition. Georgia's claim to own the Cherokee lands, which gave the bill its coercive force, was simply unfounded, in the view of many. Senator Theodore Frelinghuysen of New Jersey, for one, strongly assailed both the bill and the state's claim of ownership. The Indians were "fully sustain[ed] in their rights," he argued.

> By immemorial possession, as the original tenants of the soil, they hold a title beyond and superior to the British Crown and her colonies, and to all adverse pretensions of our confederation and subsequent Union. . . . In all our public intercourse with the Indians, ever since the first colonies of white men found an abode on these Western shores, we have distinctly recognized their title; treated with them, as owners, and in all our acquisitions of territory, applied ourselves to these ancient proprietors, by purchase and cession alone, to obtain the right of soil. . . . I challenge the record of any other or different pretension.[21]

"Discovery . . . confers no claim or right against the natives, the persons discovered," Maine's Peleg Sprague echoed, "but only as between discoverers." Discovery had brought not title to discovered lands, but a preemption right to those lands. "It is the same as if five or six persons, being about to go in search of sugar lands in South America, should mutually engage that they would not interfere with each other in their purchases." Aboriginal title had always been respected by the United States, he contended: "The rights which the United States have claimed with respect to the territory of the aborigines have been two-fold—pre-emptive and reversionary; a right to purchase, to the exclusion of all others; and to succeed the natives, should they voluntarily leave the country or become extinct." The Indians "cannot indeed transfer their country to others," he admitted—this was the consequence of the preemption right—"but this does not impair their title, although it may diminish its value in the market."[22] The fact that the tribes could sell their lands only to the United States, and the likely diminished price that circumstance promised, did not mean that they did not own them.

These arguments were solid and in an earlier era had been successful. In 1830, however, the majority were of a different mind, and they had in their arsenal a useful Supreme Court opinion. Frelinghuysen himself provided the Jacksonians the occasion for spotlighting this opinion. "When, or where," he asked, "did any assembly or convention meet which proclaimed, or even suggested to these tribes, that the right of discovery contained a superior efficacy over all prior titles?" His new colleague, former Georgia governor John Forsyth, happily provided the answer: "The Supreme Court of the United States has pronounced upon the condition of the Indians and the Indian lands—the Indians are subject to the United States or the States—the Indian lands owned in fee simple by the Government of the United States, or the State Governments." These were the consequences of discovery. For authority, John McKinley of Alabama, himself soon to be elevated to the Supreme Court, provided the citation: *Johnson v. M'Intosh*, "reported in the 8th of Wheaton."[23]

Jackson supporters outnumbered opponents in the Senate, and the result was foregone. On a party vote, the Senate passed the bill on April 26.[24] Debate then passed to the House, where it faced more serious opposition.[25] John Bell, whose Committee on Indian Affairs had already reported a similar bill, spoke in favor of the Senate bill for seven hours on May 13 and 14. When he was done, William Storrs of Connecticut echoed Frelinghuysen in contending that "whatever may have been the theories on which the [British] Government . . . asserted its supremacy, . . . our English ancestors, who first colonised these States, [n]ever countenanced that disregard of Indian rights, or carried into practice that system of injustice to the native inhabitants, which has been asserted in the report of the Committee on Indian Affairs." "As a nation, from the first," William W. Ellsworth of Connecticut argued, the United States had admitted the Indians' "independent existence, and their full right to the soil." Isaac C. Bates of Massachusetts denied that the Cherokees were "the tenants of Georgia" or "subject to her jurisdiction; they are the sole proprietors of the territory they occupy . . . and are sovereign." As in the Senate, however, removal proponents were well armed to meet such representations. On May 17, Georgia's congressman Thomas F. Foster "beg[ged] leave to refer to the decision of the Supreme Court of the United States in Johnson vs. McIntosh." Two days later, Richard H. Wilde of Georgia reiterated the reference. On May 26, by a vote of 103 to 97, with amendments, the removal bill passed the House. The bill was immediately returned to the Senate, which acceded to the House amendments the same day.[26] President Jackson signed the bill into law two days later.[27]

The Supreme Court had adjourned its January 1830 session on March 22,[28] and John Marshall was riding circuit in Virginia and North Carolina during the whole of the debate on the Indian removal bill. Newspaper coverage, however, was widespread, and key opponents of removal, including Frelinghuysen and Congressman Edward Everett of Massachusetts, forwarded Marshall copies of their speeches.[29] Marshall was distressed at Congress's cooperation in completing "the coercive measures begun by the states" of Georgia, Alabama, and Mississippi,[30] and he privately denounced the Removal Act in a letter to Virginia judge Dabney Carr, lamenting, "Humanity must bewail the course which is pursued."[31] His distress was no doubt enhanced by feelings of culpability. The degree to which he had developed in *Johnson v. M'Intosh* the legal theory on which the "coercive measures" were grounded was apparent on the public record. Four months after the enactment of the removal bill, the source of these measures became even more obvious—and no doubt more painful—when a convention of Georgia's circuit judges used *Johnson v. M'Intosh* to crush the first major judicial challenge to Georgia's imposition of its civil and criminal jurisdiction over the Cherokees.

George Tassells was a Cherokee charged with having murdered another Cherokee inside the Cherokee Nation. A state judge, asserting Georgia's claim to jurisdiction over criminal offenses within the Cherokee Nation, sentenced him to death, and he appealed his conviction on the grounds of lack of jurisdiction. In September 1830, the Georgia judicial convention upheld the legality of Georgia's statutory claim of jurisdiction over the Cherokee Nation. The validity of the assertion, the convention found, depended on the relation between Georgia and the Cherokees. This relation depended in turn "upon the principles established by England towards the Indian tribes occupying that part of North America which that power colonized." These principles had been "ably elucidated by the decision of the Supreme Court in the case of Johnson vs. McIntosh." As Chief Justice

Marshall then stated, "'Discovery gave . . . a right to such degree of sovereignty, as the [circumstances of the] people would allow them to exercise.'" The plea to jurisdiction was overruled.[32]

Tassells applied to the Supreme Court for relief, and on December 12, three days after the text of the convention's opinion appeared in the *Richmond Enquirer*, John Marshall directed the State of Georgia to appear and defend itself. On December 22, two days before Tassells's slated execution, Governor George Gilmer submitted Marshall's citation to the state legislature, informing them that, as far as he was concerned, "orders received from the Supreme Court, for the purpose of staying, or interfering with the decisions of the Courts of the State, in the exercise of their constitutional jurisdiction," would be disregarded, "and any attempt to enforce such orders" would be "resisted with whatever force the laws" had "placed at [his] command."[33] The legislature, characterizing the citation as "a flagrant violation" of Georgia's rights, resolved that the governor "communicate to the Sheriff of Hall County, by express, . . . such orders as are necessary to ensure the full execution of the laws, in the case of George Tassells."[34] The governor dispatched a rider at midnight on December 23, and Georgia hanged George Tassells, as scheduled, on Christmas Eve.[35]

The Tassells case might have provoked a constitutional showdown had not the Cherokees moved to provide Marshall a more broadly compelling case through which to invalidate Georgia's assertion of jurisdiction. On December 20, four days before Tassells's execution, Cherokee principal chief John Ross informed Gilmer that the tribe itself, by counsel, would move the Supreme Court to enjoin, or prevent, the execution of any Georgia law or the service of Georgia process within the Cherokee Nation. Contemporaneously, the Cherokee Nation commenced an original action in the Supreme Court against the state.[36]

The plaintiff in *Cherokee Nation v. Georgia* intended to offer the Court a vehicle for invalidating the Georgia laws extending jurisdiction over the Cherokee Nation. By invalidating the purported assertion of state laws, the Court would remove the teeth from the Indian Removal Act: if the states could not validly impose their laws on tribes within their limits, the tribes would have no incentive to remove. The problem was that the Cherokees lacked clear capacity to initiate an original action in the Supreme Court.

Under the Constitution, the Court could try lawsuits "between two or more States" and "between a State . . . and foreign states."[37] The Cherokees clearly were not a State of the Union. Were they a foreign state? A finding that they were would potentially invite foreign powers to enter into alliances with the tribes and oblige the United States to extend to the tribes and their members the rights of foreign nationals. This was more than Marshall was prepared to do, and more, he concluded, than was necessary to undermine the Removal Act.

When the case was called for argument, Georgia failed to appear. Attorneys John Sergeant and William Wirt argued valiantly for the tribe in a doomed cause. Marshall delivered his opinion on March 3, 1831. "Though the Indians," he declared, "are acknowledged to have an unquestionable and, heretofore, unquestioned right to the lands they occupy until that right shall be extinguished by a voluntary cession to our government, yet it may well be doubted whether those tribes which reside within the acknowledged boundaries of the United States can, with strict accuracy, be denominated foreign nations." Instead, he found, "they may, more correctly, perhaps, be denominated domestic dependent nations." The Supreme Court of the United States had no jurisdiction to entertain original actions brought by domestic dependent nations. The suit, in sum, invited the resolution of questions beyond the Court's capacity, "at least in the form in which those matters are presented." That said, these questions "might," Marshall noted, "perhaps be decided by [the] court in a proper case with proper parties."[38] The motion for an injunction was denied, but the Cherokees were invited to try again.

Two relatively new Jackson appointees sat on the Court during the 1831 term. One, John McLean of Ohio, joined Marshall's opinion. The other, Henry Baldwin of Pennsylvania, concurred, pointedly concluding, however, that *Johnson v. M'Intosh*, to which Marshall had avoided all reference in his opinion, justified Georgia's acts. In *Johnson*, Baldwin pronounced, "the nature of the Indian title to land on this continent . . . was most ably and elaborately considered; leading to conclusions satisfactory to every jurist, clearly establishing that from the time of discovery under the royal government, the colonies, the States, the confederacy and this Union, their tenure was . . . occupancy, their rights occupancy and nothing more;

that the ultimate absolute fee, jurisdiction and sovereignty was in the government, subject only to such rights; that grants vested soil and dominion and the powers of government, whether the land granted was vacant or occupied by Indians." " 'The history of America from its discovery to the present day proves, we think, the universal recognition of these principles,' " he quoted. "I feel it my duty to apply them to this case."[39]

The Jackson administration had not been idle during the months after the passage of the Indian Removal Act. After Congress adjourned, Jackson himself went to Tennessee with his secretary of war, John Eaton, and General John Coffee, then dispatched Eaton and Coffee to Mississippi, where they negotiated a cession treaty with the Choctaws. The Treaty of Dancing Rabbit Creek, signed on September 27, 1830, as the Tassells crisis was approaching its height, made clear that both parties understood the incentive to remove: "Whereas the General Assembly of the State of Mississippi," it began, "has extended the laws of the said State to persons and property within the chartered limits of the same, and the President of the United States has said that he cannot protect the Choctaw people from the operation of these laws; Now therefore that the Choctaw may live under their own laws in peace with the United States and the State of Mississippi they have determined to sell their lands east of the Mississippi." To protect against future loss of sovereignty to a surrounding state, and in accordance with the terms of the Indian Removal Act, the Choctaws received two guarantees: first, that they would receive in exchange for the eastern lands "a tract of country west of the Mississippi River, *in fee simple*"—and thus not subject to a discovery doctrine claim that they were tenants to a successor of the discovering European sovereign—and second, an explicit assurance that "no Territory or State shall ever have a right to pass laws for the government of the Choctaw Nation."[40] The treaty was ratified by the Senate and proclaimed by the president on February 24, 1831, a week before Marshall delivered the *Cherokee Nation* decision.[41] Four days later, on February 28, a group of the Seneca Nation signed a treaty exchanging their lands in Ohio for fee lands west of the Mississippi; over the summer, other Ohio groups, including Senecas, Shawnees, and Ottawa, did the same, as did the Ohio Wyandots the following January.[42] Removal was proceeding as planned.

All this activity reinforced John Marshall's commitment to arrest the process when, at the Supreme Court's February 1832 term, a "proper case with proper parties," *Worcester v. Georgia*, brought the question of the legitimacy of Georgia's acts again before the Court. The case arose when New England missionaries Samuel Worcester and Elizur Butler challenged being sentenced to hard labor by the Gwinnett County, Georgia, court for residing in the Cherokee country without a state license.[43] *Worcester* would become celebrated among Indian rights proponents for its holding the state's act imposing Georgia laws on the Cherokees invalid because the act conflicted with the U.S. Constitution and federal statutes and treaty guarantees. Of greater contemporaneous significance, however, were the implications of *Worcester* for the discovery doctrine.

The discovery doctrine had given Georgia and other eastern states a claim to the underlying fee title to the Indian lands within their borders. This claim offered these states a basis for asserting a claim to jurisdiction over these lands. The assertion, or threat of assertion, of a claim to state jurisdiction gave coercive force to the federal removal program. To frustrate the removal program, John Marshall would have to return to the source. In *Worcester*, therefore, he would dismantle the discovery doctrine by overruling that part of the doctrine assigning fee title to the discovering sovereign. *Worcester* was intended to prove *Johnson*'s undoing.

As noted, Marshall in *Worcester* held that Georgia's imposition of its laws over the Cherokee Nation violated federal statutes and treaty guarantees and was invalid under the U.S. Constitution. The Georgia court's condemnation of Worcester and Butler, therefore, the Court said, should be "reversed and annulled." But more was at stake. The treaty guarantee ruling, for example, would protect from coercion only those tribes with treaty protections (including boundary guarantees) similar to those in the Cherokee Treaty of Hopewell. Many tribes did not have such guarantees and so would continue to be theoretically vulnerable to the extension of state law on the authority of the Georgia construction of *Johnson*. Thus returning to the source, Marshall now held that the discovery doctrine construction on which Georgia relied was wrong. Discovery, Marshall now wrote, echoing Senator Peleg Sprague in the Indian Removal Bill debate, "gave to the nation making the discovery, as its inevitable consequence, [only] the sole right of acquiring the soil and of making settlements on it"—a preemption right. And though it "shut out the right of competition among those who had agreed to it," it could not "annul the previous rights of those who had not agreed to it." Although it "regulated the right given by discovery among the European discoverers," it "could not affect the rights of those already in possession, either as aboriginal occupants, or as occupants by virtue of a discovery made before the memory of man." The discovery right was not dependent on and did not result in the diminishment of tribal sovereignty. "It gave the exclusive right to purchase, but did not found that right on a denial of the right of the possessor to sell."[44] It limited the rights of individuals and states, but not the rights of tribes. It did not convey fee title.

To support this reformulation, Marshall reintroduced and (rather brazenly) discarded the lengthy historical defense of the rule he had imported in *Johnson* from his *Life of George Washington*. "Soon after Great Britain determined on planting colonies in America," he wrote in *Worcester*, "the king granted charters to companies of his subjects, who associated for the purpose of carrying the views of the crown into effect, and of enriching themselves. The first of these charters was made before possession was taken of any part of the country. They purport, generally, to convey the soil, from the Atlantic to the South Sea," which was then "occupied by numerous and warlike nations, equally willing and able to defend their possessions." What was the intended legal consequence of these charters? Certainly not "the extravagant and absurd idea" entertained by Georgia, "that the feeble settlements made on the sea-coast, or the companies under whom they were made, acquired legitimate power by [the royal charters] to govern the people, or occupy the lands from sea to sea." This idea "did not enter the mind of any man," Marshall declared. Instead, he stated, the charters "were well understood to convey the title which, according to the common law of European sovereigns respecting America, they might rightfully convey, *and no more. This was the exclusive right of purchasing such lands as the natives were willing to sell.*" To repeat: all discovery brought was a preemption right. Any other construction was ahistorical. "The crown could not be understood to grant what the crown did not affect to claim, nor was it so understood. . . . These grants asserted a title against Europeans only, and were considered as blank paper so far as the rights of the natives were concerned."[45] Under the discovery doctrine as reformulated, Georgia had no claim either to title to the Cherokee lands or to sovereignty over them.[46] Georgia's purported assertion of jurisdiction was invalid. The Indian Removal Act had no coercive force.[47]

The Jackson Administration Responds to *Worcester v. Georgia* and Removal Continues

*W*orcester v. Georgia's rejection of the *Johnson* discovery rule threatened to undermine both Georgia's efforts to dislodge the Cherokees and the Jackson administration's entire Indian removal policy. Jackson himself, as the chief proponent of that policy, reacted swiftly. In *Worcester*'s wake, the president directed Secretary of War Lewis Cass to argue, in an essay published anonymously in the administration's press organ, *The Globe*, for the restoration of the *Johnson* rule.[48] Newspapers throughout the country reprinted the piece. After identifying the salient question— whether Georgia had "a right to extend her laws over the Cherokee lands, within her boundaries"—Cass launched immediately into *Johnson v. M'Intosh*. "When the Europeans landed upon this continent," he paraphrased, "they found it inhabited by numerous tribes of savages, independent of one another, and generally engaged in hostilities." "Under such circumstances," he continued, "jurisdiction [was] well assumed, and its extent must depend upon the opinion of the dominant party." Discovery, as Marshall had held, " 'gave an exclusive right to extinguish the Indian title of occupancy, either by purchase or conquest; and gave them also a right to such a degree of sovereignty, as the circumstances of the people would allow them to exercise.' "[49] Georgia's exercise of jurisdiction was valid, and *Worcester* was wrong.

Cass's "Examination of the Cherokee Question" was Jackson's way of attempting to reestablish the *Johnson* discovery formulation without precipitating a constitutional showdown with the high court. Georgia was not so reticent. Despite *Worcester*, the state continued to enforce its laws within the Cherokee country. Worcester and Butler remained in prison, and the governor declared publicly that he would not allow their release on the authority of the expected Supreme Court mandate. Issuance of that mandate would not be possible until the Supreme Court reconvened in January, and throughout the country there was much anxious speculation as to the possible consequences of Georgia's refusal to obey. Jackson had given no indication that he would assist in the enforcement of the mandate, and indeed was on record as supporting the state against the federal judiciary. Whatever crisis resulted would therefore likely involve the federal executive as well as the Court and the State of Georgia. The continued incarceration of Worcester and Butler threatened to shake the entire federal system.[50]

That the system did not crack at this juncture owes, ironically, to the precipitous actions of South Carolinians evidently hopeful that it would. On November 24, 1832, while the nation awaited the issuance of the mandate, a convention called by the South Carolina legislature took advantage of Georgia's so far successful resistance to the federal government and issued an ordinance by which the state claimed the authority to nullify federal statutes within its borders. This proved too much for Andrew Jackson, who, though prepared to look the other way while Georgia ousted the Cherokees, was not about to preside over the dissolution of the United States.[51] Jackson immediately put a stop to the Georgia problem, pressuring Governor Wilson Lumpkin to release Worcester and Butler, which he did on the very day the Court reconvened. No mandate was therefore required from the Court, and the Georgia crisis eased. Jackson then turned his attention to the South Carolina nullifiers and they, now isolated, were also brought back into line.

Although the threat to the Union had been averted, the threat to the removal policy remained. The administration continued to press tribes for removal treaties despite *Worcester*'s invalidation of Georgia's claim to jurisdiction. Secretary of War Lewis Cass, who, as noted, drafted the administration's response to *Worcester*, simultaneously negotiated a cession treaty with the Creeks, whose delegates, prior to the Court's issuance of the *Worcester* opinion, had been sent to Washington with instructions to reach some agreement with the administration protecting them from the application of Alabama's laws. On March 24, at Cass's urging, the Creek delegates agreed, as had the Choctaws, to cede "all their land, East of the Mississippi river" in exchange for fee lands in the west and a promise that "no

State or Territory" would "ever have a right to pass laws for the[ir] govern-ment."[52] Six weeks later, Seminole representatives, who almost certainly knew nothing of the *Worcester* holding, met with federal negotiators on the Ocklawaha River in Florida and ceded their lands in exchange for a share of the Creek fee lands west of the Mississippi.[53] The Chickasaws also agreed to cede their lands in 1832. Chickasaw delegates had signed a provisional re-moval treaty after meeting with Jackson in Tennessee in August 1830 and being offered the choice to either cede or submit to state law. This treaty was never ratified by the U.S. Senate, but it opened the door to non-Indians moving to claim Chickasaw lands.[54] In October 1832, Jackson dispatched General John Coffee to push for another treaty, and Coffee persuaded the Chickasaws that, whatever they had heard about *Worcester*, it would not save them from the imposition of state law. Local courts reinforced this ar-gument, the circuit court for Monroe County, Mississippi, ruling before the end of 1832 that the federal Trade and Intercourse Act had been nullified as it applied to the Chickasaw Nation's Mississippi lands because it had been supplanted by Mississippi law.[55] Under these circumstances, the Chicka-saws yielded, their cession treaty recounting plaintively that "the Chickasaw Nation find themselves oppressed in their present situation; by being made subject to the laws of the States in which they reside. Being ignorant of the language and laws of the white man, they cannot understand or obey them. Rather than submit to this great evil, they prefer to seek a home in the west, where they may live and be governed by their own laws."[56]

Significantly, the Cherokees had not signed a removal treaty. Nor had most of the tribes that had signed such treaties based on federal representa-tions that state laws would otherwise apply to them actually removed; in-deed, many were actively resisting. The Jackson administration continued to tell tribes that *Worcester* would not protect them from state law. At the end of 1833, Jackson's home state offered support for the theory by passing its own law extending state jurisdiction over the Cherokee lands in Ten-nessee, but this position could not be sustained forever, given the opinion's clear language.[57] *Worcester* had taken the teeth out of removal by denying that discovery had given the states anything more than a preemption right. For removal to proceed on a surer legal footing, the *Johnson* formulation providing that discovery gave the discoverer fee title to discovered lands, on which the eastern states based their claims to jurisdiction over Indian lands, had to be restored. It was at this point that John Marshall lost control of his court.

The Supreme Court Restores the *Johnson* Formulation of the Discovery Doctrine

Two Jackson appointees, John McLean and Henry Baldwin, had joined the high court during the 1830 term. In the winter of 1832, Andrew Jackson was reelected to the presidency. In 1834, Justice William Johnson died, and on January 9, 1835, Jackson appointed in his place James M. Wayne, former member of the Georgia Supreme Court and from 1829 to 1835 a member of the state's congressional delegation.[58] Wayne, who took his seat on January 14, was a vigorous supporter of removal. Within hours of Wayne's swearing in, Justice Gabriel Duvall resigned, and the balance of power on the Court shifted.[59] Of the six justices, three—McLean, Baldwin, and Wayne—were Jackson appointees. Of the remaining three—Marshall, Story, and Smith Thompson—only two were fit. Chief Justice Marshall was dying. "He still possesses his intellectual powers in very high vigor," Story wrote, "but his physical strength is manifestly on the decline."[60] It was to be his last term on the Supreme Court.[61] On July 6, he died.

The 1835 term, John Marshall's last, offered the Jackson appointees a chance to restore the fee title portion of the *Johnson* formulation of the discovery doctrine. The vehicle was *Mitchel v. United States* (*Mitchel I*), which involved a claim to title to a vast tract in Florida held under an evidently publicly sanctioned Indian deed. Baldwin was assigned authorship of the Court's opinion. "As Florida was for twenty years under the dominion of Great Britain," he wrote, "the laws of that country were in force as the rule by which lands were held and sold. . . . One uniform rule seems to have prevailed from their first settlement, as appears by their laws," he continued: "that friendly Indians were protected in the possession of the lands they occupied," but that "subject to this right of possession, the ultimate fee was in the crown and its grantees, which could be granted by the crown or colonial legislatures while the lands remained in possession of the Indians, though possession could not be taken without their consent."[62] The *Johnson* discovery rule was restored: according to the Court, fee title had passed to the discovering sovereign upon discovery. The State of Georgia, by implication, did own the lands of the Cherokee Nation and so arguably had the power to impose its laws on the Cherokees. There still remained of *Worcester* the constitutional holding, in particular, that the states could not exercise this claimed power if to do so would conflict with statutory or treaty language. Statutes and treaties, however, were subject to repeal or abrogation, and this was within the control of the Jacksonians. It appeared that the states might yet successfully claim jurisdiction over the tribes.

While the Court considered the *Mitchel* case, two rival Cherokee delegations arrived in Washington. Cherokee chief John Ross's National Party delegation came to meet with the administration to insist that the Cherokees, with *Worcester* on their side, would never leave. The other party, headed by subchief John Ridge, had come prepared to negotiate for removal. Not surprisingly, the Ridge group were more warmly received. On March 14, five weeks after argument in *Mitchel* and three days before Justice Baldwin delivered the Court's opinion restoring the fee title portion of the discovery doctrine—and perhaps trying to strike a deal before much of *Worcester* evaporated—they signed a removal treaty that, in modified form, was reexecuted in December, ratified, and proclaimed by the president the following May. The Cherokee removal treaty, like most of the others, began with a recitation of the potency of the imposition of state law: "Whereas the Cherokees are anxious to make some arrangements with the Government of the United States whereby the difficulties they have experienced by a residence within the settled parts of the United States under the jurisdiction and laws of the State Governments may be terminated and adjusted," they would agree to cede all their lands east of the Mississippi River, in exchange for fee lands in the west.[63] More treaties with other tribes would follow, and physical removal—tragic and still a cause of bitter remembrance—would now begin on a large scale.

Only five justices sat during the 1836 term. With Marshall dead, the majority were Jackson appointees, a circumstance that would persist for the next eight years. Baldwin again reintroduced the *Johnson* rule in *United States v. Fernandez*, another Florida case. At issue was the validity of a grant of lands to which the Indian title had not been extinguished. "This subject was so fully and ably considered in *M'Intosh v. Johnson* [*sic*]," Baldwin wrote, "that we have only to refer to the language of the court to show that every European government claimed and exercised the right of granting lands, while in the occupation of the Indians."[64] In 1836, Jackson appointed Philip P. Barbour of Virginia and Roger B. Taney of Maryland to the seats vacated by Duvall and Marshall. Barbour had served as a member of the House in the Thirtieth Congress and voted for removal. Taney had opined in favor of removal while serving as Jackson's attorney general. In 1837, the Court was enlarged to nine members, and Jackson nominated fellow Tennesseean John Catron to the first of the two new seats.[65] Catron had established himself as a supporter of Jackson's views on removal as Tennessee's chief justice in *State v. Foreman*, decided in 1835.[66] Jackson's term expired before he had the opportunity to name a ninth justice to the high court, but his vice president and chosen successor, Martin Van Buren, no doubt had his approbation in elevating to that position John McKinley, former representative and senator from Alabama and a veteran of the Senate Indian Affairs Committee.[67] After 1837, the Court thus included seven Jacksonians. Only two members, Story and Thompson, remained from the old Marshall Court. *Worcester* was, for the foreseeable future, dead beyond redemption.

No case argued during the 1838 term offered the Jackson appointees a vehicle for reiterating *Johnson*. The following term, however, the Court finally received the case for which John Marshall had been looking. To John Catron fell the ironic task of applying the *Johnson* rule to the claim of a Virginia militia warrant holder to lands west of the Tennessee River. In *Clark v. Smith*, he denied that a patent was void because issued for "lands lying within a country claimed by Indians." According to Catron, "The colonial charters, a great portion of the individual grants by the proprietary and royal governments, and a still greater portion by the States of this Union after the Revolution, were made for lands within the Indian hunting grounds." Indeed, "North Carolina and Virginia, to a great extent, paid their officers and soldiers of the revolutionary war by such grants. . . . It was one of the great resources that sustained the war, not only by these States, but others." The *Johnson* formulation of the discovery doctrine settled the question of the grants' legitimacy. According to this doctrine, "The ultimate fee (encumbered with the

Indian right of occupancy) was in the crown previous to the Revolution, and in the States of the Union afterwards, and subject to grant. This right of occupancy was protected by the political power and respected by the courts until extinguished; when the patentee took the unencumbered fee. So this court and the State courts have uniformly and often holden."[68]

Mitchel returned to the Court in 1841. In *Mitchel v. United States* (*Mitchel II*), Justice James M. Wayne wrote for the Court that the public appropriation of Indian land would extinguish the Indian title, in accordance with "the position taken by this court in respect to the rights of European monarchs to Indian lands in North America, in *Johnson v. M'Intosh* (8 Wheat.)"[69] The following year, in *Martin v. Lessee of Waddell*, Chief Justice Taney took one last opportunity to reinforce the rule, stating, "The English possessions in America were not claimed by right of conquest, but by right of discovery. . . . The Indian tribes in the new world were regarded as mere temporary occupants of the soil, and the absolute rights of property and dominion were held to belong to the European nation by which any particular portion of the country was first discovered." In consequence, "whatever forbearance may have been sometimes practiced towards the unfortunate aborigines, wither from humanity or policy, yet the territory they occupied was disposed of by the governments of Europe at their pleasure, as if it had been found without inhabitants."[70]

In five decisions issued between 1836 and 1842—*Mitchel I*, *Fernandez*, *Clark*, *Mitchel II*, and *Martin*—the Jackson members of the Supreme Court thus hammered the *Johnson* formulation of the discovery doctrine into law.[71] Three of these decisions arose from the acquisition of Florida, one from conflicting claims to a New Jersey riverbed, and one from the Virginia militia grants. All were issued against a backdrop of ongoing state and federal efforts to coerce Indian removal. The Court's repeated citations to *Johnson* legitimized these efforts. After the removal of the southern tribes was concluded in 1842 with the defeat of resistant Seminoles in the Second Seminole War, reiteration of the *Johnson* formulation temporarily ceased, and the battle over the discovery doctrine faded from memory.[72]

Chief Justice John Marshall devised the discovery doctrine in 1823 as a means of shoring up the claims of Virginia militia bounty warrant holders to lands in the southwestern corner of the State of Kentucky. The weapon he thus forged for his former colleagues in arms was seized by expansionist Georgians and wielded against Native Americans throughout the eastern United States. The reformulation of the doctrine he engineered in *Worcester v. Georgia* proved impossible to sustain. *Johnson* was too important to removal. In 1835, Jackson appointees took control of Marshall's court and revived the *Johnson* formulation. We live today with the legacy.

AFTERWORD

———◆◆◆———

When John Marshall "traveled" beyond Robert Goodloe Harper's clever pleading to decide more than the effect on the Illinois and Wabash purchases of the Proclamation of 1763, he did not foresee that the doctrine he developed would be used to support the removal of the southeastern tribes. Indeed, when given his first real opportunity to do so in *Worcester v. Georgia*, he reversed himself, a reversal the Court subsequently ignored. The discovery doctrine survived because it facilitated Indian removal.

The southeastern tribes—the Cherokees, Creeks, Chickasaws, Choctaws, and Seminoles—were all forcibly relocated to what is now Oklahoma by 1842. Many other tribes, including the tribes that sold their lands to the Illinois and Wabash Land Companies—the Piankashaws in Indiana, the Kaskaskias, Peorias, and Cahokias in Illinois—joined them in forced western migration.[1] As is well recounted elsewhere, the human consequences of removal were tragic, with uncounted numbers dying as tribe after tribe traveled its own trail of tears.

And this was only the first unintended consequence of the Court's decision in *Johnson v. M'Intosh*. If John Marshall was surprised when the discovery doctrine was used to support removal, he can hardly have expected that more than 180 years later it would still be cited to support the assertion or retention of European-derived rights to indigenous lands, and not only in the United States. For in ways beyond the scope of the present work, *Johnson*'s reach has been global. In its 1984 decision in *Guerin v. The Queen*, for example, the Supreme Court of Canada, after citing *Johnson*, held that "Indians have a legal right to occupy and possess certain lands, the ultimate fee to which is in the Crown."[2] Under Canadian law, as under U.S. law, the tribes lost ownership of their lands by virtue of discovery. Subsequently, the High Court of Australia cited *Johnson* in a remarkable opinion—*Mabo v. Queensland*—which, while recognizing for the first time land claims of indigenous Australians, nevertheless limited those claims under a variation of the discovery doctrine.[3] There, too, the discovering European sovereign was recognized to be the owner of the underlying title to indigenous lands.

That such unexpected consequences form the decision's primary legacy is perhaps only fitting. The history of *Johnson v. M'Intosh* is replete with unexpected events and consequences. The Revolution, St. Clair's defeat, Harper's fortuitous appearance, Thomas Johnson's death, the Senate resolution of the Carver Claim, the emergence of the Virginia militia claims dispute, and the removal of the southeastern tribes all fixed in some measure the opinion's language and historical force. When courts now cite to *Johnson v. M'Intosh*, what they invoke is the repudiated product of multiple contingencies.

APPENDIX 1

———◆·◆·◆———

The 1810 Memorial

The following is the complete text (minus appendices) of the 1810 *Memorial of the United Illinois and Wabash Land Companies to the Senate and House of Representatives of the United States.*

TO THE HONORABLE
THE SENATE AND HOUSE OF REPRESENTATIVES
OF THE
UNITED STATES OF AMERICA,
IN CONGRESS ASSEMBLED,
THE UNITED
ILLINOIS AND WABASH LAND COMPANIES,
RESPECTFULLY SUBMIT THE FOLLOWING
MEMORIAL.

In the year 1773 William Murray, in conjunction with various other persons as whose agent he acted, as well as his own account, formed a plan for the purchase of lands from the Illinois Indians; a nation consisting of various tribes, who claimed and possessed a very extensive tract of country, on the Mississippi Ohio and Illinois rivers.

Murray had long been engaged in trade with these Indians, and resided in their country. In the month of June, 1773, he held several public conferences on the subject of the intended purchase, with the several tribes of the Illinois Indians, at the village of Kaskaskias, which was in their country, and had been the principal residence of one of the tribes. It was then a British settlement and military station. At these conferences, which lasted nearly a month, the civil and military officers of the British government, and all the inhabitants of the place, were invited to be present. Many persons of both descriptions did attend. And the Indians were carefully prevented from obtaining any spiritous liquors, during the whole continuance of the negociation.

On the fifth of July, 1773, the bargain was completed, by which these Indians, for a very large and valuable consideration, agreed to sell to Murray and his associates two tracts of land, which are thus bounded. The first begins on the east side of the Mississippi river, at the mouth of "Heron Creek," called by the French "The river of Mary"; being about a league below the mouth of the Kaskaskias river. From thence the line runs a straight course northward of east, about eight leagues, be it more or less, to the Hilly Plains; thence the same course in a direct line to the Crabtree Plains, seventeen leagues or thereabouts, be it more or less; thence the same course, in a direct line, to a remarkable place known by the name of the Buffaloe Hoofs, seventeen leagues or thereabouts, be it more or less; thence the same course, in a direct line, to the Salt-lick Creek, about seven leagues, be it more or less; thence crossing the creek, about one league below the ancient Shawnese town, in an easterly or a little to the north of east course, in a direct line to the river Ohio, about four leagues, be it more or less; thence down the river Ohio by its several courses, until it empties into the Mississippi, about thirty-five leagues, be it more or less; and thence up the Mississippi, by its several courses, to the place of beginning, about thirty three leagues be it more or less.

The second of these tracts begins also at the Mississippi, on the east side, at a point directly opposite to the mouth of the Missouri. From thence the line runs "up the Mississippi, by its several courses, to the mouth of the Illinois, about six leagues, be it more or less; thence up the Illinois by its several courses, in Chicagou or Garlick Creek, about ninety leagues, be it more or less; thence nearly a northerly course in a direct line, to a certain place remarkable for being the ground on which a battle was fought about forty or fifty years before that time, between the Pewaria and Renard Indians, about fifty leagues, be it more or less, thence by the same course in a direct line, to two remarkable Hills close together, in the middle of a large prairie, about fourteen leagues, be it more or less; thence a north of east course, in a direct line, to a remarkable spring, known by the Indians by the name of the Foggy Spring, about fourteen leagues, be it more or less; thence the same course, in a direct line, to a great Mountain to the northward of the White Buffaloe Plain, about fifteen leagues, be it more or less; and thence nearly a south west course, in a direct line, to the place of beginning, about forty leagues, be it more or less.

The boundaries of the land being thus settled, and the contract fully concluded, Murray, in behalf of himself and his associates, paid the stipulated consideration, and the principal Chiefs of the Illinois nation, in behalf of themselves and of their respective tribes, and with the knowledge and full assent of those tribes, by whose authority they acted, executed and delivered to him and his associates, as tenants in common in fee simple, a deed for these two parcels of land, bearing date on the fifth of July, 1773, and attested by various persons, among whom were the commandant of the British military posts in the Illinois country, and the Indian Interpreters for the British government there. Those Interpreters explained the deed to the Indians, before it was executed; and it was then duly proved and recorded, in the Office of a Notary Public at Kaskaskias, which according to the French laws, then permitted by the British government to remain in force in that county, was a public office for the registration of deeds. A copy of the deed marked No. 1, is hereto annexed by your memorialists, who are ready to produce the original whenever it may be deemed necessary. The purchasers under this deed were denominated "The Illinois Land Company."

In September 1775, Murray commenced another negociation, with the Piankishaw Indians, on behalf of himself and several other persons associated with him, for the purchase of lands on the Wabash river, then claimed and held by those Indians. In this purchase, in effecting which Louis Viviat one of the associates was employed as an agent, the same precautions were used as in the former. The Chiefs of the various tribes of Piankishaw Indians were convened in public conference, at Post Saint Vincents, or Vincennes, on the Wabash, then under the British government, and a British military post. At these conferences, as at the former, the civil and military officers of the British government, as well as the inhabitants of the place, were invited to attend. The Indians were prevented from obtaining spirituous liquors, while the business was pending. Every thing was conducted openly and fairly. And at length, on the eighteenth of October, 1775, the contract was concluded by which the Indians in question, for a large and valuable consideration, agreed to sell to Viviat Murray and their associates, as tenants in common in fee simple, two tracts of land on the Wabash, which are bounded as follows.

The first begins on the Wabash, at the mouth of a rivulet called "Riviere du Chat," or "Cat river," being about fifty-two leagues above Post Saint Vincent, and thence down the Wabash by its several courses, to a place called "Point Coupee," about twelve leagues above Post Saint Vincent, being forty leagues or thereabouts in length on the Wabash river, from the place of beginning, with forty leagues in width on the east side, and thirty on the west side of that river, to be continued from the place of beginning to Point Coupee aforesaid.

The second tract begins on the Wabash where it receives White river, about twelve leagues below Post Saint Vincent, and runs thence down the Wabash, by its several courses, 'till it empties into the Ohio, being about fifty-three leagues, be it more or less; with forty leagues in width on each side of the Wabash, to be continued from White river aforesaid to the Ohio.

For these two tracts the stipulated consideration was then paid, and a deed was executed and delivered by the Indians to the purchasers, bearing date on the eighteenth of October, 1775. This deed was publicly interpreted to the Indians before they signed it, by two sworn interpreters, and was attested by many persons present at the execution, and at the delivery of the consideration which it mentions. It was then recorded in the Office of a Notary Public, there also a public office for the registration of deeds. The purchasers under it were denominated "The Wabash Land Company." A copy of it is hereto annext, marked No. 2, and the original is in the possession of your memorialists, ready to be produced whenever required.

The war which soon afterwards broke out between Great Britain and the North American Colonies, and ended in the American Revolution, prevented the purchasers under these two deeds from taking actual possessions of their lands, or adopting any measures for making settlements on them. But in the beginning of the year 1780, these purchasers, many of whom were grantees in both deeds, resolved to unite the two Companies in one, under the name of "The United Illinois and Oubashe (or Wabash) Land Companies," and to hold the whole lands conveyed by both deeds, as a joint stock or property, according to regulations then established. This resolution was carried into effect, by an instrument of writing bearing date on the 29th of April, 1780.

The rights thus acquired by fair purchases, for valuable consideration, from the original owners of the land, whom no law did or could forbid to sell their property, are now vested in your memorialists, constituting, "The United Illinois and Wabash Land Companies"; some of whom claim as original purchasers, and the others by descent, devise or conveyance from such as were so. These rights our memorialists, and those under whom they claim, have repeatedly brought before the government of the United States. Their first application was made to congress under the old Confederation, and was reported on by a committee of that body, in 1781. On this report no further proceedings were had, and the claim rested in that situation, till the dissolution of the old government. In December 1791, your memorialists renewed their application, by a memorial to both Houses of Congress, which was in each house referred to a committee. To these committees your memorialists made a full representation of their claim, with the proofs and facts to support it, and proposed terms of compromise, which the committee of the House of Representatives, by their report, advised Congress to accept. The committee of the Senate on the 26th of March, 1792, reported differently, and consequently nothing was then dome for the relief of your memorialists.

This relief they again sought in 1797, by a memorial to Congress; which was referred to adopt the report made by the committee of the Senate, on the 6th of March, 1792.

Having thus again failed in obtaining relief, your memorialists took no further step in the affair, till the year 1804, when a petition was again presented tot the House of Representatives on their part, and was referred to a committee; whose report, unfavourable to the claim, was adopted by the House.

And lastly, this claim has been brought before the Commissioners appointed under an act of Congress to investigate claims to land within the district of Vincennes, and to report on them to Congress, through the Treasury Department. These Commissioners reported unfavorably to the claim, but this part of their report has not yet been acted on by Congress.

The reasons on which these successive rejections were founded, are various and in some instances contradictory. But your memorialists believe that they are all reducible to the following points.

    1st. That the Indian Tribes in whose names these sales were made, were not in fact the proprietors of the land sold, which is claimed by the six nations and their tributaries.

    2nd. That the grantors or individual Indians who signed and delivered the deeds, do not appear to be duly au-

thorised by their respective nations; who in their subsequent treaties with the United States, have never acknowledged these sales.

3rd. That the purchases in question were made from the
Indians by private individuals, without any public
treaty, or other act of notoriety; without any public
authority or previous liberty from the government, or
its subsequent confirmation; and therefore contrary to
the common and known usage in such cases, and to
the express prohibitions contained in the British King"
proclamation of October 7th, 1763.

4th. That one of the deeds contains merely a number of
lines, without including any land whatsoever.

5th. That the purchase of 1775, on the Wabash, was made
since the revolution, while Congress had an agent for
Indian affairs residing at Fort Pitt, who received no
notice of this purchase.

6th. That the lands comprehended in these deeds have
been ceded by the Indian tribes to the United States,
who have paid an adequate compensation for them.

And lastly, That the proceeds of all sales of lands in the Western Country,
"belonging to the United States," are appropriated towards the discharge of
the public debt.

These objections your memorialists now proceed to answer, and as they
confidently hope to remove, in the order in which they are here stated.

FIRST OBJECTION.

That the Indian tribes in whose names these sales were made, were not in fact
the owners of the land sold; which was claimed by the six nations and their
tributaries.

This objection is set up in the report made by a committee of the old
Congress, in 1781.

It might be a sufficient answer to it to say, that the United States have
since acknowledged the title of these Indians, by purchasing from them at
two several times, large portions of the land in question.

The first of these purchases was made by a treaty concluded at Vincennes on the 13th of August, 1803, from the Kaskaskias Indians, stating themselves to be all that remained of the various tribes of Illinois Indians, united into one tribe, and long known by the name of Kaskaskias; and it includes the whole of the tract first described in the deed of July 5th, 1773, from those Indians to your memorialists, with a large part of the second tract. This treaty is found in the seventh volume of the Acts of Congress, page 203. A comparison of it with the last mentioned deed to your memorialists will shew, that the tribes making the grants, and the land granted, are the same.

The second purchase was made from the Piankishaw Indians, by a treaty concluded with them at Vincennes, on the 30th of December 1805. This purchase includes a large part of the second tract granted by the same Indians, the Piankishaws, to your memorialists by the deed of October 18th, 1775.

The treaty is contained in the 8th volume of the Acts of congress, page 339. It will appear on a comparison of this treaty with the deed, that the lands granted are the same, and that the grants are made by the same tribe of Indians.

A still more solemn though less direct recognition of this right, had previously been made by the United States, in the treaty of Greenville, concluded with the north western Indians, on the 3rd of August, 1795.

This treaty is found in the second volume of the Acts of Congress, page 449. The United States claimed the lands north west of the Ohio, as having been ceded to the British Crown by the six nations, and by the British Crown to the United States, by the treaty of peace. The north western Indians resisted the claim, and from this dispute arose the bloody contest which after various turns of fortune, was terminated at the rapids of the Miami, and by the treaty of Greenville. By this treaty the United States relinquished forever their claim, with some small and particular exceptions, to all the lands north and west of the boundary line then established, which runs a little to the west of the Great Miami, and very far to the east of the lands claimed by your memorialists. The above mentioned exceptions, and all the lands to the south and east of that line, they purchased from the Indians, for a sum in hand of Twenty Thousand Dollars, and a perpetual annuity of Nine Thousand Five Hundred Dollars.

Among the Indians to whom that relinquishment was made, the Kaskaskias, including all the tribes of the ancient Illinois, and the Piankishaws are particularly named. They also received a proportionable part of the sum paid for the lands reserved, a part of which lay within their particular territories.

Your memorialists presume to expect, that after these solemn and repeated recognitions by the United States, of the title of these Indians to the lands in question, the objection now under consideration will not be again repeated. But they do not rely on these recognitions alone. On the contrary they are prepared to shew, by the most undoubted and unequivocal testimony, whenever it shall be necessary, that no Indians except those under whom they claim, ever possessed or were supposed to be entitled to the lands in question. As to the six nations it will be clearly proved, that neither they nor their tributaries or allies ever claimed any lands whatever, to the westward of a line to be drawn "up the Ohio; from the mouth of the Cherokee or Tennessee river, to the mouth of the Great Miami, and from thence up the Great Miami to its source." The lands claimed by your memorialists lie far to the west of this line.

But although your memorialists do not deem it necessary now to enter at large into the proofs of this fact, which are to be found in the history of Indian transactions from the first settlement of North America up to the American Revolution, and in all the geographical accounts of the country, especially that published by captain Hutchins to explain his map; they will nevertheless present one document of a nature so conclusive, as to remove all doubt could any exist. It is a deposition of colonel George Croghan, for more than thirty years deputy superintendent of Indian affairs, made in the year 1781, near the close of his life. This deposition is in these words—

"George Croghan, Esq. being duly sworn on the holy evangelists of Almighty God, doth depose and say, that the six nations claim by right of conquest, all the lands on the south-east side of the river Ohio down to the Cherokee river, and on the west side of the Ohio, down to the Big Miami river (otherwise called Stony river), and that the six nations never had a claim of any kind, or made any claim, to lands below the Big Miamis or Stony river, on the west side of the Ohio: but that the lands on the west side of the Ohio, below Stony river, were always supposed to belong to the Indians of the Western Confederacy. That the deponent has for thirty years been intimately acquainted with the above country, and the Indians, *and their different claims to territory*; and never heard the six nations claim, *and knows that they never did claim*, beyond the above description; nor did they ever dispute the claim of the Western Confederacy. And further saith not."

To this your memorialists will add the description given by the six nations themselves of their boundaries, at the treaty of fort Stanwicks, in November, 1768. It is contained in their final deed of cession to the king of Great Britain, dated November 5th 1768, and is in these words—

"We begin on the Ohio, at the mouth of the Cherokee river, which is our just right. And from thence we go up, *on the south side of the Ohio*, to Kittaning above Fort Pitt. From thence in a direct line to the nearest fork of the Susquehanna." Thence (by various natural boundaries and courses described in the deed) to the mouth of Canada creek, where it empties itself into Wood creek, at the end of the long carrying place beyond fort Stanwicks."

After this testimony of the best informed witness that ever lived; of the six nations themselves: of the British Government, who were parties to the deed, and under whom the United States claim; and of the United States in their recent purchases already mentioned; your memorialists presume that no more will be said of the claim of the six nations to these lands. They therefore proceed to the

SECOND OBJECTION.

That the grantors, or Individual Indians who signed and delivered these deeds, do not appear to have been duly authorised to make the sales, by their respective nations; who, in their subsequent treaties with the United States, have never acknowledged these sales.

This objection is contained in the report of a committee of the House of Representatives, in 1804. It divides itself into two branches, which will be separately considered.

    1. The want of previous authority.

    2. The want of subsequent acknowledgment.

As to the previous authority, it may be observed in the first place, that there exists the same proof of it in this case, as in all other cases of purchase from the Indians, under either the British or American Governments, by the public or individuals. The Indians who sign the deeds, are declared in the instruments to act by the authority of their respective nations or tribes. This authority is further attested, by the publicity of the act itself, and by the presence and acquiescence of many other individuals of the several tribes, who would undoubtedly oppose the act, if not done by proper authority. In the same manner have all treaties and contracts with Indians been made. A few of the chief men act on the part of the tribe, claiming to be duly authorised. The transaction is public and many other individuals of the tribe attend, who by their assent attest the authority. Finally, when the purchase money is paid, each individual of the tribe then present receives his share; and the shares of those who are absent are afterwards delivered to them. Their future silence attests the delivery, and their assent to the sale; for otherwise they would not fail speedily to complain.

This being the usual and indeed the sole manner of making purchases from the Indians, and of attesting the authority of the immediate sellers, or rather agents, your memorialists may safely challenge those who object to their title on this ground, to produce an instance in which all these formalities have been more strictly fulfilled, or all the requisites of a fair purchase more fully complied with. The conferences were held in the midst of the Indian country, and in the near neighborhood of their principal settlements. These conferences continued a month. The utmost publicity attended the transaction. Numbers of the Indians, besides those who signed the deeds, were present. All were prevented from the use of spiritous liquors. The price agreed on was very large, in comparison with what is usually or perhaps ever paid for Indian lands. It was paid on the spot, and distributed to the individuals of the several tribes as far as they were present. And no complaint has since been heard, that the sale was made without authority, or that any part of the purchase money remained unpaid.

It is to be remarked in the second place, that considering the state of society among the Indians, and the nature of their customs and institutions, it is impossible for an authority to do any act on behalf of a tribe, to be attested in any other manner. It will not as your memorialists apprehend be expected, that in such case a formal power of attorney, or a written commission, shall be produced: and short of these it is not perceived how an authority can be better attested.

On the second branch of this objection, the want of subsequent acknowledgment of these sales, by the Indians who made them in their negociations since held with the United States; your memorialists will observe in the first place, that as they were not parties to those negociations, and as their rights, though long before brought into the view of the United States, and fully understood by the government at the time of those negociations, were not represented or mentioned; they could not upon any principles of law or justice, be prejudiced by the silence of the Indians, under such circumstances, or even by their express disavowal of the sales, had they made one in the most formal manner. Such silence can only be considered as presumptive evidence that no sales were made; and your honourable body need not to be told, that such evidence cannot avail against the positive proof of the fact.

This sale, your memorialists humbly conceive, must be considered, in this respect at least, in the same manner with all other sales. And they are yet to learn that the declarations of a seller, much less his silence, while he is selling the property a second time, can affect the rights of the first purchaser.

But they contend that a very strong, though not an express, acknowledgment by the Indians of these purchases, is to be found in the price at which they made the subsequent sales to the United States. These sales include about one half of the land sold to your memorialists, for which they paid more than thirty years ago, when the country was a wilderness for many hundred miles around, the sum of fifty thousand dollars at least, on a fair valuation of the goods enumerated in the deeds, and actually delivered to the Indians. By recurring to the two treaties mentioned above (August 13th, 1803, 7 laws 205, and December 18th, 1805, 8 laws 339) it will be found, that for about one half of the same quantity of land, in the present advanced state of that country, which has increased the value of lands at least ten fold beyond what it was in 1775, the United States have paid the following sums. To the Kaskaskias, an addition to their former annuity, so as to increase it to one thousand dollars; a house for the Chief, and the enclosing of a field of one hundred acres, both of which might perhaps cost five hundred dollars; one hundred dollars a year for seven years, as a salary for a priest; three hundred dollars towards the erection of a church; and a gross sum of five hundred and eighty dollars. The former annuity being five hundred dollars, as settled by the treaty of Greenville, the increase of five hundred dollars makes a capital of eight thousand three hundred dollars. The different sums to be paid amount to two thousand dollars more; making in the whole ten thousand three hundred dollars to the Kaskaskias, who made by far the largest cession. The payment to the Piankishaws was an annuity of three hundred dollars, representing a capital of five thousand, and a sum in hand of one thousand one hundred. Thus the whole purchase money accepted by those Indians from the United States, for more than one half of the land formerly sold to your memorialists, amounted to sixteen thousand five hundred dollars; about in the proportions of one half of what your memorialists paid thirty years ago, for the same quantity of the same land.

And this price, compared with that which the United States have paid for other lands, purchased from the Indians under less favorable circumstances, appears still more inadequate.

The tract of land relinquished by the north western Indians, to the United States, by the treaty of Greenville, in the year 1795, is not more extensive than those purchased from the Kaskaskias and Piankishaws, in 1803 and 1805.

For the latter a value equal to sixteen thousand five hundred dollars was paid. A great part of the Greenville purchase was, at the time of making it, more remote from the white settlements, than the land purchased from the Piankishaws and Kaskaskias were in 1803 and 5. In point of contiguity to navigable water there is no comparison. The lands purchased from the Kaskaskias form a triangle, which is bounded on two sides by the Mississippi and Ohio. Those purchased from the Piankishaws lie on the Wabash, not far above its mouth. Those on the contrary relinquished by the treaty of Greenville, though washed on one side by the Ohio much higher up its stream, are for by far the greatest part very remote from that or any other navigable water.

And lastly, the United States had a well founded claim to those last mentioned lands, bottomed on the cessions made by the six nations to the British Government; and in support of that claim had maintained a war, in which they had recently been completely victorious.

And yet for this relinquishment, under all those circumstances unfavorable to the value of the lands, and to the right of the Indians, the United States agreed, by the treaty of Greenville, in August, 1795, to pay twenty thousand dollars in hand, and a perpetual annuity of nine thousand five hundred dollars; which represents a capital of one hundred and fifty eight thousand three hundred dollars.— Add to this the twenty thousand dollars paid down, and it gives the sum of one hundred and seventy eight thousand three hundred dollars, as the price of the Greenville purchase. In addition to which the United States relinquished their claim to the lands beyond the boundary then established, with some inconsiderable exceptions—.

And yet eight or ten years afterwards, in 1803 and 1805, when the population of the country and consequently the value of lands had very much encreased, they obtained from the Piankishaws and Kaskaskias, for the trivial sum of sixteen thousand five hundred dollars, a part of the land thus relinquished by them to those tribes, equal in extent, equal or superior in quality, and greatly superior in situation, to the Greenville cession; for which, under circumstances so much more favorable to the purchase, they had paid more than ten times as much.

The same observations apply to the purchase made at Detroit, on the 17th November, 1807 (acts of Congress, vol. 9, p. 166). The quality of land purchased was less than one half of that obtained from the Piankishaws and Kaskaskias, as may be seen by tracting the lines of all the cessions on the map. For this Detroit purchase, so much more remote from settlements and navigable water, and only one half as large, the United States paid ten thousand dollars in hand, and an annuity of two thousand four hundred. Which represents a capital of forty thousand dollars, making in the whole fifty thousand dollars: Nearly four times as much as they paid to the Kaskaskias and Piankishaws, for double the quantity of land, better situated and in every respect more valuable.—

This great inadequacy of price, your memorialists contend, must be considered as evidence, that the Indians who consented to it remembered the sales made to your memorialists, were conscious of their fairness and validity, and consequently regarded themselves as selling nothing more to the United States, than a quit claim to lands before sold.—

With these remarks your memorialists dismiss the second objection, and proceed to the third.

THIRD OBJECTION.

"That the purchases in question were made from the Indians by private individuals, without any public treaty, or other act of notoriety; without any public authority or previous licence from the Government, or its subsequent confirmation; and therefore contrary to the common and known usage established in such cases, and to the express prohibition contained in the British King's proclamation of October 7th, 1763."

This objection was first brought into view, though very imperfectly, by the report of the Committee of Congress in 1781. It remained unnoticed in all the subsequent reports on this subject, till it was brought forward in that of the Vincennes Commissioners.

That these purchases were made from the Indians, by private individuals, without any public authority or previous licence from the Government, or its subsequent confirmation, is a fact which your memorialists admit, and the legal consequences of which will be presently considered. But it is not a fact that they were made without any public treaty, or other act of notoriety. On the contrary no conferences with Indians were ever held more public or more notorious. The conferences were held at British military posts, in the view and presence of the British military and civil officers. They lasted a month each time. All the Indians, as well as the white settlers, were invited to attend. Great numbers of each description did attend—and by sworn interpreters of the British government, were attested by its civil and military officers.

Your memorialists do not perceive in what manner, such transactions could have been rendered more public or notorious.

The objection to the legal validity of these purchases, on account of their having been made without the previous authority of the Government, and not having received its subsequent confirmation, rests on one two grounds [*sic*].

1st. That the Indians in North America were divested of their right to sell their lands, by the acts of the British Government in establishing colonies whose nominal limits included those lands; or

2nd. That the British King had authority to restrain the Indians, by proclamation, from exercising the right of sale, in favor of British subjects.

Your memorialists confidently expect to shew, that both these grounds are utterly untenable.

The first question which they are to discuss is, whether the Indians in North America were divested of their right to sell their lands, by the acts of the British crown, in establishing colonies whose nominal limits included those lands.

Your memorialists say "nominal limits," because as to lands *actually occupied* by British subjects, or included within the bounds of *actual settlements*, the question, could it at this day arise, might depend on different principles. But the present question is, whether the British Government, by establishing a colony of a few thousand or a few hundred persons, on the Atlantic coast of North America, and describing its limits in a charter or a commission to its Governors, so as to extend from the Atlantic to the south sea, and to include the territories and habitations of many independent states, over whom it neither could exercise or did claim any jurisdiction right or power whatever, did or could divest those states of their property in the soil, which they had held as sovereigns from time immemorial, or of the right of alienation which is one of the inherent and essential ingredients of property.

Surely to state so extravagant a proposition is to refute it.— And yet it is for this proposition, in all its extent, that they who oppose the claim of your memorialists do and must contend.

But certain it is that the British Government never set up such a claim. It incorporated companies, indeed, for the settlement of colonies in America, and gave them charters describing the limits within which they might make settlements.

After settlements were made it established Governments, and prescribed their limits by its charters or commissions. But these acts were considered merely as conferring powers of government, over colonies composed of British subjects, and as defining the limits within which those powers might be exercised, when settlements should be made. It never entered into the head of any man in England, that the Indians included within the limits of those grants became British subjects, were deprived of their property in the soil, or in any manner restricted in its use or disposition. On the contrary the British Government, and the Governments and people of the colonies thus established, always considered and treated these Indians as independent nations, and absolute owners of the land; from whom individuals or colonies might purchase, and did purchase, as convenience or inclination happened to direct.

This appears from the whole history of the New England establishments; of which more authentic and particular accounts exist than of any others, and from which your memorialists will select two very noted and remarkable instances, by way of illustration.

The first is the Indian deed in New Hampshire, to Whelewright and others.

James I. on the 3d of November, 1620, granted to the Council of Plymouth, all the country from the Atlantic to the South Sea, and from the fortieth to the forty-eighth degree of north latitude. This Charter included all the country which now composes the New England states, and much more.

On the 10th of August, 1622, the Council of Plymouth granted to Mason and Gorges all the country lying between the rivers Merrimack and Sagadahock, and extending back to the great Lakes, and the river of Canada. This grant included the greater part of New Hampshire and Vermont, besides a considerable portion of the District of Maine.

On the 17th of May, 1629, John Whelewright and others, without any permission for any person whatever, purchased from the Pisquataqua Indians, by deed, the lands between the Merrimack and Pisquataqua rivers, extending back to lines drawn in various directions, from the Pantucket falls in the Merrimack, to Newishwannock falls in the Pisquataqua. The whole of the land lay within the grant from the Plymouth Company to Mason and Gorges.

On the 7th of November, 1629, Mason alone obtained from the Plymouth Company a new grant, of the country lying between the Merrimack and Pisquataqua, and lines drawn west from the head of Merrimack, and northwest from the head of Pisquataqua, sixty miles. This grant included all the land purchased by Whelewright and others from the Indians.

Mason was a man of fortune and influence in England, as well as in the Colony. He possessed great energy enterprize and activity of character—and he and his descendants and representatives were constantly engaged, from the year 1629 till the American revolution in 1775, more than one hundred and fifty years, in efforts to recover those lands under his grant from the Plymouth Company. But all these efforts were unavailing. The lands continued to be held, and are at this day held, under the Indian Deed, in opposition to the preemptive right of soil claimed under the Crown of Great Britain, thro' its Charter to the Council of Plymouth. Since the revolution a quit claim, for the purpose of putting an end to a troublesome dispute, has been obtained, for some trifling or nominal consideration, from the persons who had purchased the claim.[1]

The other case is that of Major Mason's purchase within the limits of Connecticut, from the Moheagen Indians.

The country which now composes the state of Connecticut, was also included within the Charter of James I. to the Council of Plymouth. On the 17th of March, 1631, it was granted by the Company to Lord Say and Seale Lord Brooke and others; who in their turn made grants to persons inclined to undertake settlements.

But these persons never supposed themselves to have any right till they had purchased from the Indians. Such purchases were sometimes made by the colonies, to whom the patents had been granted, and very often by individuals, on their own account, who had obtained no patents.

A large portion of the lands belonged to the Moheagen Indians; whose chief Uncas, on the 1st of September, 1640, made a deed to the Colony, of all

---

[1] See Belknop's History of New Hampshire, vol. 1st, pages 4, 8, 11, 13, et passim.

his lands situated within its limits, reserving parts for himself and his nation, among which was the land now composing the Township of Norwich.

In June 1659, Uncas and his two sons sold and conveyed by a formal deed this township, a tract of country about nine miles square, to Thomas Leffingwell, Major Mason and others; who do not appear to have asked or had any permission from any person whatever, to make this purchase, under which the lands have ever since been held.

There can be no doubt that in the history of the other New England states, and of New York and New Jersey, many similar instances might be found. But these suffice to shew that the Indians were never considered as being restrained from the power of selling, or individuals from the power of buying from them, by the royal grants merely, unaccompanied by any treaty or compact with the Indians themselves, transferring their rights to the Government of Great Britain.

As to a very large part of New York, almost the whole of Pennsylvania, all the western part of Tennessee, and all the country north west of the Ohio, as low down as the great Miami, the British Government claimed the right of preemption in the soil, as well as of jurisdiction, under a cession made by the six nations, the acknowledged proprietors of all that country, at Albany in the year 1679. Their deed of cession was made to Governor Dungan of New York, in trust for the Crown, and is now of record in Albany. They confirmed it four years afterwards, September 26, 1683—at another treaty held in Albany, at which the agents of William Penn attended. Penn had obtained the grant of his province from the Crown, on the 4th day of March, A.D. 1681, previously to this final cession by the Indians of the preemptive right to their lands. Part of those lands lay within his province. The preemptive right to that part he wished to obtain from the Indians; and for that purpose sent agents to the treaty held at Albany in September 1683. But the Indians having considered his proposals, refused to accede to it; alledging that they had before sold the right to the Crown. Penn therefore, to secure this preemptive right, was compelled to obtain a deed of conveyance from Governor Dungan, which was executed at London, no doubt with the assent of the King, in January 1696.

There cannot be a clearer proof that the Crown did not claim this preemptive right, independently of any cession by the Indians. Otherwise, as the Crown had granted these lands to Penn, before the final cession at Albany in 1683 the right would have passed to him by the grant, and he need not afterwards have applied for it to the Indians, or Governor Dungan.

On this cession by the six nations, in 1679, 1683, is founded the right claimed by Virginia under the British Crown, and by the United States under Virginia, to the country North West of the Ohio.

The claim was disputed by the North Western Indians, and gave rise to the war with them, which after the bloody and decisive victory of August 20, 1794, near the Miami of the lake, was terminated by the treaty of Greenville in August 1795.

But this claim never extended to the lands purchased by your memorialists, from the Illinois and Piankishaw Indians, who until the year 1763, were so far from owing any allegiance to the Crown of Great Britain, or acknowledging any dependance on it or connection with it, that they were in a state of war against it, and the six nations its allies.— They were the allies of France in the war of 1756, which arose out of disputes about boundaries in America, and was terminated by the treaty of Paris in 1763.

In the conferences and negocations which preceded that war, it was acknowledged by both the contending powers, France and Great Britain, "that there were intermediate nations between Canada and Louisiana, and between Virginia and Louisiana (that is between the territories claimed by the two powers), who were independent of the sovereignty of both Crowns, and to be considered as a barrier between them."

These "intermediate nations" were the North Western Indians, of whom the Illinois and Piankishaw made a part; and whose complete independence was thus formally acknowledged by both crowns.

The treaty of Paris settled what should ever afterwards be the line of division between the two powers; not for the purpose of appropriating to themselves, and dividing between them the country of these Independent nations, which they neither had or pretended to have a right to do, but merely for that of designating the limits, within which each should in future be permitted by the other to form colonies, under its own laws and Government, with the consent of the Indians, whenever it could be obtained.

The treaty did not operate, and was not intended to operate, as a mutual cession of territory; but as a covenant, by which each party was restrained from attempting to acquire territory from the Indians, beyond certain limits. So far, and so far only, as territory had been already obtained beyond these limits, as in the cases of military posts and actual settlements, it operated as a mutual cession.—This treaty then left the Indians as it found them, independent nations, and absolute proprietors of the soil; with full and complete powers of alienation.

Of this power of alienation they might divest themselves, as the six nations had done, by a treaty or a sale; but until they did so divest themselves it remained in them, as an inherent and essential part of the right of property, and of the attributes of sovereignty.

That they were viewed in this light by the British Government, and had made no such cession or treaty, is proved by the proclamation of October 7th, 1763, in which the British King declared that although they "lived under his protection, their territory was their own; having never been ceded to or purchased by him."

How indeed, your memorialists would ask, could it have ceased to be their own? not by conquest; for Great Britain never did conquer them or their country. She gained indeed such general advantages in the war against France, whose allies these Indians were, has induced that power to yield to the adjustment of limits in America which she had claimed; but she never over ran this country in the course of the war, or obtained possession of any posts or settlements in it, till the peace. Not by the cession of France; for France was not, and did not pretend to be, the sovereign of this country. The Indians to whom it belonged were not her subjects, but her allies; and were acknowledged and treated by her as independent States. She held, by previous cessions from them, some military posts and trading stations in their country. These she could cede and did cede to Great Britain. But as to the country itself she neither had nor claimed a right to cede it. She merely agreed to withdraw from it, as far as a certain line established by the treaty; and not in future to attempt settlements or establishments in it, beyond that line: but this withdrawal and agreement could not transfer a right which she did not possess. That she possessed no right to the country, and claimed none further than related to her posts and stations, held under cessions from the Indians, is abundantly manifest from all her acts and declarations, and from the nature of her connexion with these Indians.

But if France had been the sovereign of this country, and had as such ceded it to Great Britain, this cession would have transferred merely the jurisdiction and powers of Government, and not the right of property in the soil. This right is a private right, and is never affected by the cession of a country, from one sovereign to another. The Indians, if they were not sovereigns of the country, but subjects of France, were certainly proprietors of the soil, and as such were invested with all the rights incident to property; of which the right to sell is one. This right and power to sell therefore, as it existed under the French Government, before the cession, was not and could not be affected by the cession; but still remained in the Indians, the original proprietors.

Whether therefore these Indians are considered as sovereign States in alliance with France, or as the subjects of that power, their right of property in the soil, and their power of alienation as an inseparable ingredient of that right, remained equally unaffected by the cession from France to Great Britain. As little could this right be affected by conquest, admitting them to have been conquered by Great Britain. It is a well known and undeniable principle, that the conquest of a country does not deprive the individual owners of the soil of their rights of property. It merely affects the sovereignty and powers of Government. The new sovereign may, if he please, confiscate the property of his new subjects; but this is an exercise of the powers of legislation and government which he has acquired by his conquest, not a direct or immediate effect of the conquest itself. If therefore these Indians be considered as having been conquered by Great Britain, either in the war of 1756 or at any former period, still they continued to be the owners and proprietors of the land. They became by the conquest the subjects of the British Crown, but did not lose their rights of private property. Nor could they be divested of these rights, except by an act of the Supreme legislative authority.

This authority, according to the British Constitution, to the protection of which they were in that case entitled, resided not in the King, but in Parliament. No act of Parliament having passed on this subject, it follows undeniably that the rights of private property, and among them the ownership of the land, and the right to sell it, which were vested in the Indians before the conquest, admitting a conquest to have been made, still continued in them.

If after the conquest their country was included within the limits of any colony, they might by this inclusion become members of the colony, or its subjects; but could not be deprived of their rights of private property.

Your memorialists therefore trust that on this first branch of the objection, viz. "that the Indians in North America were divested of their right to sell their lands by the acts of the British Government, in establishing colonies whose nominal limits included those lands," no doubt can remain.

It is manifest, as your memorialists conceive, that such limits can be regarded by no person, and never were regarded by the British Government, or by the people of the colonies, in any other light, than as mere designations of the extent to which settlements might be made under each colony, when the land could be purchased from the Indians; and of the Government to which such settlements when made should belong; the Indians being in the meantime the sovereigns of the country, and the absolute proprietors of the soil. This brings your memorialists to the second branch of the objection which they now proceed to consider, viz. "that the British King had a right to restrain the Indians by proclamation, from exercising the right of sale in favour of British subjects."

Or in other words that the British King, without the authority of Parliament, or any act of the legislature, had the power, under the English constitution, of restraining British subjects, from purchasing from those who had a right to sell.

It might be expected that they who contend for such a proposition would support it by some authority; but your memorialists will waive this advantage, and proceed to shew that the proposition is wholly unfounded. It embraces two questions, which shall be separately considered:

     1st. Whether the king of England possessed such a power
          to restrain the Indians from selling?

    2nd. Whether he possessed such a power to restrain British
          subjects from buying?

As to the first, it has already been shewn, conclusively, that the Indians were not British subjects, but independent nations; and consequently that no acts of the British Government, however clearly within its constitutional powers, could affect them. But admit them to be British subjects; they were still the owners of the land, and had all the rights of British subjects. One of these rights was the right of sale, unless restrained not by a proclamation but by law. That the proclamations of the British King, in matters of property, cannot have the force of laws, is a proposition which none will deny or doubt; and however competent it might have been to the British Parliament, in the exercise of its supreme Legislative powers, to enact that certain persons, subjects of the British Government, should be restrained from selling their lands, except on certain conditions, it is very clear that the King alone had no such power; and that any attempt to exercise such a power was absolutely void. What would be thought in England of a proclamation forbidding British land-holders, or any class or description of them, to sell their estates? In what manner would such an act be viewed by the Courts in Westminster Hall?

The same observations apply to the second question, relative to the power of restraining by proclamation British subjects from purchasing land.

As the territory within which these lands were situated was acknowledged by the British Government, through the King, its constitutional organ for making such acknowledgements, to be an independent territory, over which that Government neither exercised nor claimed any jurisdiction; it may well be doubted whether any act of Parliament could produce the effect contended for. It certainly is not easy to imagine how the legislative or other acts of a Government, can operate in a foreign territory. But admitting that in this case an act of Parliament might produce such an effect, it is an effect to be produced by a law, and not by a proclamation, which was not a law, in England or her colonies then, more than it now is in the United States. To restrain British subjects from the exercise of so dear and natural a right, as that of making purchases, is surely an effect to which by the British Constitution, the power of Parliament is alone competent. What, let it again be asked, would be thought in England or in Jamaica, of a proclamation forbidding all persons, or a particular class of persons, from making purchases of land?

That the proclamation of October 7th, 1763, did produce and could produce no such effect, is further manifest from an opinion given officially to the King, nine years after its date, by three of the greatest lawyers that England ever produced, Prat, Yorke and Dunning, who were then the Crown Lawyers, and two of whom, Yorke and Prat, afterwards the famous Lord Camden, became Lord Chancellors of England. Being consulted by the King in Council, in the year 1772, as to the legal effects of Indian Grants and Royal Patents, they gave the following answer, on the 1st of August, 1772.

"In respect to such places as have been or shall be acquired by treaty or grant from any of the Indian Princes or Governments, your Majesty's letters patent are not necessary, the property of the soil vesting in the grantee by the Indian Grants, subject only to your Majesty's right of sovereignty over the settlements as English settlements, and over the inhabitants as English subjects; who carry with then your Majesty's Laws, wherever they form colonies and receive your Majesty's protection, by virtue of your Royal Charters."

This opinion not only supports the validity of Indian sales to individuals, made after the proclamation; but shews the true use and operation of the Royal Charters: which was not to transfer the right of soil, or even the preemptive right; but to establish Governments, and extend to the settlements the privileges of British subjects, and the protection of the British Crown. It clearly proves that the proclamation of October 7th, 1763, was not considered in England as restraining the power of the Indians to sell, or the right of British subjects to buy.

That it was viewed in the same light in America, both by private persons and by those holding the highest offices under the British Government, is perfectly manifest. Among the grantees in the deeds under which your memorialists claim, are found the names of some of the most eminent lawyers of that day, both in Pennsylvania and Maryland, of some of the best informed merchants in both places, and of the Earl of Dunmore then Governor of Virginia. These men cannot be supposed to have been ignorant of what was the law and practice of the British Government, on a subject of so much importance, where they were about to expend such large sums of money. Still less can it be supposed that they would knowingly violate the rules prescribed on such a subject, by a Government whose displeasure would have produced effects so serious to some of them: and when they were sanctioned in their proceedings by such an opinion as your memorialists have cited, surely they cannot now be considered as having acted illegally.

Your memorialists on these grounds humbly trust, that they have destroyed the second branch of the objection, as well as the first, and have proved "that the British King had no authority to restrain the Indians by proclamation, from exercising the right of sale, in favor of British subjects." Hence it results that the third objection to the claim of your memorialists, founded on the proclamation of October 7th, 1763, must fall to the ground.

They further take the liberty to suggest, on this head, that it may well be doubted whether the British King intended by this proclamation, to forbid purchases *from the Indians* by individuals. An intent so clearly repugnant to the first principles of the British Constitution, ought to be very clearly made out, before it is admitted.

The parts of the proclamation which relate to this subject are in the following words.

> 1st. "And whereas it is just and reasonable and essential to our interest, and the security of our Colonies, that the several nations or tribes of Indians, with whom we are connected, and who live under our protection should not be molested or disturbed, in the possession of such parts, of our dominions and territories as not having been ceded to or purchased by us, are reserved to them

or any of them as their hunting grounds; we do there-fore, with the advice of our privy council, declare it to be our royal will and pleasure, that no Governor or Commander in Chief, in any of our colonies of Que-bec, East Florida or West Florida, do presume, upon any pretence whatever, to grant warrants of survey or patents, for lands beyond the bounds of their respec-tive Governments, as described by their Commissions: as also that no Governor or Commander in Chief, of our other colonies or plantations in America do pre-sume, for the present, and until our further pleasure shall be known, to make grants, warrants of survey, or pass patents for any lands beyond the heads or sources of any of the rivers which fall into the Atlantic Ocean from the west or north-west; or upon any lands what-ever, which not having been ceded to, or purchased by us as aforesaid, are reserved to the said Indians or any of them."

2nd. "And we do further declare it to be our royal will and pleasure, for the present as aforesaid, to reserve under our sovereignty, protection, and dominion, for the use of the said Indians, all the lands and territories not in-cluded within the limits of our said three new Govern-ments, nor within the limits of the territory granted to the Hudson's Bay Company, as also all the lands and territories lying to the westward of the sources of the rivers, which fall into the sea from the west and north-west as aforesaid; and we do hereby strictly forbid on pain of our displeasure, all our loving subjects from making any purchases or settlements whatever, or tak-ing possession of any of the lands above reserved, without our special leave and licence for that purpose first obtained."

3rd. "And we do further strictly enjoin and require all per-sons whatever, who have either wilfully or inadvertently seated themselves, upon any lands within the territories above described, or upon any other lands which, not

having been ceded to or purchased by us, are still reserved to the said Indians, as aforesaid, forthwith to
remove themselves from such settlements."

4th. "And whereas great frauds and abuses have been committed, in the purchasing land *of the Indians*, to the
great prejudice of our interest and to the great dis-
satisfaction of the said Indians; in order therefore to
prevent such interruption for the future, and to the
end that the Indians may be convinced of our justice,
and determined resolutions to remove all reasonable
cause of discontent, we do with the advice of our privy
Council strictly enjoin and require that no private
person do presume to make any purchase from the
said Indians, of any lands reserved to the said Indians
within those parts of our colonies, where we have
thought proper to allow settlements; but that if at any
time, any of the said Indians should be inclined to dispose of the said lands, the same shall be purchased
only for us, in our name, at some public meeting or
assembly of the said Indians, to be held for that purpose, by the Governor or Commander in Chief of our
colony respectively within which they lie."[2]

The prohibition in question is supposed to be contained in the second of
the clauses here cited, and in this part of it; "and we do hereby strictly forbid,
on pain of our displeasure, all our loving subjects from making any purchases or settlements whatever, or taking possession of any of the lands above
reserved, without our special licence, for that purpose first obtained."

The words undoubtedly contain a prohibition to make purchases; but the
question is whether that prohibition extends to purchases from the *Indians*;
or is confined to purchases from the King's Governors? He has in the next
preceding clause forbidden his Governors, "for the present," to grant warrants of survey or pass patents for lands situated as these were. This he clearly
had a right to do; because those Governors were his own officers, deriving

2 See the proclamation at large in Marshal's History of Washington, vol. 5, Appendix—
And in Chalmers's collection of State Papers respecting the Colonies.

their whole authority from him; which authority he might therefore limit at his pleasure. It may well be supposed that in order to render the prohibition more complete and effectual, he went on in the next clause, and forbid all his subjects under pain of his displeasure, to buy from those officers, not only by warrants or survey or patents, but in any manner whatever.

This construction would satisfy the words of the proclamation, and would reconcile it with the constitutional powers of the King. And it is very much strengthened by the fifth clause; the object of which was to regulate purchases from the Indians, and to prohibit them unless made in the mode prescribed. The purchases "from the Indians," are expressly mentioned. But that clause, does not extend to the lands now in question; which lay, "to the westward of the sources of the rivers falling into the Atlantic from the west and north-west" and not "within those parts of the colonies where settlements were allowed."

It being therefore at least doubtful, whether this proclamation was intended to prohibit such purchases from the Indians as those made by your memorialists; and a plain and clear intent being necessary, to establish a construction contrary to the principles of the British Constitution; your memorialists humbly insist that on this ground also the objection founded on this proclamation ought to be disregarded. They now proceed to the

FOURTH OBJECTION.

That one of the deeds from the Indians to them, contains only a number of lines, without comprehending any land whatever. This objection is contained in the report of the Committee of Congress in the year 1781.

It applies to the second tract described in the deed of 1773, from the Illinois Indians; which begins at the mouth of the Illinois river.

On this objection your memorialists would observe in the first place, that whatever may be its validity, it cannot affect their right to the other tracts, which are in no manner connected with it, except that one of them is conveyed by the same deed. It relates therefore not to their right of recovery, which is a matter of distinct and subsequent consideration.

They observe in the second place, that it is an invariable rule in surveying, and in the granting of lands, that where lines are declared in the instrument to run a certain course and distance, to natural and fixed boundaries, which are described and can be found, such lines shall terminate at those boundaries although the course may be found to be different, and the distance greater or less. In other words, that the boundary or fixed object, or "the call," as it is sometimes denominated, shall controul the course and distance.— This rule is founded on the most obvious principles of common sense, justice and convenience; it being manifest that a fixed object in the country, such as a tree, a rock, a river, a spring, a mountain, or a battle ground, is a much more certain, obvious and permanent indication of boundary than a course depending on the compass or on conjecture, or a distance to be ascertained by measurement. The rule therefore is believed to be universal in its application; and it is more completely and properly applicable to Indian grants than to any others. As they never sell by actual measurement, and the direction of the lines is never ascertained by the compass, it follows that their courses and distances must always be conjectural, and very often erroneous. But they are well acquainted with the natural objects in their country, and describe them with great accuracy. All their lines are terminated by such objects; to which they constantly appeal, when any question about boundary arises.

Let this rule be applied to the case in question, and your memorialists apprehend that all difficulty will disappear. The natural objects described in this deed can no doubt be easily found. Let the line be drawn through them, as directed by the deed, and if it includes no land, your memorialists admit that they will be entitled to none. But their title to whatever land it may be found to include rests, as they apprehend, on the most solid foundation. They proceed to the

FIFTH OBJECTION.

That the purchase of 1775, from the Piankishaws on the Wabash, was made since the revolution, while Congress had an Agent for Indian affairs residing at Fort Pitt, who had no notice of this purchase.

This objection also is contained in the report of 1781. It is a sufficient answer to it to say, that the revolution had not taken place in October, 1775, when this purchase was made. The colonies indeed were in arms, to resist oppression, but they had not separated themselves from the mother Country, or declared a change of Government. The powers of the British Government, moreover, so far as they extended to the country where these lands lay, were in full vigour and operation at the time of peace in 1783. Till then the British remained in the actual and legal possession of all their posts and establishments in that country; and those Indians were their allies in the war.

There is therefore no pretence for saying that the United States had any right or claim to this country in October, 1775, when the purchase in question was made, or that their Agent at Fort Pitt, if in fact there was one, had any thing to do with the affair.

SIXTH OBJECTION.

The lands comprehended in these deeds have been since ceded by the Indian tribes to the United States; who have paid an adequate compensation for them.

This objection is set up by the Committee of 1804. It is true in part, as your memorialists have already explained in their answer to the second objection. The United States have purchased a part of these lands; first from the Kaskaskias in 1803, and afterwards from the Piankishaws in 1805. The part thus purchased constitutes about one half of the lands sold your memorialists; whose right to the remaining half remains, of course, unaffected by these purchases of the United States.

But upon what presence can it be said, that their right to the part subsequently purchased by the United States, is affected by those purchases? They were not parties to the contracts. They had no notice or knowledge of them, till after they were made. They never in any manner assented to them. Their claim had been repeatedly and fully brought into the view of the Government of the United States, before those purchases were made; and if the Government, with that notice, chose to go on, and purchase land from the Indians which those Indians had before sold, can the rights of the prior purchasers be affected by such a transaction? This your memorialists presume will not be seriously contended for. They therefore dismiss this objection, and proceed to

THE SEVENTH AND LAST.

That the proceeds of sales of land in the Western Country, "belonging to the United States," are appropriated towards the discharge of the public debt.

This objection is urged in the report made by a Committee of the Senate, in 1792. The fact stated in the objection and which is its whole foundation, is true, as relates to lands *belonging to the United States*. But the lands now claimed by your memorialists, never did belong to the United States, having been sold by the legal owners before the United States were in existence, as an independent or separate Government; while no law forbidding such sales existed, and while the powers of the British Government, under which the United States claim, through the State of Virginia, were in as full operation as they could be in that country. This objection therefore does not affect the case of your memorialists; who trust that they have now proved their claim, to be fair, legal and valid.—

But although they feel a perfect confidence in the legal and equitable grounds of their claim, they are ready to admit, that the measures adopted by the Government for the defence and settlement of the neighboring country, have greatly enhanced the value of this property; and that it may be inconvenient to the public, for individuals to hold so large a body of land. They are therefore willing to compromise with the United States, on terms liberal and mutually advantageous.

With this view they take the liberty of suggesting two modes of compromise, either of which they are ready to offer, and one or the other of which they pray Congress to accept.

First that Congress shall confirm to them all that part of the land described in and conveyed to them by the deed of October the 18th, 1775, which lies east of the Wabash, and south of the tract of land called the Vincennes tract; with permission to make all necessary arrangements with the Indians for the settlement of the country, and to sell the lands according to the plan and on the terms which may be adopted by the United States, with respect to the lands west of the Wabash; in consideration of which confirmation they will relinquish and transfer to the United States all their claim, to the rest of the land described and conveyed by both deeds. Or secondly, that the United States shall issue to them certificates of debt, transferable and bearing interest, to the amount of what the above mentioned body of land east of the Wabash would sell for, at the price of two dollars the acre; the interest of these certificates to be annually paid, and the principal ultimately extinguished, out of the funds to arise from such parts of the lands included in both deeds as the United States shall first sell: in consideration of which your memorialists will relinquish and transfer to the United States all their right and title under both deeds.

This body of land, east of the Wabash, and south of the Vincennes tract, is not included in any of the purchases made by the United States from the Indians. Should the first proposition suggested by your memorialists be accepted, they would take on themselves the risk of obtaining from the Indians a recognition of the sales on which their claim is founded. Should they fail in this object, they will neither gain, nor the United States lose, by the confirmation proposed; but every thing will remain in the present situation. If, on the other hand, the recognition should be made by the Indians, it will extend to the whole sales of 1773 and 1775, and will operate as an extinguishment of the Indian title, in a very extensive tract of country not heretofore purchased by the United States. The title of the United States to those large tracts which they purchased from the Kaskaskias and Piankishaws, in 1803 and 1805, would moreover be quieted and confirmed.

Should the second proposition be accepted, the United States will have their title in the same manner quieted and confirmed, in the lands purchased by them in 1803 and 1805, and will moreover acquire the Indian title in very large tracts, which have not yet been ceded to the Government. This Indian title which they will thus acquire, will enable them to extinguish the Indian claim in all these lands, at a very slight additional expence, and probably without any, while they would have nothing to pay to your memorialists, till it should be received from the sale of the lands themselves.

Your memorialists therefore hope that the compromise which they propose, will be deemed advantageous to the United States, and pray that it may be accepted by your honourable body; or that they may receive such other relief in the premises, as in the wisdom and justice of Congress the merits and circumstances of their case may seem to require.

And they will ever pray and so forth.

By authority and on behalf of the *United Illinois and Wabashe Land Companies.*

ROB. G. HARPER, }
SOLOMON ETTING, } *Agents.*
BENJAMIN STODDERT. }

Baltimore, December 10th, 1810.

APPENDIX 2

———◆◆◆———

The Agreed Statement
of Facts and Objections
to the Claims

In the United Illinois and Wabash Land Companies' 1810 memorial, Robert Goodloe Harper summarized the universe of objections raised against the claims by congressional committees and land commissions as follows:

> 1st. That the Indian Tribes in whose names these sales were made, were not in fact the proprietors of the land sold, which is claimed by the six nations and their tributaries.
>
> 2nd. That the grantors or individual Indians who signed and delivered the deeds, do not appear to be duly authorized by their respective nations; who in their subsequent treaties with the United States, have never acknowledged these sales.
>
> 3rd. That the purchases in question were made from the Indians by private individuals, without any public treaty, or other act of notoriety; without any public authority or previous liberty from the government, or its subsequent confirmation; and therefore contrary to the common and known usage in such cases, and to the express prohibitions contained in the King's proclamation of October 7th, 1763.

4th. That one of the deeds contains merely a number of lines, without including any land whatsoever.

5th. That the purchase of 1775, on the Wabash, was made since the Revolution, while Congress had an agent for Indian affairs residing at Fort Pitt, who received no notice of this purchase.

6th. That the lands comprehended in these deeds have been ceded by the Indian tribes to the United States, who have paid an adequate compensation for them.

[7th.] And lastly, That the proceeds of all sales of lands in the Western country, "belonging to the United States," are appropriated towards the discharge of the public debt."[1]

The first objection was readily suited to elimination by stipulation. Harper dispensed with it by stipulating in paragraph 8 of the agreed statement:

8th. That among the tribes of Indians, thus holding and inhabiting the territory north of the Ohio, east of the Mississippi, and west of the Great Miami, within the limits of Virginia, as described in the letters patent of May 23d, 1609, were certain independent tribes or nations, called the Illinois or Kaskaskias, and the Piankeshaw or Wabash Indians; the first of which consisted of three several tribes united into one, and called the Kaskaskias, the Pewarias, and the Cahoquias; *that the Illinois owned, held, and inhabited, as their absolute and separate property, a large tract of country within the last mentioned limits, and situated on the Mississippi, Illinois, and Kaskaskias rivers, and on the Ohio below the mouth of the Wabash; and the Piankeshaws, another large tract of country within the same limits, and as their absolute and separate property, on the Wabash and Ohio rivers; and that these Indians remained in the sole and absolute ownership and possession of the country in question, until the sales made by them,* in the manner herein after set forth.[2]

The second objection, relating to the authority of the signatories, he addressed in paragraphs 11, 12, 15, and 16, concurrently addressing the remainder of the conveyancing requisites:

11th. That from time immemorial, and always up to the present time, all the Indian tribes, or nations of North America, and especially the Illinois and Piankeshaws, and other tribes holding, possessing, and inhabiting the said countries north and northeast of the Ohio, east of the Mississippi, and west of the Great Miami, held their respective lands and territories each in common, the individuals of each tribe or nation holding the lands and territories of each tribe in common with each other, and there being among them no separate property in the soil; and that *their sole method of selling, granting, and conveying their lands, whether to governments or individuals, always has been, from time immemorial, and now is, for certain chiefs of the tribe selling, to represent the whole tribe in every part of the transaction; to make the contract, and execute the deed, on behalf of the whole tribe; to receive for it the consideration, whether in money or commodities, or both; and, finally, to divide such consideration among the individuals of the tribe: and that the authority of the chiefs, so acting for the whole tribe, is attested by the presence and assent of the individuals composing the tribe, or some of them, and by the receipt by the individuals composing the tribe, of their respective shares of the price, and in no other manner.*

12th. That on the 5th of July, 1773, certain chiefs of the Illinois Indians, *then jointly representing, acting for, and being duly authorized by that tribe, in the manner explained above,* did, by their deed poll, duly executed and delivered, and bearing date on that day, . . . for and on behalf of the said Illinois nation of Indians . . . grant, bargain, sell, alien, lease, enfeoff, and confirm, to [the Illinois Company, the Illinois lands]. . . .

13th. That *the consideration in this deed expressed . . . was paid and delivered,* at the time of the execution of the deed, . . . to the Illinois Indians, who freely accepted it, and divided it among themselves: that the conferences in which the sale of these lands was agreed on and made, and in which it was agreed that the deed should be executed, . . . were attended by many individuals of all the tribes of Illinois Indians, besides the chiefs, named as grantors in the deed.. . .

15th. That on the 18th of October, 1775, Tabac, and certain other Indians, all being *chiefs of the Piankeshaws, and jointly representing, acting for, and duly authorized by that nation, in the manner stated above,* did, by their deed poll, . . . at a public council held . . . by them, for and on behalf of the Piankeshaw Indians, . . . grant, bargain, sell, alien, enfeoff, release, ratify, and confirm to [the Wabash Company, the Wabash lands].

16th. That *the consideration in this deed expressed . . . was paid and delivered* at the time of the execution of the deed . . . to the Piankeshaw Indians, who freely accepted it, and divided it among themselves: that the conferences in which the sale . . . was agreed upon and made, and in which it was agreed, that the deed should be executed, . . . were attended by many individuals of the Piankeshaw nation of Indians, besides the chiefs named as grantors in the deed. . . .[3]

The factual portions of the third objection Harper addressed in paragraphs 12, 13, 15, and 16:

12th. That on the 5th of July, 1773, certain chiefs of the Illinois Indians . . . did, by their deed poll, . . . at the post of Kaskaskias, then being a British military post, and *at a public council* there held by them . . . [sell the Illinois lands] . . . as will more fully appear by the said deed poll, . . . *duly recorded at Kaskaskias,* on the 2d of September, 1773, *in the office of Vicerault Lemerance, a notary public, duly appointed and authorized.*

13th. . . . That *the conferences* in which the sales of these lands was agreed on and made . . . *were publicly held,* for the space of a month, at the post of Kaskaskias . . . ; that *the whole transaction was open, public, and fair.* . . .

15th. That on the 18th of October, 1775, Tabac, and certain other Indians, being chiefs of the Piankeshaws, . . . did, by their deed poll, . . . at the post of Vincennes, otherwise called post St. Vincent, then being a British military post, and *at a public council held there by them*, . . . [sell the Wabash lands] . . . , as will more fully appear by the deed itself, . . . *duly recorded at Kaskaskias*, on the 5th of December, 1775, *in the office of Louis Bomer, a notary public, duly appointed and authorized.*

16th. . . . That *the conferences* in which the sale of these two tracts of land was agreed on and made . . . *were publicly held* for the space of a month, at the post of Vincennes, or post St. Vincent . . . ; that *the whole transaction was open, public, and fair.*[4]

As to the remaining portions of the third objection, Harper had argued in the 1810 memorial that they rested on two grounds: that the Indians were divested of their right to sell their lands by virtue of the establishment of colonies in whose nominal limits those lands lay, and that the Crown had the power to restrain the Indians by proclamation from selling to British subjects. The first of these he addressed in paragraphs 3, 5, 7, 8, 13, and 16:

3d. That at the time of granting these letters patent, and of the discovery of the continent of North America by the Europeans, and during the whole intermediate time, *the whole of the territory*, in the letters patent described, except a small district on James River, where a settlement of Europeans had previously been made, was *held, occupied, and possessed, in full sovereignty*, by various independent tribes or nations of Indians, *who were the sovereigns of their respective portions of the territory, and the absolute owners and proprietors of the soil*; and who neither acknowledged nor owed any allegiance or obedience to any European sovereign or state whatever: and that *in making settlements within this territory, and in all the other parts of North America*, where settlements were made, under the authority of the English government, or by its subjects, *the right of*

*soil was previously obtained by purchase or conquest,
from the particular Indian tribe or nation by which the
soil was claimed and held;* or the consent of such tribe
or nation was secured. . . .

5th. That some time previous to the year 1756, *the French
government*, laying a claim to the country west of the
Allegheny or Appalachian mountains, on the Ohio
and Mississippi rivers, and their branches, *took possession of certain parts of it, with the consent of the several
tribes or nations of Indians possessing and owning them;*
and, with like consent, established several military
posts and settlements therein, particularly at Kaskaskias, on the river Kaskaskias, and at Vincennes, on the
river Wabash, within the limits of the colony of Virginia, as described and established in and by the letters
patent of May 23d, 1609. . . .

7th. That at and before the commencement of the war in
1756, and during its whole continuance, and at the
time of the treaty of February 10th, 1763, *the Indian
tribes or nations*, inhabiting the country north and
northwest of the Ohio, and east of the Mississippi, as
far east as the river falling into the Ohio called the
Great Miami, were called and known by the name of
the Western Confederacy of Indians, and *were the allies
of France in the war, but not her subjects, never having
been in any manner conquered by her, and held the
country in absolute sovereignty, as independent nations,
both as to right of jurisdiction and sovereignty, and the
right of soil* except a few military posts, and a small territory around each, which they had ceded to France,
and she held under them, and among which were the
aforesaid posts of Kaskaskias and Vincennes; and that
*these Indians, after the treaty, became the allies of Great
Britain*, living under her protection as they had before
lived under that of France, but were *free and independent, owing no allegiance to any foreign power whatever,
and holding their lands in absolute property;* the territo-

ries of the respective tribes being separated from each other, and distinguished by certain natural marks and boundaries to the Indians well known; and *each tribe claiming and exercising separate and absolute ownership, in and over its own territory, both as to the right of sovereignty and jurisdiction, and the right of soil.*

8th. . . . That *the Illinois owned, held, and inhabited, as their absolute and separate property, a large tract of country* . . . situated on the Mississippi, Illinois, and Kaskaskias rivers, and on the Ohio below the mouth of the Wabash; *and the Piankeshaws, another large tract of country* within the same limits, and *as their absolute and separate property*, on the Wabash and Ohio rivers; and that these Indians remained *in the sole and absolute ownership and possession of the country in question, until the sales made by them*, in the manner herein after set forth. . . .

13th. . . . That *the two tracts of parcels of land which [the 1773 deed] describes, and purports to grant, were then part of the lands held, possessed, and inhabited by the Illinois Indians, from time immemorial*, in the manner already stated. . . .

16th. . . . That *these tracts of land [conveyed in 1775] were then part of the lands held, possessed, and inhabited by the Piankeshaw Indians, from time immemorial*, as is stated above.[5]

The fourth objection related solely to the upper Illinois tract, which would not be at issue in the present case. The fifth rested on a factual predicate—the date of commencement of the Revolution—that was not amenable to stipulation. Last, objections six and seven were factually incontrovertible—six, in fact, was in part essential to the ejectment action—and Harper left them alone as well.

NOTES

PREFACE

1. WESTLAW search, "Johnson /2 (M'Intosh or McIntosh)" in JLR database, 5 July 2003, conducted by the author.

2. Perhaps the most powerful of the intellectual histories of the case is Robert A. Williams Jr., *The American Indian in Western Legal Thought: The Discourses of Conquest* (New York: Oxford University Press, 1990). Only a few authors have offered a glimpse at contemporaneous primary materials relating to the claim. See, e.g., Eric Kades, "History and Interpretation of the Great Case of *Johnson v. M'Intosh*," *Law & History Review* 19 (2001): 67.

CHAPTER 1

1. William M. Meigs, *The Life of Charles Jared Ingersoll* (Philadelphia: J. B. Lippincott, 1897), 123–24, 126.

2. The land approximates 43,000 square miles, or approximately 27.5 million acres, based on the dimensions of the tracts as defined in the deeds at issue in the litigation. Henry Murray's conversational estimate of 70 million acres con-

verts to approximately 109,000 square miles. England is indeed smaller, at 93,000 square miles.

3. Gilmer to Carr, 12 January 1822, Gilmer Collection, Virginia State Library, Richmond, Virginia.

4. Wilcomb E. Washburn, comp., *The American Indian and the United States: A Documentary History* (New York: Random House, 1973), 3: 2137, 2138. If the land lay within the limits of a proprietary government, it was to be purchased in the name and for the use of the proprietaries, "conformable to such instructions as we or they shall think proper to give for that purpose" (3: 2138).

5. Murray's background is something of a mystery. See Anna Edith Marks, "William Murray, Trader and Land Speculator in the Illinois Country," *Transactions of the Illinois State Historical Society* 26 (1919): 188.

6. For a fascinating discussion of the prevailing theories, see Jack M. Sosin, *Whitehall and the Wilderness: The Middle West in British Colonial Policy, 1760–1775* (Lincoln: University of Nebraska Press, 1961), 259–67.

7. Quoted in Williams, *The American Indian in Western Legal Thought*, 276–77.

8. These merchants included, in addition to Murray and Franks, Moses and Jacob Franks of London, Moses Franks of Philadelphia, John Inglis, Barnard and Michael Gratz, Alexander Ross, David Sproat, James Milligan, Andrew and William Hamilton, and Edmund Milne, also of Philadelphia, Joseph Simons and Levi Andrew Levi of Lancaster, and Thomas Minshall of York County. *Johnson v. M'Intosh*, 21 U.S. (8 Wheat.) 543, 550–51 (1823).

9. Sosin, *Whitehall and the Wilderness*, 232, quoting Murray to Michael and Bernard Gratz, 15 May 1773, Ohio Company Papers, 1: 102, Historical Society of Pennsylvania, Philadelphia (hereafter, HSP). At Pittsburgh, Murray added three new members to the company: Robert Callendar and William Thompson of Cumberland County and John Campbell of Pittsburgh. Over the next two months, he would add two more, George Castles and James Ramsey of the Illinois country, for a total of twenty-two shareholders. *Johnson v. M'Intosh*, 551.

10. Lord to Haldimand, 3 July 1773, British Library, Additional MSS 21730: 131.

11. United Illinois and Wabash Land Companies, *An Account of the Proceedings of the Illinois and Ouabache Companies, in Persuance [sic] of their Purchases Made of the Independent Natives, July 5th, 1773, and 18th October, 1775* (Philadelphia, 1796). The first tract was bounded by a line "on the east side of the Mississippi, beginning at the mouth of the Heron creek, . . . about a league below the mouth of the Kaskaskias river," and running "thence, a northward of east course, in a direct line," through the Hilly Plains, the Crab

Tree Plains and "a remarkable place known by the name of the Big Buffalo Hoofs," to the Salt Lick Creek, an estimated forty-nine leagues; thence crossing the Salt Lick Creek "about one league below the ancient Shawanese town, in an easterly, or a little to the north of east course, in a direct line" to the Ohio River, about four leagues; "then, down the Ohio, by [its] several courses . . . , until it empties into the Mississippi," a distance of "about thirty-five leagues"; then up the Mississippi "thirty-three leagues or thereabouts" back to the mouth of Heron Creek. The second tract was bounded by a line beginning on the Mississippi at a point "directly opposite to the mouth of the Missouri," then running up the Mississippi to the mouth of the Illinois, estimated to be about six leagues, then running up the Illinois "about ninety leagues" to "Chicagou or Garlic creek," then "nearly . . . northerly" an estimated sixty-four leagues through "a certain place, remarkable, being the ground on which a battle was fought, about forty or fifty years before that time, between the Pewaria and Renard Indians," to a place marked by "two remarkable hills close together, in the middle of a large prairie or plain;" then in a "north of east course" an estimated twenty-nine leagues through "a remarkable spring, known by the Indians by the name of Foggy Spring, . . . to a great mountain to the northward of the White Buffalo Plain"; then in "nearly a southwest course" "about forty 40 leagues" back to the mouth of the Missouri. *American State Papers: Public Lands* 2: 117–18. "Consideration for the conveyance consisted of 260 shrouds, 250 blankets, 350 shirts, 150 pairs of stroud and half thick stockings, 150 stroud breech cloths, 500 lbs. of gunpowder, 4,000 lbs. of lead, 1 gross of knives, 30 lbs. of vermillion, 2,000 gun flints, 200 lbs. of brass kettles, 200 lbs. of tobacco, 3 dozen gilt looking-glasses, 1 gross gun-worms, 2 gross awls, 1 gross of fire steels, 16 dozen garterings, 10,000 lbs. of flour, 500 bushels of Indian corn, 12 horses, 12 horned cattle, 20 bushels of salt, and 20 guns" (2: 117). See Maps 3 through 6 in the front matter of this book.

12. Sosin, *Whitehall*, 233, quoting Dartmouth to Haldimand, 1 December 1773, Public Archives of Canada (Ottawa) Transcripts Addit. MSS 21695: 53.

13. Frederick Haldimand's Proclamation, 10 March 1774, in Sir William Johnson, *The Papers of Sir William Johnson* (Albany: University of the State of New York, 1933), 8: 1076.

14. Sosin, *Whitehall*, 233.

15. Clarence Walworth Alvord, *The Mississippi Valley in British Politics* (Cleveland: Arthur H. Clark Company, 1917), 2: 203; Petition of David Franks, John Mur-

ray, and John Campbell to Dunmore, 19 April 1774, Public Record Office, Colonial Office (hereafter PRO, CO) 5 1352: 141.

16. Alvord, *Mississippi Valley*, 2: 204, citing Murray to Gratz, 16 May 1774, Ohio Company Papers, 2: 27, HSP.

17. Ibid., quoting Dunmore to Dartmouth, 16 May 1774, PRO, CO 5 1352: 141.

18. Thomas P. Abernethy, *Western Lands and the American Revolution* (New York: Appleton-Century, 1937), 120.

19. Quebec Act, 14 Geo. 3, c. 83.

20. The Maryland members of the Wabash Company were Thomas Johnson Jr. and John Davidson of Annapolis; William Russel, Matthew Ridley, Robert Christie Sr., and Robert Christie Jr. of Baltimore; Peter Campbell of Piscataway; and William Geddes, the customs collector in Newtown Chester. Other members included Illinois Company shareholders David Franks and Moses Franks of Philadelphia; Daniel Murray, Nicholas St. Martin, and Joseph Page of the Illinois country; Francis Perthuis of Vincennes; and Moses Franks and Jacob Franks of London. *Johnson v. M'Intosh*, 21 U.S. (8 Wheat.) 543, 555 (1823).

21. See Maps 5 and 6 in the front matter of this book. The first of these tracts was defined by a line beginning at the mouth of the "riviere du Chat, or Cat river, where it empties itself into the Wabash river," running down the Wabash "forty leagues or thereabouts" to Point Coupee, "about twelve leagues above" Vincennes, and consisted of all lands within forty leagues of this line on the east side of the river and forty leagues of the line on the west. The spine of the second tract was a line running from the mouth of White River, where it emptied into the Wabash "about twelve leagues below" Vincennes, down the Wabash "fifty three leagues . . . or thereabouts" to the Ohio, the tract consisting of all lands within forty leagues of the line on the east side of the river and within thirty leagues of the line on the west. *American State Papers: Public Lands* 2: 119–20.

22. Virginia, Convention, *The Proceedings of the Convention of Delegates* [May 6–July 5, 1776] (Williamsburg: Alexander Purdie, 1776), 40 (hereafter, *Proceedings*); Abernethy, *Western Lands*, 164–65.

23. *Proceedings*, 124; Abernethy, *Western Lands*, 125.

24. *Proceedings*, 66–67.

25. Ibid., 125.

26. William Waller Hening, comp., *The Statutes at Large; Being a Collection of All the Laws of Virginia, from the First Session of the Legislature in 1609* (1819–23; reprint, Charlottesville: University Press of Virginia, 1969), 3: 464–66.

27. *Proceedings*, 154, emphasis added.

28. William S. Lester, *The Transylvania Colony* (Spencer, IN: Guard, 1935), 231.

29. "Memorial of William Murray et al., Purchasers and Proprietors of Lands on the Ouabache River in the Illinois Country, to the Governor, the Council, the Senate, and Burgesses of Virginia," 26 December 1778, in William P. Palmer et al., eds., *Calendar of Virginia State Papers and Other Manuscripts Preserved in the Capitol at Richmond* (Richmond, 1875), 1: 314.

30. In its 1776 constitution, Virginia rejected Parliament's 1774 transfer of these lands to the Province of Quebec.

31. Virginia, Convention, *Journal of the House of Delegates* [May 3–June 26, 1779] (Williamsburg: Clarkson & Davis, 1779), 45–46; Hening, *Statutes*, 10: 97–98, emphasis added.

32. Hening, *Statutes*, 10: 97; Kate M. Rowland, *The Life of George Mason* (New York: Putnam's, 1892), 1: 439.

33. Merrill Jensen, "Early Reaction and Ratification," in *The Articles of Confederation* (Madison: University of Wisconsin Press, 1962); Peter S. Onuf, *The Origins of the Federal Republic: Jurisdictional Controversies in the United States, 1775–1787* (Philadelphia: University of Pennsylvania Press, 1983).

34. Enclosure in Samuel Huntington to Thomas Jefferson, 10 September 1780, in Thomas Jefferson, *The Papers of Thomas Jefferson*, ed. Julian P. Boyd (Princeton: Princeton University Press, 1950), 3: 627.

35. Mason to Lee, 12 April 1779, in Rowland, *George Mason*, 1: 321–22.

36. Hening, *Statutes*, 11: 567–69.

37. Abernethy, *Western Lands*, 245.

38. *Journals of the Continental Congress, 1774–1789*, ed. Worthington C. Ford et al. (Washington, DC, 1909), 22 (1782): 230 (hereafter, *JCC*). These last two grounds were based on the common law requisites of a valid alienation by deed: "that there be persons able to contract and be contracted with, for the purposes intended by the deed; and also a thing, or subject matter to be contracted for; all of which must be expressed by sufficient names." William Blackstone, *Commentaries on the Laws of England* (1766; reprint, Chicago: University of Chicago Press, 1979), 2: 296. An additional ground was also cited: that "the Wabash purchase has been made since the present revolution, when Congress had an agent for Indian affairs residing at Fort Pitt, who had no notice thereof." This point was introduced to establish Congress's jurisdiction over the question of the deeds' validity by asserting a breach of a supposed duty to notify the confederation of any private treaties with Native Americans. *JCC*, 22 (1782): 230.

39. *JCC*, 22: 406, 25 (1783): 554–64.

40. Ibid., 25 (1783): 562–64.

41. Merrill Jensen, "The Creation of the National Domain, 1781–1784," *Mississippi Valley Historical Review*, 11 (December 1939): 341.

42. Mason to Delegates in Virginia Assembly, 30 May 1783, reprinted in Rowland, *George Mason*, 2: 51.

43. Paul W. Gates, *History of Public Land Law Development* (Washington, DC: Zenger, 1968), 61.

44. Henry Steele Commager, ed., *Documents of American History*, 3rd ed. (New York: F.S. Crofts, 1944), 123–24; see also Peter S. Onuf, *Statehood and Union* (Bloomington: Indiana University Press, 1987); Payson Jackson Treat, *The National Land System, 1785–1820* (New York: E. B. Treat, 1910).

45. *Statutes at Large of the United States of America, 1789–1873* (Washington, DC, 1850–73), 1 (1845): 137 (hereafter, *Stats. at Large of USA*). The prohibition was renewed in 1793, 1796, 1799, 1802, and 1834, when it became a permanent part of the U.S. Code (1: 329, 469, 743; 2 [1845]: 139; 4 [1850]: 729). On the Trade and Intercourse Acts generally, see Francis Paul Prucha, *American Indian Policy in the Formative Years: Indian Trade and Intercourse Acts, 1790–1834* (Cambridge, MA: Harvard University Press, 1962).

46. See Harvey Lewis Carter, *The Life and Times of Little Turtle: First Sagamore of the Wabash* (Urbana: University of Illinois Press, 1987). See also materials collected in *Annals of the Congress of the United States, 1789–1824* (Washington, D.C., 1834–56), 2d Cong., 1st sess., 1052–59.

47. *Annals of Congress*, 2d Cong., 1st sess., 247, 1052, 48, 50.

48. Minutes, 17 December 1791, United Illinois and Wabash Land Companies Papers, University of Oklahoma Law Library.

49. *American State Papers: Public Lands*, 1: 27.

50. *Annals of Congress*, 2d Cong., 1st sess., 524.

51. *American State Papers: Public Lands*, 1: 27. The committee "g[a]ve no opinion" on the Companies' allegations that "the considerations specified in the said deeds were paid to the Indians, and were, at least, as valuable, as any that were given on similar occasions, and that the Indians, named in the said deeds, were owners of the land" (1: 27).

52. *Annals of Congress*, 2d Cong., 1st sess., 121.

53. Ibid., 674.

54. Minutes, 20 December 1792, Illinois and Wabash Papers.

55. *Annals of Congress*, 2d Cong., 2d sess., 624, 628.

56. Edward Burd to Jasper Yeates, 4 August 1796, quoted in Charles Page Smith, *James Wilson: Founding Father, 1742–1798* (Westport, CT: Greenwood, 1956), 380.

57. *Annals of Congress*, 4th Cong., 2d sess., 1530, 1531.

58. Ibid., 2064; Ross and Jeremiah Smith to William Smith, 2 February 1797, Illinois and Wabash Papers.

59. *Annals of Congress*, 4th Cong., 2d sess., 1540, 1551, 2064.

60. Chase had purchased a share in the Companies prior to July 1780. Samuel Chase, Power of Attorney, 23 March 1781, Illinois and Wabash Papers.

61. George L. Haskins and Herbert A. Johnson, *Foundations of Power: John Marshall, 1801–15*, vol. 2 of *History of the Supreme Court of the United States*, (New York: Macmillan, 1981), 129–33.

62. Jefferson to John Dickinson, 19 December 1801, in Thomas Jefferson, *The Writings of Thomas Jefferson*, ed. Albert Ellery Bergh (Washington, DC: Thomas Jefferson Memorial Association of the United States, 1907), 10: 302.

63. The Supreme Court confirmed that appeals would not lie from territorial courts in *Clarke v. Bazadone*, 5 U.S. (1 Cranch) 212 (1803). See John R. Wunder, "Constitutional Oversight: *Clarke v. Bazadone* and the Territorial Supreme Court as the Court of Last Resort," *The Old Northwest* 4 (September 1978): 259–84.

64. *Annals of Congress*, 7th Cong., 1st sess., 199, 1163; George Logan to William Smith and John Shee, 12 March 1802, Illinois and Wabash Papers.

65. Jefferson, *The Writings of Thomas Jefferson*, 3: 353–54; *Stats. at Large of USA* 7 (1846): 79.

66. *Annals of Congress*, 8th Cong., 1st sess., 496, 27.

67. *Stats. at Large of USA*, 7: 75. This tract contained lands to which the Indian title had allegedly been extinguished (i.e., nullified by purchase or conquest) under the British and French governments, and the rights of the United States to the tract had been confirmed at Greenville in 1795. The treaty of Greenville, however, failed to identify the boundaries of the tract, and this problem was addressed in the June 1803 treaty.

68. U.S. *House Journal*, 8th Cong., 1st sess., 1 December 1803, 156; *Annals of Congress*, 8th Cong., 1st sess., 639; U.S. *House Journal*, 8th Cong., 1st sess., February 1804, 414.

69. Stoddert to Harper, 19 January 1810, Illinois and Wabash Papers.

70. *Stats. at Large of USA*, 2: 277–83.

71. Ibid., 7: 83.

72. Ibid., 2: 343–45.

73. Brinton to Samuel Chase Jr., 26 January 1809, Illinois and Wabash Papers.

74. *American State Papers: Public Lands*, 1: 267.

75. Ibid., 279; Stoddert to Harper, 19 January 1810, Illinois and Wabash Papers.

76. Brinton to Chase Jr., 26 January 1809, Illinois and Wabash Papers.

77. *American State Papers: Public Lands*, 2: 126ff.

78. Ibid., 113.

CHAPTER 2

1. C. Peter Magrath, *Yazoo: Law and Politics in the New Republic* (Providence, RI: Brown University Press, 1966), 6, 7, 13.

2. Ibid., 15.

3. On the pleading strategy and its ethical implications, see Lindsay G. Robertson, "'A Mere Feigned Case': Rethinking the *Fletcher v. Peck* Conspiracy and Early Republican Legal Culture," *Utah Law Review* 2000 (2000): 249.

4. Magrath, *Yazoo*, 54.

5. Ibid., 54–55.

6. *Fletcher v. Peck*, 10 U.S. (6 Cranch) 87, 127 (1810).

7. J. G. de R. Hamilton, "Robert Goodloe Harper," *Dictionary of American Biography*, ed. Dumas Malone (New York: Charles Scribner's Sons, 1932), 8: 285–86; Joseph W. Cox, *Champion of Southern Federalism: Robert Goodloe Harper of South Carolina* (Port Washington, NY: Kennikat Press, 1972), *passim*.

8. Harper to Stoddert, 10 January 1810, Illinois and Wabash Papers; Stoddert to Etting, 28 February 1810, Illinois and Wabash Papers. For Turner's service, see Committee on Publication and the Recording Secretary, comp., *Records of the Columbia Historical Society, Washington, D.C.* (Washington, DC: Columbia Historical Society, 1906), 9: 231. Stoddert to Harper, 16 January 1810, Illinois and Wabash Papers.

9. Harper to Brinton and Simon Gratz, 26 January 1810, Illinois and Wabash Papers.

10. Etting to Simon Gratz, 26 January 1810, Illinois and Wabash Papers.

11. Malcolm J. Rohrbough, *The Land Office Business* (New York: Oxford University Press, 1968), 33.

12. Freeman Cleaves, *Old Tippecanoe: William Henry Harrison and His Time* (New York: Charles Scribner's Sons, 1939), 26–27; C. W. Sommerville, *Robert Goodloe Harper* (Washington, DC: Neale, 1899), 7; Magrath, *Yazoo*, 4.

13. Cleaves, *Old Tippecanoe*, 27.

14. Heister to Brinton, 18 December 1809, Illinois and Wabash Papers.

15. Harper to Brinton and Simon Gratz, 26 January 1810, Illinois and Wabash Papers.

16. Magrath, *Yazoo*, 69.

17. *Fletcher v. Peck*, 127, 143. On May 25, Jefferson, in retirement at Monticello, denounced the decision as a "twistification." Jefferson to James Madison, 25 May 1810, in Thomas Jefferson, *The Works of Thomas Jefferson*, ed. Paul Leicester Ford (New York: G. P. Putnam's Sons, 1905), 11: 141.

18. *Annals of Congress*, 11th Cong., 2d sess., 1881.

19. Congressman George Troup of Georgia, for example, subsequently excoriated the method of pleading from the House floor. The claimants had found "in the law books of England," he pronounced, "a maxim which suited them; two of the speculators combined and made up a fictitious case, a feigned issue for the decision of the Supreme Court," and "presented precisely those points for the decision of the Court which they wished the Court to decide, and the Court did actually decide them as the speculators themselves would have decided them if they had been in the place of the Supreme Court" (ibid., 12th Cong., 2d sess., 857–58). Troup's colleague, Samuel Farrow of South Carolina, railed even more pointedly: "The case . . . was a feigned issue made up between Fletcher and Peck, with the aid of their counsel, for the purpose of obtaining a judgment of the Court against Fletcher, the plaintiff," and "I never did hear of one who wished to lose his suit, but what he was by some means accommodated. I never did see a Judge who had talents and energy enough to overrule and defeat both parties and their attorneys, and award judgment to the plaintiff, contrary to their united efforts" (1896).

20. John Quincy Adams, *Memoirs of John Quincy Adams, Comprising Portions of His Diary from 1795–1848*, ed. Charles Francis Adams (Philadelphia: J. B. Lippincott, 1874), 1: 546.

21. *Fletcher v. Peck*, 147–48.

22. Stoddert to Etting, 28 February 1810, Illinois and Wabash Papers. The bill was introduced to provide a route to the Supreme Court for the dispute over title to the Batture in New Orleans, on which controversy see Ronan E. Degnan, "Livingston v. Jefferson: A Freestanding Footnote," *California Law Review* 75 (January 1987): 115.

23. When the bill failed, the Batture claimant, Edward Livingston, brought suit on a legal fiction in the U.S. Circuit Court for the District of Virginia. *Livingston v. Jefferson*, 15 F.Cas. 660 (C. D.Va. 1811).

24. *American State Papers: Public Lands*, 2: 108–109.

25. Ibid., 112.

26. Ibid.

27. Ibid.

28. *Annals of Congress*, 11th Cong., 3d sess., 415.

29. Ibid., 416; U.S. *House Journal*, 11th Cong., 3d sess., 21 December 1810, 64; Heister to Brinton, 21 December 1810, Illinois and Wabash Papers.

30. Report of the Committee on Public Lands, undated, Illinois and Wabash Papers; U.S. *House Journal*, 11th Cong., 3d sess., 13 January 1811, 16, 178; *Annals of Congress*, 11th Cong., 3d sess., 839.

31. *Annals of Congress*, 11th Cong., 3d sess., 839.

32. Etting to Simon Gratz, 14 February 1811, Etting to Simon Gratz and Brinton, 22 February 1811, Etting to Jacob Gratz, 25 February 1811, Brinton Papers; Jacob Gratz to Joseph Gratz, 10 March 1811, Gratz Family of Philadelphia Papers, American Jewish Historical Society, Waltham, MA.

33. Etting to Simon Gratz and Brinton, 22 February 1811, Illinois and Wabash Papers.

34. Clarence E. Carter, ed., *The Territorial Papers of the United States* (Washington, DC: U.S. Government Printing Office, 1939), 8: 95.

35. Jones to Harper, 17 February 1811, Etting to Simon Gratz and Brinton, 22 February 1811, Illinois and Wabash Papers. Jones may already have been an Illinois and Wabash shareholder prior to his retention by Harper. An unsigned, undated Illinois and Wabash Companies memorandum states, "John Rice Jones and James Morrison purchased [original Illinois Company member] Joseph Page's share." Bernard Gratz (1738–1801) and Michael Gratz (1740–1811) Papers, 1753–1814, American Jewish Historical Society, Waltham, MA.

36. Etting to Jacob Gratz (with enclosure), 3 April 1811, Illinois and Wabash Papers; Carter, *Territorial Papers*, 8: 79, 84. Jones's campaign to unseat Harrison was unsuccessful, and he ultimately abandoned Indiana for Missouri. In 1820, he unsuccessfully ran against Thomas Hart Benton for the U.S. Senate; that same year, he was appointed one of three judges of Missouri's new supreme court. He died in office on February 1, 1824, at the age of sixty-four. "Biography of John Rice Jones (1759–1824)," William H. English Papers, Indiana Historical Society, Indianapolis.

37. Harper to Etting (copy) enclosed in Etting to Jacob Gratz, 3 April 1811, Illinois and Wabash Papers.

38. Jacob Gratz to Joseph Gratz, 10 March 1811, Gratz Family of Philadelphia Papers.

39. Henry Adams, *History of the United States of America during the First Administration of James Madison* (1890; reprint, New York: Antiquarian Press, 1962), 116.

40. *Annals of Congress*, 20th Cong., 2d sess., 1925, 2817. The indemnification bill passed the Senate on February 28 (643).

41. Brinton[?] to Harper and Etting, 19 December 1815, Illinois and Wabash Papers.

42. Curtis W. Garrison, "Benjamin Stoddert," in *Dictionary of American Biography*, ed. Dumas Malone (New York: Charles Scribner's Sons, 1943), 18: 62; Brinton[?] to Harper and Etting, 19 December 1815, Illinois and Wabash Papers.

43. Law to Hurst, 25 October 1815, Illinois and Wabash Papers. Harper considered other possible agents, including General Van Ness, "who is a great favorite with the majority and the Government," and "Col. Lear," who "would perhaps do still better." In addition, Harper encouraged Etting to contact his friend Robert Smith, Jefferson's former navy secretary, who "could," Harper suggested, "give some useful hints about suitable agents." Harper to Etting, 28 December 1815, Illinois and Wabash Papers. Stephen Decatur, then the premiere U.S. naval hero, was evidently considered for agency as well. Brinton, Simon Gratz, and Callender Irvine to Etting and Harper, 10 January 1816, Illinois and Wabash Papers.

44. Senate votes and proceedings, p. 3, of the House, p. 8, December Session, 1816, cited in Sommerville, *Robert Goodloe Harper*, 28.

45. *Annals of Congress*, 14th Cong., 1st sess., 104–105.

46. Law to Hurst, 25 October 1815, Illinois and Wabash Papers.

47. Harper to Etting, 28 December 1815, Illinois and Wabash Papers.

48. United Illinois and Wabash Land Companies, *Memorial of the United Illinois and Wabash Land Companies, to the Senate and House of Representatives of the United States* (Baltimore: Joseph Robinson, 1816), 46. The "Opinion of Counsellor Dagge of London on the Indian Grant of Lands to William Trent and others" and endorsements, copied verbatim from the final pages of a pamphlet, "View of the Title to Indiana, a Tract of Country on the River Ohio," submitted to the Continental Congress in support of the claim of the Indiana Company, another land speculation concern, concluded that a grant by the Six Nations of the Iroquois Confederacy to Trent and his Indiana associates had conveyed "a good, lawful and sufficient title . . . subject only to the King's sovereignty over the settlements to be established" on the deeded lands (46).

49. *Annals of Congress*, 14th Cong., 1st sess., 19, 95.

50. Brinton, Simon Gratz, and Irvine to Harper and Etting, 28 February 1816, Illinois and Wabash Papers.

51. Ibid.

52. *Annals of Congress*, 14th Cong., 1st sess., 372.

53. Ibid., 31.

54. Ibid., 315, 1373.

55. Brinton, Simon Gratz, and Irvine to Etting, 1 February 1816, Illinois and Wabash Papers.

56. Sommerville, *Robert Goodloe Harper*, 30.

57. *Annals of Congress*, 14th Cong., 2d Sess., 1348, 1337.

58. Carter, *Territorial Papers*, 8: 451 n.48.

CHAPTER 3

1. Specifically, the Act provided "that the district court in Kentucky shall, besides the jurisdiction [of a district court], have jurisdiction of all other causes, except of appeals and writs of error, hereinafter made cognizable in a circuit court, and shall proceed therein in the same manner as a circuit court and writs of error and appeals shall lie from decisions therein to the Supreme Court in the same causes, as from a circuit court to the Supreme Court." *Stats. at Large of USA*, 1 (1846): 77–78.

2. Ibid., 3 (1846): 390–91, 1 (1846): 77–78.

3. The Gratzes had extensive real estate holdings in Kentucky, including Mammoth Cave.

4. Benjamin Gratz to [?], 8 February 1819, Benjamin Gratz Papers, American Jewish Historical Society, Waltham, MA.

5. Ingersoll to Benjamin Gratz, 20 March 1819, Benjamin Gratz Papers. Ingersoll had only collected $80 on the latest assessment since Gratz left Philadelphia and advised that Gratz "not promise Mr. Dewey a very great fee" (ibid.).

6. Charles W. Taylor, comp., *Biographical Sketches and Review of the Bench and Bar of Indiana* (Indianapolis: Bench and Bar, 1895), *seriatim*; Leander J. Monks, ed., *Courts and Lawyers of Indiana* (Indianapolis: Federal Publishing Co., 1916), 198–99; William Wesley Woollen, *Biographical and Historical Sketches of Early Indiana* (Indianapolis: Hammond, 1883), 360–65.

7. *Stats. at Large of USA*, 1: 278–79.

8. Ingersoll to Benjamin Gratz, 20 March 1819, Benjamin Gratz Papers.

9. Parke was no doubt relieved that the Companies did not press their claim. He was not eager to be placed in such an uncomfortable situation in the future and almost certainly was involved in the introduction of the bill enacted on March 3, 1821, to amend section 11 of the 1792 Process Act to authorize conflicted judges in states with no circuit court to certify actions "to the most convenient circuit court in an adjacent state." *Stats. at Large of USA*, 3: 643.

10. *Annals of Congress*, 15th Cong., 2d sess., 2548, 2514.

11. *Stats. at Large of USA*, 3: 503.

12. Clarence Walworth Alvord, *The Illinois Country 1673–1818* (Chicago: A. C. McClurg, 1922), 429.

13. Monroe Johnson Jr., "The Johnson Family Genealogy," 1987, Frederick County Historical Society, Frederick, MD. John Pope married Eliza Johnson in 1811. Nathaniel Pope's wife, Lucretia, was the daughter of former land office commissioner and (as will be seen) anti-Harrison activist Elijah Backus. Elizabeth Breckenridge Ellis, "Nathaniel Pope," *Dictionary of American Biography*, ed. Dumas Malone (New York: Charles Scribner's Sons, 1943), 15: 78.

14. Woollen, *Biographical and Historical Sketches of Early Indiana*, 379.

15. M'Intosh was a bit casual in this claim. The lands are described in the agreed statement of facts filed with the lawsuit. Most are in southwestern Illinois and clearly outside the lower Wabash purchase. See, e.g., Eric Kades, "History and Interpretation of the Great Case of *Johnson v. M'Intosh*," *Law & History Review* 19 (2001): 67. By the Companies' reckoning, however, many of the lands did overlap. The lower Wabash purchase was defined as "situated and lying on both sides of the Ouabache River . . . , beginning from the mouth of White River where it empties itself into the Ouabache River (about twelve leagues below Post St. Vincent), thence down the Ouabache River by the several courses thereof until it empties itself into the Ohio River, being from said White River to the Ohio, fifty three leagues in length or thereabouts, be the same more or less, with forty leagues in width or breadth on the east side, and thirty leagues in width or breadth on the west side of the Ouabache River aforesaid, to be continued along from White River aforesaid to the Ohio River aforesaid." United Illinois and Wabash Land Companies, *Memorial of the United Illinois and Wabash Land Companies, to the Senate and House of Representatives of the United States* (Baltimore: Joseph Robinson, 1810), 42. An English league measured three statute miles (each 5,280 feet). The distance esti-

mated from Vincennes (Post St. Vincent) to the mouth of the White River is off—it is not twelve leagues, but approximately eight leagues, or twenty-four miles—as is the estimated distance from the White to the Ohio, which is approximately fifteen leagues, or forty-five miles, far short of the estimated fifty-three leagues. That said, the east-west lines of the tract were not bounded by natural objects and so one might justly construe the distances as intended. A line running thirty leagues, or ninety miles, due west from the mouth of the White River extends approximately two-thirds of the way across Illinois, and a line running due west thirty leagues from the juncture of the Ohio and the Wabash Rivers reaches all the way to the Mississippi River. When the end points are connected, it is clear that many of M'Intosh's tracts do lie within the purchase area. Louis Viviat, who negotiated the treaty, was of course French, and it is possible that he intended that the distances be measured in French leagues, or *lieues*, which measured approximately 2.4 statute miles, rather than three. In this case, the lines would run not ninety but seventy-two miles west from the White and the Ohio—a closer call, but still it appears that M'Intosh had lands within the area sufficient for the federal court to have jurisdiction to hear the case.

16. See William Henry Harrison to Thomas Jefferson, 20 November 1805, Papers of William Henry Harrison, Library of Congress.

17. [Vincennes] *Indiana Gazette*, 27 August 1804, 11 September 1804. See, e.g., 18 September 1804.

18. [Frankfort, KY] *Western World*, 31 December 1807, 4; 7 January 1808, 4.

19. *Western World*, 3 March 1808, 6.

20. *Stats. at Large of USA*, 7: 113–15.

21. *Dawson's Harrison*, 176, quoted in Elmore Barce, "Tecumseh's Confederacy," *Indiana Magazine of History* 12 (June 1916): 165. According to this account, "Two-thirds of his property" was "returned to McIntosh and the remaining part given to some of the orphan children of those distinguished citizens who fell a sacrifice to their patriotism in the last war" (165). An 1812 deed to non-war orphan James Kyle effecting the transfer of one hundred acres of M'Intosh's land levied upon by the sheriff of Knox County, Indiana, pursuant to the defamation judgment renders this representation at best somewhat suspect. Myron Boehm, "An Old Kyle Deed Uncovered," *Vincennes Shopper*, 21 July 1971, p. 1.

22. See, e.g., *United States v. Lydia, a woman of color*, Knox County, Indiana, Minute Book A, 1811–1817, 146, 155, and *State of Indiana v. Lydia, a woman of*

color, ibid., 407, 413. M'Intosh and Lydia had to overcome more than local prejudice to preserve their relationship. In 1814, they contested a legal challenge that Lydia was in fact the property of Simon Vanarsdal, assignee of Peter and Henry Keykendal, the heirs and executors of John and Elizabeth Keykendal of Virginia. See, e.g., *United States and M'Intosh v. Vanarsdal*, ibid., 198, 207, 240, and *M'Intosh v. Vanarsdal*, ibid., 299, 340.

23. These fictional tenants were invariably identified by name in the pleadings. Usually, they were called John Doe and Richard Roe. Occasionally, however, more inventive names were chosen. In *Martin v. Hunter's Lessee*, 14 U.S. (1 Wheat.) 304 (1816), for example, the fictional lessee of the defendant in error was identified in the initial pleading as "Timothy Trittite." Albert J. Beveridge, *The Life of John Marshall* (New York: Houghton Mifflin, 1919), 4: 148. As the example above suggests, the plaintiff's tenant appeared by title as the nominal plaintiff in the action: a typical case might be styled, for example, *DiFonzo's Lessee v. Shaw*. For the history of the development of the ejectment action, see Sir William Holdsworth, *A History of English Law*, 2nd. ed. (1937; reprint, London: Methuen, 1966), 7: 3–23, 57–81.

24. Harper may have worked, of course, from the more recent 1816 resubmission of the 1810 memorial. The Companies' files, and presumably Harper's as well, contained multiple copies of both (Illinois and Wabash Papers). The 1810 memorial is somewhat easier to read, in that it contains fewer typographical errors.

25. The paragraphs were not numbered when the agreed statement was presented to the district court, but were by the time the case reached the Supreme Court. The Supreme Court version, materially identical, is far more accessible, and the numbering of the paragraphs a convenient aid. Accordingly, the discussion herein follows the Supreme Court version.

26. This paragraph was obviously added after Johnson's death. See below.

27. For a full analysis of Harper's method, see Appendix 2.

28. Lord Mansfield's opinion in *Campbell v. Hall*, 98 Eng. Rep. 1045, 1 Cowp. Rep. 204 (1774); see chapter 6.

29. Grahame was the son of Johnson's daughter Ann Jennings Johnson and Maj. John Colin Grahame. M. Johnson, "The Johnson Family Genealogy."

30. Frederick County, Maryland, Register of Wills, Record of Wills, H.S. 2, 312–23.

31. *Johnson and Graham's Lessee v. McIntosh*, Record Group 21, U.S. District Court, Southern District of Illinois, Complete Record Book, 1819–1842, National Archives, Great Lakes Region, Chicago, 18.

32. Ibid.

33. Writ of Error, *Johnson and Graham's Lessee v. McIntosh*, 8 Wheat. 543 (1823), reprinted in National Archives Microfilm Publications, Case No. 1105, 3.

34. Ibid.

35. Ingersoll to Brinton, 26 February 1822, Illinois and Wabash Papers.

36. Ibid.

37. Ingersoll to Simon Gratz, Brinton, and Callender Irvine, 19 February 1823, Illinois and Wabash Papers. This compensation consisted of an unknown set fee plus a contingent fee of $1,000. Harper was to receive the same (ibid.).

38. Ingersoll to Brinton, 26 February 1822, Illinois and Wabash Papers. Winder, at age forty-seven a seasoned advocate but the equal of neither Harper nor Webster, was still smarting from the damage to his reputation done when, in a patriotic foray into military service during the War of 1812, he commanded the routed American forces at the Battle of Bladensburg and, many believed, made possible the British burning of the Capitol. Murray, whose sister was married to former U.S. attorney general Richard Rush, was relatively new to the bar and had never argued a case before the Supreme Court.

39. Ibid.

40. For the history of the Carver Grant, see Daniel Steele Durrie, "Jonathan Carver and Carver's Grant," *Wisconsin Historical Collections* 91(1872): 220; Milo M. Quaife, "Jonathan Carver and the Carver Grant," *Mississippi Valley Historical Review* 7(1920): 3.

41. *Annals of Congress*, 17th Cong., 1st sess., 826.

42. *American State Papers: Public Lands*, 2: 551.

43. *Annals of Congress*, 17th Cong., 2nd sess., 47, 97, 152–53; *American State Papers: Public Lands*, 2: 611.

44. *Annals of Congress*, 17th Cong., 2d sess., 159.

45. Gilmer to Wirt, 30 December 1822, Gilmer Collection.

46. Minutes, 23 January 1823, Illinois and Wabash Papers.

47. The Companies' records show 1/2 share sold to Mrs. Mary Anne Patterson of Baltimore, widow, for $460; 1/2 share sold to David Winchester, president of the Baltimore Insurance Company, for $640; 1/2 share sold to John McTavish for $820; and 1/2 share sold to L. Kimball for $810. Deed, 4 February 1823, Illinois and Wabash Papers, and Note, 2 February 1823, Illinois and Wabash Papers.

48. Ingersoll to Simon Gratz, Brinton, and Irvine, 11 February 1823, Illinois and Wabash Papers.

49. Ingersoll to Jacob Gratz, 13 February 1823, Gratz Collection, HSP. Neither

Harper nor Webster argued that the Quebec Act validated the Wabash purchase, probably because the argument would have been difficult to win. The Wabash lands were clearly within the Province of Quebec at the time of the Wabash purchase, and the Quebec Act had indeed repealed much of the Proclamation of 1763 as it applied to Quebec, but the prohibition on individual purchases of Indian lands remained. Quebec Act, 14 Geo. 3, c. 83.

50. Ingersoll to Jacob Gratz, 13 February 1823, Gratz Collection, HSP. The book Webster sought was George Chalmers's *Opinions of Eminent Lawyers on Various Points of English Jurisprudence, Chiefly Concerning the Colonies, Fisheries, and Commerce, of Great Britain*, 2 vols. (London: Reed and Hunter, 1814).

51. *Fletcher v. Peck*, 88, 121, 146, 142–43.

52. George Bridges Rodney, *Diary of George Bridges Rodney* (National Society of the Colonial Dames of America in the State of Delaware, n.p., n.d.), 28.

53. Wheaton's report erroneously states that the argument lasted from February 17 through February 19, 1823. Correspondence and contemporary newspaper accounts prove that Harper and Webster opened on February 15. See, e.g., [Washington, DC] *Daily National Intelligencer*, 17 February 1823, p. 3; 18 February 1823, p. 3; and 19 February 1823, p. 3; *Washington Gazette*, 20 February 1823, p. 2.

54. *Johnson v. M'Intosh*, 21 U.S. (8 Wheat.) 543, 562 (1823).

55. Ibid., 562–63.

56. Hugo Grotius, *The Rights of War and Peace*, trans. A. C. Campbell (Washington, DC: M. Walker Dunne, 1901), 91.

57. *Johnson v. M'Intosh*, 563.

58. *Fletcher v. Peck*, 142.

59. *Jackson v. Wood*, 7 Johns. Rep. 290, 295 (1810).

60. *Johnson v. M'Intosh*, 563.

61. Ibid., 563–64.

62. *Campbell v. Hall*, 98 Eng. Rep. 1045, 1 Cowp. Rep. 204 (1774); *Johnson v. M'Intosh*, 564.

63. *Johnson v. M'Intosh*, 564–65.

64. Ibid., 565–66.

65. Ibid., 566–67.

66. Rodney, *Diary*, 28.

67. *Daily National Intelligencer*, 18 February 1823, p. 3.

68. *Johnson v. M'Intosh*, 567.

69. The appended material was John Glynn's concurrence to Dagge's opinion on the validity of the Indiana grant.

70. United Illinois and Wabash Land Companies, *Memorial of the United Illinois and Wabash Land Companies, to the Senate and House of Representatives of the United States* (Baltimore: Joseph Robinson, 1816), 46.

71. *Johnson v. M'Intosh*, 568, emphasis in original.

72. Ibid., 569. This phrase comes from Vattel, who employed it, however, to refer not to indigenous peoples, but to a class recognized by modern immigration law: permanent resident aliens. Emmerich de Vattel, *The Law of Nations*, ed. Edward D. Ingraham (Philadelphia: T. & J. W. Johnson, 1855), 101. The irony is apparent.

73. *Johnson v. M'Intosh*, 569.

74. Ibid., 571.

75. Ingersoll to Simon Gratz, Brinton, and Irvine, 19 February 1823, Illinois and Wabash Papers.

76. Rodney, *Diary*, 29.

77. Ingersoll to Simon Gratz, Brinton, and Irvine, 19 February 1823, Illinois and Wabash Papers. Harper's "argument," Ingersoll wrote his colleagues, "has been everything that could be desired[,] full, powerful and eloquent. I do not believe a better was ever heard in this, or any other, Court. If he has not ensured success he has at least deserved it" (ibid.).

78. Ingersoll to Brinton, 20 February 1823, Illinois and Wabash Papers.

79. Ingersoll to Simon Gratz, Brinton, and Irvine, 19 February 1823, Illinois and Wabash Papers. Adams had been co-counsel with Harper in the first *Fletcher* appeal and well knew his pleading habits.

80. Harper to Simon Gratz, Brinton, and Irvine, 22 February 1823, Gratz Papers, HSP.

81. The date of delivery given in the official reports, March 10, is incorrect, as is made evident by contemporary newspaper accounts. See, e.g., [Philadelphia] *National Gazette and Literary Register*, 3 March 1823, p. 2.

82. *Johnson v. M'Intosh*, 594, 585.

83. Most of the *Johnson* protagonists vanished remarkably soon after the judgment was announced. Indeed, within twenty-two months of John Marshall's delivery of the Court's opinion, the United Illinois and Wabash Land Companies were dissolved and three of the four attorneys who argued the case before the Supreme Court were dead. Henry Murray was the first to go. On April 18, 1824, fourteen months after dining at the White House, he was fatally injured when the boiler on the steamboat *Eagle* exploded on Chesapeake Bay. He died in Baltimore ten days later ([Annapolis] *Maryland Gazette and State Register*,

29 April 1824, p. 3). The following month, on May 24, 1824, William H. Winder died unexpectedly at his Baltimore home at the age of forty-nine (*Niles' Weekly Register*, 29 May 1824, p. 202). Robert Goodloe Harper survived him by eight months. On January 14, 1825, Harper collapsed while reading a newspaper before his fireplace and was dead probably before he hit the floor. William Wirt to [?] Wirt, 16 January 1825, quoted in John P. Kennedy, *Memoirs of the Life of William Wirt*, rev. ed. (Philadelphia: Blanchard and Lea, 1854), 2: 169. Daniel Webster alone survived to witness *Johnson*'s apotheosis into a landmark. A year after *Johnson*, Judge Nathaniel Pope attempted to leave the Illinois federal district court bench, campaigning unsuccessfully for appointment to the U.S. Senate seat vacated by retired Illinois senator Ninian Edwards. Two years later, in the wake of Associate Justice Thomas Todd's demise, he was back in Washington unsuccessfully lobbying for appointment to the Supreme Court. Twice frustrated, Pope remained Illinois's lone federal judge until his death on January 22, 1850 (E. Ellis, "Nathaniel Pope," 15: 77–78). Pope's courtroom in Springfield, to which Illinois's capital was removed in 1839, is open to the public. It shares a building with the restored law offices of Abraham Lincoln, who appeared before him often. Pope's son, John, enjoyed a rather different relationship with Lincoln. Named to command of the Union Army of Virginia in the summer of 1862, he led his troops to decisive defeat at the Second Battle of Manassas. Oliver L. Spaulding Jr., "John Pope," in *Dictionary of American Biography*, ed. Dumas Malone (New York: Charles Scribner's Sons, 1943), 15: 76–77. Judge Benjamin Parke was named first president of the Indiana Historical Society in 1830. Parke presided over the Indiana federal district court until his death on July 12, 1835. Charles Dewey, trial counsel for the Illinois and Wabash Companies, delivered his eulogium. George S. Cottman, "Benjamin Parke," in *Dictionary of American Biography*, ed. Dumas Malone (New York: Charles Scribner's Sons, 1943), 14: 209–10. Dewey himself was elected to the Indiana legislature in 1821. In 1836, after two unsuccessful runs for Congress, he was appointed judge of the Indiana Supreme Court, a position he held until 1847. He died in 1862. Woolen, *Biographical and Historical Sketches of Early Indiana*, 360–65. William M'Intosh, cantankerous and socially beleaguered, lived out his life in semi-exile at his home at the Grand Rapids of the Wabash. On February 9 and 10, 1824, two young residents of the recently established alternative community at New Harmony, Indiana, immediately downriver from the Grand Rapids, visited M'Intosh and his family and later provided a telling portrait. Thirty-two-year-old Donald Mcdonald, who

had sailed from Scotland with utopian Robert Owen and his family to take possession of New Harmony, recorded in his journal:

> Mr. McIntosh received us kindly, and as the following day proved very rainy detained us at his house. He has a black housekeeper by whom he has several children. His partiality for the Blacks procures the assistance of one who comes from Mount Carmel distant two miles. His house is a frame building containing two rooms. There are some small out buildings. He has very little land cleared or cultivated around his house which is shut in on all sides by the forst [*sic*] except next to the river the opposite bank of which, however is thickly covered with wood and a very low bottom.—In consequence of Mr. McIntosh's connection with this black female, his character is lost among the Americans, and he lives quite retired from all society. Our time was passed in conversation. He spoke of the fall of the value of land & his embarrassments therefrom: of the advantageous situation he resided upon for the site of a mill, & his want of capital; of his life while he resided at Vincennes. He was a Major & public treasurer under General Harrison, and had much intercourse with the French & Indians. He came from Inverness, held a British commission in Canada, resigned it as he could not live on his pay. He gave us an account of the proceedings of the Americans in purchasing & getting possession of the lands of the Indians, and the wars which had taken place. On this subject he had a misunderstanding with General Harrison and resigned his public office. . . . Mr. McIntosh frequently spoke of his intention of sending his children to Mr. Owen's Society; but we said nothing on the subject as we did not know how far it would be wise, in the first instance, so decidedly opposed to the feelings of the American People.

Donald Mcdonald, "The Diaries of Donald Mcdonald, 1824–1826," *Indiana Historical Society Publications* (Indianapolis: Indiana Historical Society, 1942), 14: 285–86.

Mcdonald's companion, Robert Owen's twenty-two-year-old son, William, noted in his own diary that on arriving at M'Intosh's house, "we found a fine old man. His house is pretty large, but only partly finished in side. . . . We were introduced to a black woman as his housekeeper but who seems to answer to all the purposes of a wife, as he has three black children by her. Two of them are fine children. Mrs. J. McIntosh [a neighbor, not related], who is from New Jersey, had informed us of them before, saying she would go often to see him, were it not that he had a black woman and that he fondled the little black things as if they were white as snow. . . . We had a good deal of conversation with him and he seemed much inclined to go all together with us. He appeared to be a deist." The following day, Owen noted: "Rain all day, almost without interruption. We found we could not leave Mr. McIntosh's that day. We therefore remained talking to him all day. Of course it was very dull." William Owen, "Diary of William Owen from November 10, 1824, to April 20, 1825," ed. Joel W. Hiatt, *Indiana Historical Society Publications* (Indianapolis: Bobbs-Merrill, 1906), 4: iii, 113–14. When M'Intosh died sometime before March 1834, his wife and three children were left destitute (J. B. McCall to John Tipton, 12 March 1834, John Tipton Collection, Indiana State Library, Indianapolis; Woolen, *Biographical and Historical Sketches*, 381). They did not remain so. McIntosh had given his son "a good education in the English and Latin languages and mathematics," and he became a distinguished minister in the African Methodist Episcopal Church.

84. *Johnson v. M'Intosh*, 574.

CHAPTER 4

1. *Johnson v. M'Intosh*, 21 U.S. (8 Wheat.) 543, 604.

2. U.S. (1 Cranch) 137 (1803).

3. Perhaps the best summary account of the *Cohens* dispute and its political fallout is G. Edward White, *The Marshall Court and Cultural Change, 1815–1835*, vols. 3 and 4 of *The Oliver Wendell Holmes Devise History of the Supreme Court of the United States* (New York: Macmillan, 1988), 504–24. For a more extensive treatment, see W. Ray Luce, *Cohens v. Virginia (1821): The Supreme Court and State Rights, a Reevaluation of Influences and Impacts* (New York: Garland, 1990). See also Mark A. Graber, "The Passive-Aggressive Virtues: *Cohens v. Virginia* and the Problematic Establishment of Judicial Power," *Constitutional Commentary* 12 (1995): 67.

4. *Cohens v. Virginia*, 19 U.S. (6 Wheat.) 264, 290 (1821).

5. *Stats. at Large of USA*, 1: 73, 85–86.

6. G. White, *The Marshall Court and Cultural Change*, 505, citing *Niles' Weekly Register*, 20 January 1821 and 4 February 1821.

7. *Cohens v. Virginia*, 344. Ironically, in light of subsequent events, three days later Marshall declined an invitation to serve as an ex officio vice president of "[a] new society for the benefit of Indians organized, at the City of Washington," based on his having "the most entire conviction of [his] inability to contribute in any manner to the success of this institution." Marshall to Jedidiah Morse, 21 February 1822, John Marshall Papers, Library of Congress.

8. Marshall to H. Wheaton, 2 June 1821, Henry Wheaton Papers, Pierpont Morgan Library, New York, New York, quoted in G. White, *The Marshall Court and Cultural Change*, 521.

9. Story to J. Mason, 10 January 1822, in *The Life and Letters of Joseph Story*, ed. William Wetmore Story (Boston: Charles C. Little and James Brown, 1851), 1: 411–12, quoted in G. White, *The Marshall Court and Cultural Change*, 523.

10. *Green v. Biddle*, 21 U.S. (8 Wheat.) 1 (1823).

11. Hening, *Statutes*, 12: 789, 13:9.

12. *Green v. Biddle*, 17–18.

13. *Richmond Enquirer*, 9 February 1822, p. 3.

14. Ibid.

15. Ibid., 2 March 1822, p. 2, 5 March 1822, p. 3.

16. Hening, *Statutes*, 10: 50, 54–55.

17. Ibid., 10: 465–67; *Richmond Enquirer*, 9 February 1822, p. 4.

18. Hening, *Statutes*, 11: 309–10.

19. *Richmond Enquirer*, 9 February 1822, p. 4.

20. Ibid.

21. *Stats. at Large of USA*, 7: 192–95. The treaty was proclaimed on January 15, 1819. For an account of the treaty negotiation, see Robert V. Remini, *Andrew Jackson and His Indian Wars* (New York: Viking, 2001), 168–79.

22. Kentucky General Assembly, *Acts Passed at the First Session of the Twenty-Seventh General Assembly for the Commonwealth of Kentucky* (Frankfort: Kendall and Russells, 1819), 606.

23. Kentucky General Assembly, *Acts Passed at the First Session of the Twenty-Eighth General Assembly for the Commonwealth of Kentucky* (Frankfort: Kendall and Russells, 1820), 947.

24. Kentucky General Assembly, *Acts Passed at the First Session of the Twenty-Ninth General Assembly for the Commonwealth of Kentucky* (Frankfort: Kendall and Russells, 1821), 197–200.

25. Kentucky General Assembly, *Acts Passed at the First Session of the Thirtieth General Assembly for the Commonwealth of Kentucky* (Frankfort: Kendall and Russell, 1821), 384.

26. Ibid., 409–15.

27. *Richmond Enquirer*, 2 March 1822, p. 1.

28. *Hoofnagle v. Anderson*, 20 U.S. 96 (1822). Such transferees included speculators.

29. Lowell H. Harrison, *Kentucky's Road to Statehood* (Lexington: University of Kentucky Press, 1992), 88ff.

30. According to his foremost early biographer, "It is more than probable that Marshall drew this important statute." Albert J. Beveridge, *The Life of John Marshall* (New York: Houghton Mifflin, 1916), 2: 55 n.5.

31. Jefferson to Henry Knox, 10 August 1791, in Thomas Jefferson, *The Papers of Thomas Jefferson*, ed. Charles T. Cullen (Princeton: Princeton University Press, 1986), 22: 27.

32. *Marshall v. Clark*, 8 Va. (4 Call) 268, 272 (1791).

33. See *Gilman v. Brown*, 10 Fed. Cas. 392, 399 (Cir. Ct., D. Mass, 1817), *aff'd* 17 U.S. (4 Wheat.) 255 (1819).

34. [Lexington, KY] *Western Monitor*, 26 March 1822, p. 3.

35. *Richmond Enquirer*, 5 March 1822, p. 3; *Western Monitor*, 26 March 1822, p. 3.

36. *Western Monitor*, 21 May 1822, p. 2.

37. Ibid., p. 3.

38. *Western Monitor*, 5 November 1822, p. 2.

39. Ibid., 19 November 1822, p. 3, 22 November 1822, p. 3. The legislature may have been moved to agree to a commission in part by weak sales: despite a provision in the act of December 21, 1821 entitling any purchaser whose title was subsequently judicially lost to him to a full refund, during the first three days after sales began in September, only twelve quarter sections were sold, and sales were subsequently suspended. Kentucky General Assembly, *Acts Passed at the First Session of the Thirtieth General Assembly*, 409–15; *Richmond Enquirer*, 27 September 1822, p. 3.

40. *Richmond Enquirer*, 22 October 1822, p. 3.

41. Ibid., 27 December 1822, p. 3; *Western Monitor*, 10 January 1823, p. 1.

42. *Richmond Enquirer*, 2 January 1823, p. 3.

43. Ibid., 11 January 1823, p. 3.

44. Ibid., 4 January 1823, p. 3.

45. Ibid., 14 January 1823, p. 2.

46. Ibid., 21 January 1823, p. 3.

47. Gilmer to Wirt, 30 January 1823, Gilmer Collection.

48. *Richmond Enquirer*, 25 January 1823, p. 3.; *Western Monitor*, 11 February 1823, p. 3.

49. *Richmond Enquirer*, 28 January 1823, p. 3, 30 January 1823, p. 3.

50. Ibid., 1 February 1823, p. 3.

51. Ibid., 8 February 1823, p. 3; *Western Monitor*, February 11, 1823, p. 1, 18 February 1823, p. 3.

52. *Richmond Enquirer*, 28 January 1823, p. 2. Prior to January 7, White had declined to accept his appointment, and Clay and Rowan were authorized to appoint a replacement (ibid., 25 January 1823, p. 3).

53. Ibid., 11 February 1823, p. 2.

54. *Western Monitor*, 6 May 1823, p. 3.

55. Jefferson to Johnson, 12 June 1823, in Jefferson, *The Writings of Thomas Jefferson*, 15: 447, 448.

CHAPTER 5

1. G. White, *The Marshall Court*, 373 n.397.

2. *Johnson v. M'Intosh*, 21 U.S. (8 Wheat.) 543, 571–72 (1823).

3. Ibid, 572, emphasis added.

4. Ibid., 572–73.

5. Ibid., 573.

6. Ibid., 573–74, emphasis added.

7. Ibid., 574, emphasis added.

8. *Johnson* was not the first opinion in which Marshall gilded questionable propositions in the rhetorical fool's gold of self-evidence.

9. Thomas Jefferson, *Notes on the State of Virginia* (1784; reprint, Chapel Hill: University of North Carolina Press, 1955), 96.

10. St. George Tucker, *Blackstone's Commentaries* (Philadelphia: William Young Birch and Abraham Small, 1803), 2: appendix 4–5, emphasis added.

11. [Thomas Hart Benton, ed.,] *Abridgment of the Debates of Congress from 1789 to 1856* (New York: Appleton, 1857), 1: 578.

12. Lindsay G. Robertson, "John Marshall as Colonial Historian: Reconsidering the Origins of the Discovery Doctrine," *Journal of Law & Politics* 13 (1997): 759–77. Charles F. Hobson writes, "The public did not receive Marshall's 'Introduction' well . . . , and even Marshall recognized it as a patchwork of passages lifted from published sources." Republican reviewers criticized that "'whatever may be the professional talents of Chief-Justice Marshall, it is feared that, as an historian, he will add nothing to our literary reputation as a nation,'" while Marshall expressed himself "'mortified beyond measure to

find that it has been so carelessly written," its "inelegancies . . . more numerous than I had supposed could have appeared in it.'" Charles F. Hobson, ed., *The Papers of John Marshall* (Chapel Hill: University of North Carolina Press, 1990), 6: 223, and sources cited therein.

13. For a line-by-line comparison, see Robertson, "John Marshall as Colonial Historian," 759–77.

14. *Johnson v. M'Intosh*, 574, 576, 576–77, 579.

15. John Marshall, *The Life of George Washington, Commander in Chief of the American Forces, During the War Which Established the Independence of His Country, and First President of the United States* (Philadelphia: C. P. Wayne, 1804), 1: xi.

16. Ibid., xii; see xiii–xiv.

17. *Johnson v. M'Intosh*, 584.

18. Ibid, emphasis added.

19. Ibid., 584–85, emphasis added.

20. Francis Paul Prucha, *American Indian Treaties: The History of a Political Anomaly* (Berkeley: University of California Press, 1994), 46, 47, quoting *The Olden Time; a Monthly Publication, Devoted to the Preservation of Documents and Other Authentic Information in Relation to Early Explorations, and the Settlement and Improvement of the Country around the Head of the Ohio*, ed. Neville B. Craig (Pittsburgh, 1848; reprint, Millwood, NY: Kraus Reprint Company, 1976), 2: 423–27.

21. Prucha, *Treaties*, 49–50, quoting "Memorandum of the Proceedings at Treaty of Fort McIntosh," Timothy Pickering Papers, as quoted in Randolph C. Downes, *Council Fires on the Upper Ohio: A Narrative of Indian Affairs in the Upper Ohio Valley Until 1795* (Pittsburgh: University of Pittsburgh Press, 1940), 203.

22. Prucha, *Treaties*, 54–55, citing *JCC*, 31: 490–93, 66–69.

23. Prucha, *Treaties*, 57.

24. *Glasgow's Lessee v. Smith and Blackwell*, 2 Tenn. 144 (1805). See also *Weiser's Lessee v. Moody*, 2 Yeates 126 (1796), in which the Supreme Court of Pennsylvania affirmed that if Pennsylvania's colonial government had knowingly granted Indian lands, "the patent would enure for the benefit of the grantee, when the lands came afterwards to be purchased from the Indians; and the proprietaries could not pass the title to a stranger. *It might be compared to a person's selling lands without title, and afterwards obtaining a right thereto, where the vendor would hold in trust for the vendee*" (emphasis added).

25. *American State Papers: Indian Affairs*, 1: 36–46, 95–98, 48–50.

26. *American State Papers: Public Lands*, 1: 108.

27. [Benton, ed.,] *Abridgment of the Debates of Congress*, 1: 577, 578, 577, 579, 579–80.

28. Ibid., 578. Blount countered that he "did not know of one purchase made in Carolina. It was all conquest, and so were nine-tenths of all the lands held by the white people in America" (580).

29. Ibid., 579.

30. U.S. *House Journal*, 3d Cong., 1st sess., 30 January 1795, pp. 309–11, emphasis added. One congressman who might have profited by attending the Persons petition debate missed the best of it. Robert Goodloe Harper of South Carolina arrived and took his seat on February 9. Ibid., p. 317.

31. *American State Papers: Public Lands*, 1: 624.

32. U.S. *House Journal*, 5th Cong., 2d sess., 9 April 1798, p. 392, emphasis added. See also 23 January 1798, p. 160; *American State Papers: Public Lands*, 1: 25–26, 80–81. A similar petition submitted to the House in February 1793 by John Rogers was implicitly denied via the House's rejection of the Russell and Nelson petitions. See *American State Papers: Public Lands*, 1: 80–81.

33. *Laws of the Colonial and State Governments Relating to Indians* (Washington, DC: Thompson, 1832), 186.

34. Magrath, *Yazoo*, 3.

35. Jefferson to Knox, 10 August 1791, in Jefferson, *The Papers of Thomas Jefferson*, ed. Cullen, 22: 27, emphasis added.

36. *American State Papers: Indian Affairs*, 4: 533ff.; see also *Laws of the Colonial and State Governments Relating to Indians*, 186.

37. See *American State Papers: Public Lands*, 1: 132–64.

38. *Fletcher v. Peck*, 10 U.S. (6 Cranch) 87, 146–47 (1810).

39. *Johnson v. M'Intosh*, 585–86. Marshall failed to say that the lands possessed by the Cherokees, whom the Virginians likely believed to be the principal Indian nation within Kentucky at the time, were expressly exempted from the grant.

40. Ibid., 586.

41. Ibid., 587.

42. Ibid., 587–88, emphasis added.

43. Ibid., 588, 588–89, 591–92.

44. Ibid., 592.

45. Ibid., 593–94.

46. Ibid., 595–96, 597.

47. Ibid., 601, 598, 601–3, 604.

48. Ibid., 599–600.

CHAPTER 6

1. Paul W. Gates, "Tenants of the Log Cabin," *Mississippi Valley Historical Review* 49 (1962): 24–26.

2. Kentucky General Assembly, *Acts Passed at the First Session of the Thirty-Second General Assembly for the Commonwealth of Kentucky* (Frankfort: J. H. Holeman, 1824), 396.

3. *Richmond Enquirer*, 5 February 1828, p. 3, 12 February 1828, p. 3, 14 February 1828, p. 3, 11 May 1830, p. 3; [Washington, DC] *United States Telegraph*, 4 March 1830, p. 2, 11 May 1830, p. 3, 10 May 1830, p. 3; *Stats. at Large of USA*, 4 (1846): 422–24.

4. *Hawkins v. Barney's Lessee*, 30 U.S. (5 Peters) 457 (1831).

5. On Georgia's motives, see generally Mary Young, "The Exercise of Sovereignty in Cherokee Georgia," *Journal of the Early Republic* 10 (1990): 43.

6. *Register of Debates in Congress*, 21st Cong., 1st sess., 1056.

7. James Monroe, Message to Congress, 30 March 1824, in *Compilation of the Messages and Papers of the Presidents, 1789–1897*, ed. James D. Richardson (Washington, DC: U.S. Government Printing Office, 1898), 2: 235.

8. Ibid.

9. [Milledgeville, GA] *Southern Recorder*, 9 November 1824, p. 2.

10. Ibid.

11. The sale document, the Treaty of Indian Springs, was ratified by the U.S. Senate and proclaimed by President John Quincy Adams but ultimately, as noted below, superseded by the 1826 Treaty of Washington, under which the Muscogee (Creek) Nation kept its Alabama lands. Many of the signatories to the Treaty of Indian Springs, including McIntosh, were executed pursuant to Creek law by order of the Creek National Council. See generally Michael D. Green, *The Politics of Indian Removal: Creek Government and Society in Crisis* (Lincoln: University of Nebraska Press, 1982).

12. William G. McLoughlin, *Cherokee Renascence in the New Republic* (Princeton: Princeton University Press, 1986), 397.

13. *Southern Recorder*, 19 November 1827, p. 4.

14. Georgia General Assembly, *Acts of the General Assembly of the State of Georgia, Passed in Milledgeville at an Annual Session in November and December 1827* (Milledgeville: Camak & Ragland, 1827), 249, 250, 249, emphasis in original.

15. Georgia General Assembly, *Acts of the General Assembly of the State of Georgia, Passed in Milledgeville, at an Annual Session in November and December 1828* (Milledgeville: Camak & Ragland, 1829), 88–89.

16. Alabama General Assembly, *Acts Passed at the Tenth Annual Session of the General Assembly of the State of Alabama* (Tuscaloosa: M'Guire, Henry and M'Guire, 1829), 65–66.

17. Andrew Jackson, First Annual Message, in *Compilation of the Messages and Papers of the Presidents, 1789–1897*, 2: 457–59.

18. *Southern Recorder*, 19 December 1829, p. 3.

19. Mississippi General Assembly, *Acts Passed at the Thirteenth Session of the General Assembly of the State of Mississippi* (Jackson: Peter Isler, 1830), 7–8.

20. *Southern Recorder*, 6 March 1830, p. 2.

21. *Congressional Debates*, 21st Cong., 1st sess., 1830, pp. 305, 307, 309, 311–12.

22. Ibid., 345, 352.

23. Ibid., 312, 337, 353.

24. Ibid., 383.

25. Robert Remini, *Andrew Jackson and the Course of American Freedom, 1822–1832* (New York: Harper & Row, 1981), 261.

26. *Congressional Debates*, 21st Cong., 1st sess., 1830, pp. 456, 988, 993–94, 1007, 1029, 1051, 1032, 1090, 1135.

27. *Stats. at Large of USA*, 4: 411–12.

28. *United States Telegraph*, 25 March 1830, p. 3.

29. Marshall to Frelinghuysen, 22 May 1830, in Charles F. Hobson, ed., *The Papers of John Marshall* (Chapel Hill: University of North Carolina Press, 1990), 11: 374; ibid., Marshall to Everett, 5 June 1830, 11: 379.

30. Ibid., Marshall to Everett, 5 June 1830.

31. Ibid., Marshall to Dabney Carr, 26 June 1830, 11: 381.

32. *State v. Tassells*, reprinted in *Richmond Enquirer*, 9 December 1830, p. 4.

33. *Richmond Enquirer*, 4 January 1831, p. 2.

34. Ibid., 4 January 1831, p. 2.

35. Ibid., 11 January 1831, p. 2.

36. Ibid.

37. U.S. Constitution, art. 3, sec. 2.

38. *Cherokee Nation v. Georgia*, 30 U.S. (5 Peters) 1, 17, 20 (1831).

39. Ibid., 48, 49. There was almost certainly an intended irony in Baldwin's tone. Baldwin was inordinately contentious during the 1831 term. See G. White, *The Marshall Court*, 298. In 1833, Story wrote that Baldwin's "distaste for the Supreme Court and especially for [Chief Justice Marshall] is so familiarly known to us that it excites no surprise" (ibid., quoting Story to Joseph Hopkinson, 9 May 1833, Joseph Hopkinson Papers, HSP). Two justices, Smith Thompson and Joseph Story, were unwilling to defer resolution of the issues raised by Georgia's imposition of state law and dissented. Both were prepared to find the Cherokees a foreign state for purposes of jurisdiction under Article 3, Section 2 and to invalidate certain of the challenged laws (*Cherokee Nation*, 50–80). Marshall achieved a majority in favor of deferral because Justice William Johnson was reluctant to precipitate a crisis. He concurred in the decision, but "in pursuance of [his] practice in giving an opinion on all constitutional questions," issued a separate opinion denying that the Cherokees were a foreign state under the Constitution (20). Gabriel Duvall was absent and took no part.

40. Charles J. Kappler, *Indian Affairs: Laws and Treaties* (Washington, DC: U.S. Government Printing Office, 1904), 2: 310–11, emphasis added.

41. Grant Foreman, *Indian Removal* (Norman: University of Oklahoma Press, 1953), 29.

42. Kappler, *Indian Affairs*, 2: 325–41.

43. *Worcester v. Georgia*, 31 U.S. (6 Peters) 515, 528–33 (1832).

44. Ibid., 562–63, 597, 544.

45. Ibid., 546, emphasis added. Marshall's language is telling. The phrase "did not enter the mind of any man" is cavalier, even for Marshall, and plainly designed to dissuade prying too deeply into the truth of the recitation it introduces. The phrase is not one typically associated with Marshall. Indeed, prior to *Worcester*, he had used it only twice before in a reported opinion. In *Cherokee Nation v. Georgia*, Marshall wrote, "At the time the constitution was framed, the idea of appealing to an American court of justice for an assertion of right or a redress of wrong, had perhaps never entered the mind of an Indian or of his tribe" (18). Twenty-one years earlier, in *Oneale v. Thornton*, 10 U.S. (6 Cranch) 53, 69 (1810), he had written, "Consequently it could never enter the mind of the commissioners, or of the legislature, that one of these lots resold would not command a much higher price than the estimate made of it in the original contract." A variant of the phrase appears prominently, however, in the Illinois and Wabash Companies' 1810/1816 memorial to Congress. In his

refutation of the "Third Objection, that the purchases in question were made from the Indians by private individuals, without any public treaty, or other act of notoriety; without any public authority or previous licence from the Government, or its subsequent confirmation; and therefore contrary to the common and known usage established in such cases, and to the express prohibition contained in the British King's proclamation of October 7th, 1763," Robert Goodloe Harper wrote: "*It never entered into the head of any man* in England, that the Indians included within the limits of those grants became British subjects, were deprived of their property in the soil, or in any manner restricted in its use or disposition. On the contrary the British Government, and the Governments and people of the colonies thus established, always considered and treated these Indians as independent nations, and absolute owners of the land; from whom individuals or colonies might purchase, and did purchase, as convenience or inclination happened to direct" (see appendix 1; emphasis added). The use of the phrase and the context in which it appears suggests that in drafting *Worcester*, at least that part of *Worcester* rejecting *Johnson*'s conclusion that fee title to discovered lands vested in the discovering sovereign, Marshall consulted and borrowed from the Illinois and Wabash Companies' 1810/1816 memorial.

It is also worth observing that the section in *Worcester* overruling the fee title portion of the *Johnson* formulation of the discovery doctrine does not once mention *Johnson* overtly. John Marshall, superintending a Court that was still fragile, never expressly overruled himself. *Worcester* was intended to *erase* the former opinion by making the new rule, as was Marshall's wont, appear self-evident.

46. Because discovery did not convey anything more than the preemptive right, the Virginia militia grants were again made suspect. By 1832, however, as discussed above, this did not matter.

47. Three justices—Duvall, Thompson, and Story—joined Marshall in abandoning the *Johnson* formulation of the discovery doctrine. Not surprisingly, Justice Baldwin dissented, mostly on procedural grounds, then rather heroically declined to deliver his opinion to Court Reporter Richard Peters for publication: Baldwin wished to give Georgia no grounds for disobeying the Court's expected mandate directing the state to release Worcester and Butler (*Worcester*, 596). For the text of this opinion and an account of the circumstances of its nondelivery, see Lindsay G. Robertson, "Justice Henry Baldwin's 'Lost Opinion' in *Worcester v. Georgia*," *Journal of Supreme Court History* 23 (1999):

50–75. Justice John McLean issued an almost certainly politically motivated centrist concurrence, in which he sided with the majority on the ultimate issue—the Georgia acts, he agreed, violated the laws, treaties, and Constitution of the United States—but effectively invited Georgia expansionists to press on, opining that "if a contingency shall occur which shall render the Indians who reside in a State incapable of self-government, either by moral degradation or a reduction of their numbers, it would undoubtedly be in the power of a State government to extend to them the *aegis* of its laws" (*Worcester*, 593–94). Justice Johnson, who was absent, took no part in the decision.

48. W. L. G. Smith, *Fifty Years of Public Life: The Life and Times of Lewis Cass* (New York: Derby & Jackson, 1856), 248–49.

49. *Southern Recorder*, 19 April 1832, pp. 1, 2.

50. See, generally, Joseph C. Burke, "The Cherokee Cases: A Study in Law, Politics, and Morality," *Stanford Law Review* 21 (February 1969): 500; Jill Norgren, *The Cherokee Cases: The Confrontation of Law and Politics* (New York: McGraw-Hill, 1996).

51. Richard E. Ellis, *The Union at Risk: Jacksonian Democracy, States' Rights, and the Nullification Crisis* (New York: Oxford University Press, 1987), 75–76, *seriatim*.

52. Foreman, *Indian Removal*, 110; Kappler, *Indian Affairs*, 2: 341–43.

53. Kappler, *Indian Affairs*, 2: 344–45.

54. Foreman, *Indian Removal*, 193, 197; Vine Deloria Jr. and Raymond J. DeMallie, *Documents of American Indian Diplomacy* (Norman: University of Oklahoma Press, 1999), 2: 752–56.

55. Foreman, *Indian Removal*, 201. For a history of the role state courts played in removal, see Tim Alan Garrison, *The Legal Ideology of Removal: The Southern Judiciary and the Sovereignty of Native American Nations* (Athens: University of Georgia Press, 2002).

56. Kappler, *Indian Treaties*, 356.

57. *Public Acts Passed at the First Session of the Twentieth General Assembly of the State of Tennessee* (Nashville: Republican and Gazette Office, 1833), 10–12.

58. Carl Brent Swisher, *The Taney Period, 1836–64*, vol. 5 of *The Oliver Wendell Holmes Devise History of the Supreme Court of the United States* (New York: Macmillan, 1974), 53–54.

59. Alexander A. Lawrence, *James Moore Wayne, Southern Unionist* (Chapel Hill: University of North Carolina Press, 1943), 61–62. Duval's replacement, Jackson appointee Philip P. Barbour, would not join the court until 1837.

60. Story to [?] Fay, 2 March 1835, in *The Life and Letters of Joseph Story*, ed. William Wetmore Story (Boston: Charles C. Little and James Brown, 1851), 2: 192, quoted in Charles Warren, *The Supreme Court in United States History*, rev. ed. (Boston: Little, Brown, 1926), 1: 803.

61. Of the thirty-nine opinions reported that term, Marshall delivered only fifteen. Story delivered ten, McLean seven, Thompson five, and Baldwin and Wayne each one.

62. *Mitchel v. United States*, 34 U.S. (9 Peters) 711, 746 (1835).

63. Kappler, *Indian Treaties*, 439–40.

64. *United States v. Fernandez*, 35 U.S. (10 Peters) 303, 304 (1836).

65. Catron was confirmed four days into the Van Buren administration. Henry J. Abraham, *Justices and Presidents: A Political History of Appointments to the Supreme Court*, 2nd ed. (New York: Oxford University Press, 1985), 101, 103.

66. Swisher, *The Taney Period, 1836–64*, 61, citing, inter alia, Catron to Martin Van Buren, 12 December 1835, Martin Van Buren Papers, Library of Congress and Georgia Historical Society, Savannah. *Foreman*, like *Tassells*, involved the application to an Indian of state criminal laws. Catron's opinion constituted a twenty-three-page declaration that, as far as discovery was concerned, *Worcester* was wrong and *Johnson* was right. *State v. Foreman*, 16 Tenn. (8 Yerger) 256 (1835). After he was elevated to the Supreme Court of the United States, Catron himself issued a writ of error to bring *Foreman* before the high court, with the aim of providing a vehicle for reversing *Worcester*. The case was never argued, however, possibly because Foreman escaped (Swisher, *The Taney Period, 1836–64*, 61).

67. Abraham, *Justices and Presidents*, 103.

68. *Clark v. Smith*, 38 U.S. (13 Peters) 195, 201 (1839).

69. *Mitchel v. United States*, 40 U.S. (15 Peters) 52, 89 (1841).

70. *Martin v. Lessee of Waddell*, 41 U.S. (16 Peters) 367, 409 (1842).

71. *Worcester*, by contrast, was cited by the Court only once during the antebellum period. In *The Mayor, Aldermen, and Commonalty of the City of New York v. Miln*, 36 U.S. (11 Peters) 102 (1836), Justice Thompson cited *Worcester* for the proposition that in cases where the Court had held a state law unconstitutional, "there [had been] an actual conflict between the legislation of Congress and that of the States, upon the right drawn in question" (145). After *Miln*, the Court did not cite *Worcester* again for thirty years, until its opinion in *United States v. Holliday*, 70 U.S. (3 Wall.) 407, 420 (1865) (decided March 5, 1866).

72. Four years after delivering his opinion in *Martin v. Lessee of Waddell*, 41 U.S. (16 Peters) 367 (1842), Chief Justice Roger Taney reaffirmed the *Johnson* formulation without citation to *Johnson* in *United States v. Rogers*, 45 U.S. (5 How.) 567, 572 (1846). Over the next thirteen years, the Court returned to the rule (with citation) twice in opinions by Justice John Catron, in *Marsh v. Brooks* 49 U.S. (8 How.) 223, 232 (1850) and *Doe v. Wilson*, 64 U.S. 457, 463 (1859), the rule's last antebellum appearance.

AFTERWORD

1. Some members of the southeastern tribes successfully resisted removal, and their descendants reside today in their traditional homelands. The Kaskaskia, Peoria, and Cahokia were given a tract of land in Kansas next to the Wea and Piankashaw tribes. These five tribes subsequently consolidated and in 1867 sold their lands in Kansas to the United States and moved to the Indian Territory. Today, numbering 2,677, they are organized as the Peoria Tribe of Indians of Oklahoma. Sharon Malinowski and Anna Sheets, eds., *The Gale Encyclopedia of Native American Tribes* (New York: Gale Research, 1998), 1: 71–72; *Dictionary of Indian Tribes of the Americas* (Newport Beach, CA: American Indian Publishers, 1995), 3: 756.

2. *Guerin v. The Queen*, 2 S.C.R. 335 (1984) (Supreme Court of Canada).

3. *Mabo v. Queensland*, 107 A.L.R. (1992) (Australian High Court).

APPENDIX 2

1. *American State Papers: Public Lands*, 2: 109.

2. *Johnson v. M'Intosh*, 21 U.S. (8 Wheat.) 543, 548–49 (1823), emphasis added.

3. Ibid., 549–54, 555–57, emphasis added.

4. Ibid., 550–53, 554, 555–58, emphasis added.

5. Ibid., 544–45, 546, 547–49, 554, 558, emphasis added.

BIBLIOGRAPHY

MANUSCRIPTS AND ARCHIVAL COLLECTIONS

English, William H. Papers. Indiana Historical Society, Indianapolis.

Gilmer Collection. Virginia State Library, Richmond, VA.

Gratz, Benjamin. Papers. American Jewish Historical Society, Waltham, MA.

Gratz, Bernard (1738–1801) and Michael Gratz (1740–1811). Papers, 1753–1814. American Jewish Historical Society, Waltham, MA.

Gratz Collection. Historical Society of Pennsylvania, Philadelphia.

Gratz Family of Philadelphia. Papers. American Jewish Historical Society, Waltham, MA.

Gratz Papers. Historical Society of Pennsylvania, Philadelphia.

Harrison, William Henry. Papers. Library of Congress.

Lasselle, Charles B. Papers. Indiana State Library, Indianapolis.

McLean, John. Papers, 1785–1861. Library of Congress.

Public Archives of Canada (Ottawa).

Tipton, John. Papers. Indiana State Library, Indianapolis.

United Illinois and Wabash Land Companies. Papers. University of Oklahoma Law Library (on loan from Jasper Brinton).

United Kingdom. British Library.

United Kingdom. Public Record Office. Colonial Office Series 5.

Alabama General Assembly. *Acts Passed at the Tenth Annual Session of the General Assembly of the State of Alabama.* Tuscaloosa, AL: M'Guire, Henry and M'Guire, 1829.

American State Papers: 2, Indian Affairs; 8, Public Lands.

Annals of the Congress of the United States, 1789–1824. 42 vols. Washington, DC, 1834–56.

[Benton, Thomas Hart, ed.]. *Abridgment of the Debates of Congress from 1789 to 1856.* Vol. 1. New York: Appleton, 1857.

Carter, Clarence E., ed. *The Territorial Papers of the United States.* Vol. 8. Washington, DC: U.S. Government Printing Office, 1939.

Compilation of the Messages and Papers of the Presidents, 1789–1897. Edited by James D. Richardson. Vol. 2. Washington, DC: U.S. Government Printing Office, 1898.

Continental Congress. *Journals of the Continental Congress, 1774–1789.* Edited by Worthington C. Ford et al. 34 vols. Washington, DC, 1904–37.

Elliott, Jonathan. *Debates in the Several State Conventions on the Adoption of the Federal Constitution.* Vol. 3. Philadelphia, 1866.

Frederick County, Maryland, Register of Wills, Record of Wills, H.S. 2.

Georgia General Assembly. *Acts of the General Assembly of the State of Georgia, Passed in Milledgeville at an Annual Session in November and December 1827.* Milledgeville, GA: Camak & Ragland, 1827.

———. *Acts of the General Assembly of the State of Georgia, Passed in Milledgeville,* at *an Annual Session in November and December 1828.* Milledgeville, GA: Camak & Ragland, 1829.

Hening, William Waller, comp. *The Statutes at Large; Being a Collection of All the Laws of Virginia, from the First Session of the Legislature in 1609.* 1819–23; reprint, Charlottesville: University Press of Virginia, 1969.

Johnson and Graham's Lessee v. McIntosh. Record Group 21, U.S. District Court, Southern District of Illinois, Complete Record Book, 1819–1842. National Archives, Great Lakes Region, Chicago.

Kappler, Charles J. *Indian Affairs: Laws and Treaties.* Vol. 2. Washington, DC: U.S. Government Printing Office, 1904.

Kentucky General Assembly. *Acts Passed at the First Session of the Twenty-Seventh General Assembly for the Commonwealth of Kentucky.* Frankfort, KY: Kendall and Russells, 1819.

———. *Acts Passed at the First Session of the Twenty-Eighth General Assembly for the Commonwealth of Kentucky*. Frankfort, KY: Kendall and Russells, 1820.

———. *Acts Passed at the First Session of the Twenty-Ninth General Assembly for the Commonwealth of Kentucky*. Frankfort, KY: Kendall and Russells, 1821.

———. *Acts Passed at the First Session of the Thirtieth General Assembly for the Commonwealth of Kentucky*. Frankfort, KY: Kendall and Russells, 1821.

———. *Acts Passed at the Second Session of the Thirtieth, and the First Session of the Thirty-First General Assembly for the Commonwealth of Kentucky*. Frankfort, KY: J. H. Holeman, 1823.

———. *Acts Passed at the First Session of the Thirty-Second General Assembly for the Commonwealth of Kentucky*. Frankfort, KY: J. H. Holeman, 1824.

Knox County, Indiana. Minute Book A, 1811–1817.

Laws of the Colonial and State Governments Relating to Indians. Washington, DC: Thompson, 1832.

Mississippi General Assembly. *Acts Passed at the Thirteenth Session of the General Assembly of the State of Mississippi*. Jackson, MS: Peter Isler, 1830.

New York. *Journals of the Provincial Congress, Provincial Convention, Committee of Safety and Council of Safety*. Vol. 1. Albany, NY: Weed, 1842.

Palmer, William P., et al., eds. *Calendar of Virginia State Papers and Other Manuscripts Preserved in the Capitol at Richmond*. Vol. 1. Richmond, 1875.

Register of Debates in Congress. 14 vols. Washington, DC, 1824–38.

Statutes at Large of the United States of America, 1789–1873. 17 vols. Washington, DC, 1850–73.

Tennessee General Assembly. *Public Acts Passed at the First Session of the Twentieth General Assembly of the State of Tennessee*. Nashville: Republican and Gazette Office, 1833.

U.S. Constitution, art. 3, sec. 2.

U.S. Congress. *Congressional Debates*, 21st Cong., 1st sess.

U.S. *House Journal*.

U.S. *Senate Journal*.

Virginia. Convention. *The Proceedings of the Convention of Delegates [May 6–July 5, 1776]*. Williamsburg, VA: Alexander Purdie, 1776.

———. House of Delegates. *Journal of the House of Delegates [May 3–June 26, 1779]*. Williamsburg, VA: Clarkson & Davis, 1779.

———. *Journal of the House of Delegates [October 1–December 28, 1792]*. Richmond, VA: Davis, 1792.

Campbell v. Hall, 98 Eng. Rep. 1045, 1 Cowp. Rep. 204 (1774).

Cherokee Nation v. Georgia, 30 U.S. (5 Peters) 1 (1831).

Clark v. Bazadone, 5 U.S. (1 Cranch) 212 (1803).

Clark v. Smith, 38 U.S. (13 Peters) 195 (1839).

Cohens v. Virginia, 19 U.S. (6 Wheat.) 264 (1821).

Doe v. Wilson, 64 U.S. (23 How.) 457 (1859).

Fletcher v. Peck, 10 U.S. (6 Cranch) 87 (1810).

Gilman v. Brown, 10 Fed. Cas. 392 (Cir. Ct., D. Mass, 1817), *aff'd* 17 U.S. (4 Wheat.) 255 (1819).

Glasgow's Lessee v. Smith and Blackwell, 2 Tenn. 144 (1805).

Green v. Biddle, 21 U.S. (8 Wheat.) 1 (1823).

Guerin v. The Queen, 2 S.C.R. 335 (1984) (Supreme Court of Canada).

Hawkins v. Barney's Lessee, 30 U.S. (5 Peters) 457 (1831).

Hoofnagle v. Anderson, 20 U.S. (7 Wheat.) 212 (1822).

Hughes v. Union Ins. Co. of Baltimore, 21 U.S. (8 Wheat.) 292 (1823).

Jackson v. Wood, 7 Johns. Rep. 290 (N.Y. 1810).

Johnson and Graham's Lessee v. McIntosh, 8 Wheat. 543 (1823). National Archives Microfilm Publications, Case No. 1105.

Johnson v. M'Intosh, 21 U.S. (8 Wheat.) 543 (1823).

Livingston v. Jefferson, 15 F.Cas. 660 (C. D.Va. 1811).

Mabo v. Queensland, 107 A.L.R. (1992) (Australian High Court).

Marsh v. Brooks, 49 U.S. (8 How.) 223, 232 (1850).

Marshall v. Clark, 8 Va. (4 Call) 268 (1791).

Martin v. Lessee of Waddell, 41 U.S. (16 Peters) 367 (1842).

Maryland Ins. Co. v. Le Roy, 11 U.S. (7 Cranch) 26 (1812).

The Mayor, Aldermen, and Commonalty of the City of New York v. Miln, 36 U.S. (11 Peters) 102 (1836).

Meigs v. M'Clung's Lessee, 13 U.S. (9 Cranch) 11 (1815).

Mitchel v. United States, 34 U.S. (9 Peters) 711 (1835).

Mitchel v. United States, 40 U.S. (15 Peters) 52 (1841).

Oneale v. Thornton, 10 U.S. (6 Cranch) 53, 69 (1810).

State v. Foreman, 16 Tenn. (8 Yerger) 256 (1835).

United States v. Fernandez, 35 U.S. (10 Peters) 303 (1836).

United States v. Holliday, 70 U.S. (3 Wall.) 407 (1865).

United States v. Rogers, 45 U.S. (5 How.) 567 (1846).

Weiser's Lessee v. Moody, 2 Yeates 127 (Pa. 1796).

Worcester v. Georgia, 31 U.S. (6 Peters) 515 (1832).

NEWSPAPERS

[Annapolis] *Maryland Gazette and State Register.*

Daily National Intelligencer.

[Frankfort, KY] *Western World.*

Illinois Intelligencer.

[Lexington, KY] *Western Monitor.*

[Milledgeville, GA] *Southern Recorder.*

Niles' Weekly Register.

[Philadelphia] *National Gazette and Literary Register.*

Richmond Enquirer.

[Vincennes] *Indiana Gazette.*

[Washington, DC] *Daily National Intelligencer.*

Washington [DC] *Gazette.*

[Washington, DC] *United States Telegraph.*

BOOKS AND ARTICLES

Abernethy, Thomas P. *Western Lands and the American Revolution.* New York: Appleton-Century, 1937.

Abraham, Henry J. *Justices and Presidents: A Political History of Appointments to the Supreme Court.* 2nd ed. New York: Oxford University Press, 1985.

Adams, Henry. *History of the United States of America during the First Administration of James Madison.* 1890; reprint, New York: Antiquarian Press, 1962.

Adams, John Quincy. *Memoirs of John Quincy Adams, Comprising Portions of His Diary from 1795–1848.* Edited by Charles Francis Adams. Vol. 1. Philadelphia: J. B. Lippincott, 1874.

Alvord, Clarence Walworth. *The Illinois Country 1673–1818.* Chicago: A. C. McClurg, 1922.

———. *The Mississippi Valley in British Politics.* Vol. 2. Cleveland, OH: Arthur H. Clark, 1917.

Barce, Elmore. "Tecumseh's Confederacy." *Indiana Magazine of History* 12 (June 1916): 161.

Beveridge, Albert J. *The Life of John Marshall*. Vol. 2. New York: Houghton Mifflin, 1916.

———. *The Life of John Marshall*. Vol. 4. New York: Houghton Mifflin, 1919.

Blackstone, William. *Commentaries on the Laws of England*. Vol. 2. 1766; reprint, Chicago: University of Chicago Press, 1979.

Boehm, Myron. "An Old Kyle Deed Uncovered." *Vincennes Shopper*, 21 July 1971, p. 1.

Burke, Joseph C. "The Cherokee Cases: A Study in Law, Politics, and Morality." *Stanford Law Review* 21 (February 1969): 500.

Carter, Harvey Lewis. *The Life and Times of Little Turtle: First Sagamore of the Wabash*. Urbana: University of Illinois Press, 1987.

Chalmers, George. *Opinions of Eminent Lawyers on Various Points of English Jurisprudence, Chiefly Concerning the Colonies, Fisheries, and Commerce, of Great Britain*. 2 vols. London: Reed and Hunter, 1814.

Chilton, W. B. "The Brent Family." *The Virginia Magazine of History and Biography*, 19 (1911): 206.

Cleaves, Freeman. *Old Tippecanoe: William Henry Harrison and His Time*. New York: Charles Scribner's Sons, 1939.

Clinton, Robert N. "The Proclamation of 1763: Colonial Prelude to Two Centuries of Federal-State Conflict over the Management of Indian Affairs." *Boston University Law Review* 69 (1989): 329.

Commager, Henry Steele, ed. *Documents of American History*, 3rd ed. New York: F. S. Crofts, 1944.

Committee on Publication and the Recording Secretary, comp. *Records of the Columbia Historical Society, Washington, D.C.* Vol. 9. Washington, DC: Columbia Historical Society, 1906.

Cottman, George S. "Benjamin Parke." *Dictionary of American Biography*. Edited by Dumas Malone. Vol. 14. New York: Charles Scribner's Sons, 1943.

Cox, Joseph W. *Champion of Southern Federalism: Robert Goodloe Harper of South Carolina*. Port Washington, NY: Kennikat Press, 1972.

Davis, Richard Beale. *Francis Walker Gilmer: Life and Learning in Jefferson's Virginia*. Richmond, VA: Dietz Press, 1939.

Day, Richard. *Vincennes: A Pictorial History*. St. Louis, MO: G. Bradley, 1994.

Degnan, Ronan E. "*Livingston v. Jefferson*: A Freestanding Footnote." *California Law Review* 75 (January 1987): 115.

Deloria, Vine, Jr. "Revision and Reversion." In *The American Indian and the Problem of History*. Edited by Calvin Martin. New York: Oxford University Press, 1987.

Deloria, Vine, Jr., and Raymond J. DeMallie, *Documents of American Indian Diplomacy*. Vol. 2. Norman: University of Oklahoma Press, 1999.

Downes, Randolph C. *Council Fires on the Upper Ohio: A Narrative of Indian Affairs in the Upper Ohio Valley Until 1795*. Pittsburgh, PA: University of Pittsburgh Press, 1940.

Duckett, Alvin Laroy. *John Forsyth: Political Tactician*. Athens: University of Georgia Press, 1962.

Durrie, Daniel Steele. "Jonathan Carver and Carver's Grant." *Wisconsin Historical Collections* 91 (1872): 220.

Ellis, Elizabeth Breckenridge. "Nathaniel Pope." *Dictionary of American Biography*. Edited by Dumas Malone. Vol. 15. New York: Charles Scribner's Sons, 1943.

Ellis, Richard E. *The Union at Risk: Jacksonian Democracy, States' Rights, and the Nullification Crisis*. New York: Oxford University Press, 1987.

Foreman, Grant. *Indian Removal*. Norman: University of Oklahoma Press, 1953.

Garrison, Curtis W. "Benjamin Stoddert." *Dictionary of American Biography*. Edited by Dumas Malone. Vol. 18. New York: Charles Scribner's Sons, 1943.

Garrison, Tim Alan. *The Legal Ideology of Removal: The Southern Judiciary and the Sovereignty of Native American Nations*. Athens: University of Georgia Press, 2002.

Gates, Paul W. *History of Public Land Law Development*. Washington, DC: Zenger, 1968.

———. "Tenants of the Log Cabin." *Mississippi Valley Historical Review* 49 (1962): 3.

Graber, Mark A. "The Passive-Aggressive Virtues: *Cohens v. Virginia* and the Problematic Establishment of Judicial Power." *Constitutional Commentary* 12 (1995): 67.

Green, Michael D. *The Politics of Indian Removal: Creek Government and Society in Crisis*. Lincoln: University of Nebraska Press, 1982.

Grotius, Hugo. *The Rights of War and Peace*. Translated by A. C. Campbell. Washington, DC: M. Walker Dunne, 1901.

Hamilton, J. G. de R. "Robert Goodloe Harper." *Dictionary of American Biography*. Edited by Dumas Malone. Vol. 8. New York: Charles Scribner's Sons, 1932.

Harden, Edward J. *The Life of George M. Troup*. Savannah, GA: E. J. Purse, 1859.

Harrison, Lowell H. *Kentucky's Road to Statehood*. Lexington: University of Kentucky Press, 1992.

Haskins, George L., and Herbert A. Johnson. *Foundations of Power: John Marshall, 1801–15*, vol. 2 of *History of the Supreme Court of the United States*. New York: Macmillan, 1981.

Hobson, Charles F., ed. *The Papers of John Marshall.* Vols. 6, 11. Chapel Hill: University of North Carolina Press, 1990.

Holdsworth, Sir William. *A History of English Law.* 2nd ed. Vol. 7. 1937; reprint, London: Methuen, 1966.

Jefferson, Thomas. *Notes on the State of Virginia.* 1784; reprint, Chapel Hill: University of North Carolina Press, 1955.

———. *The Papers of Thomas Jefferson.* Edited by Julian P. Boyd. Vol. 1. Princeton, NJ: Princeton University Press, 1950.

———. *The Writings of Thomas Jefferson.* Edited by Albert Ellery Bergh. Vol. 10. Washington, DC: Thomas Jefferson Memorial Association of the United States, 1907.

———. *The Works of Thomas Jefferson.* Edited by Paul Leicester Ford. Vol. 11. New York: G. P. Putnam's Sons, 1905.

———. *The Papers of Thomas Jefferson.* Edited by Charles T. Cullen. Vol. 22. Princeton: Princeton University Press, 1986.

Jensen, Merrill. *The Articles of Confederation.* Madison: University of Wisconsin Press, 1962.

———. "The Creation of the National Domain, 1781–1784." *Mississippi Valley Historical Review,* 11 (December 1939): 323.

Johnson, Monroe, Jr. "The Johnson Family Genealogy." 1987. Frederick County Historical Society, Frederick, MD.

Johnson, Sir William. *The Papers of Sir William Johnson.* Vol. 8. Albany: University of the State of New York, 1933.

Kades, Eric. "History and Interpretation of the Great Case of *Johnson v. M'Intosh,*" *Law & History Review* 19 (2001): 67.

Kennedy, John P. *Memoirs of the Life of William Wirt.* Rev. ed. Vol. 2. Philadelphia: Blanchard and Lea, 1854.

Laub, C. H. "Revolutionary Virginia and the Crown Lands." *William and Mary Quarterly,* 2nd ser., 11 (October 1931): 304.

Lawrence, Alexander A. *James Moore Wayne, Southern Unionist.* Chapel Hill: University of North Carolina Press, 1943.

Lester, William S. *The Transylvania Colony.* Spencer, IN: Guard, 1935.

Lewis, George E. *The Indiana Company, 1763–1798.* Glendale, CA: Arthur H. Clark, 1941.

Luce, W. Ray. *Cohens v. Virginia (1821): The Supreme Court and State Rights, a Reevaluation of Influences and Impacts.* New York: Garland, 1990.

Madison, James. *The Papers of James Madison,* Presidential Series. Edited by J. C. A Stagg. Vol. 2. Charlottesville: University Press of Virginia, 1992.

Magrath, C. Peter. *Yazoo: Law and Politics in the New Republic.* Providence, RI: Brown University Press, 1966.

Malinowski, Sharon, and Anna Sheets, eds. *Dictionary of Indian Tribes of the Americas.* Vol. 3. Newport Beach, CA: American Indian Publishers, 1995.

———, eds. *The Gale Encyclopedia of Native American Tribes.* Vol. 1. New York: Gale Research, 1998.

Marcus, Maeva, ed. *Origins of the Federal Judiciary.* New York: Oxford University Press, 1992.

Marks, Anna Edith. "William Murray, Trader and Land Speculator in the Illinois Country." *Transactions of the Illinois State Historical Society* 26 (1919): 188.

Marshall, John. *The Life of George Washington, Commander in Chief of the American Forces, During the War Which Established the Independence of His Country, and First President of the United States. Compiled Under the Inspection of the Honorable Bushrod Washington, from Original Papers Bequeathed to Him by His Deceased Relative, and Now in Possession of the Author. To Which is Prefixed, an Introduction, Containing a Compendious View of the Colonies Planted by the English on the Continent of North America, from Their Settlement to the Commencement of That War Which Terminated in Their Independence.* Philadelphia: C. P. Wayne, 1804.

Mcdonald, Donald. "The Diaries of Donald Mcdonald, 1824–1826." *Indiana Historical Society Publications.* Vol. 14. Indianapolis: Indiana Historical Society, 1942.

McLoughlin, William G. *Cherokee Renascence in the New Republic.* Princeton, NJ: Princeton University Press, 1986.

Meigs, William M. *The Life of Charles Jared Ingersoll.* Philadelphia: J. B. Lippincott, 1897.

Monks, Leander J., ed. *Courts and Lawyers of Indiana.* Indianapolis: Federal Publishing Co., 1916.

Newcomb, Steven T. "The Evidence of Christian Nationalism in Federal Indian Law: The Doctrine of Discovery, *Johnson v. M'Intosh*, and Plenary Power." *New York University Review of Law & Social Change* 20 (1993): 303.

Norgren, Jill. *The Cherokee Cases: The Confrontation of Law and Politics.* New York: McGraw-Hill, 1996.

Onuf, Peter S. *The Origins of the Federal Republic: Jurisdictional Controversies in the United States, 1775–1787.* Philadelphia: University of Pennsylvania Press, 1983.

———. *Statehood and Union.* Bloomington: Indiana University Press, 1987.

Owen, William. "Diary of William Owen from November 10, 1824, to April 20, 1825." Edited by Joel W. Hiatt. *Indiana Historical Society Publications.* Vol. 4. Indianapolis: Bobbs-Merrill, 1906.

Papenfuse, Eric Robert. *The Evils of Necessity: Robert Goodloe Harper and the Moral Dilemma of Slavery.* Philadelphia: American Philosophical Society, 1997.

Perkins, Dexter. "Richard Rush." *Dictionary of American Biography.* Edited by Dumas Malone. Vol. 16. New York: Charles Scribner's Sons, 1943.

Prucha, Francis Paul. *American Indian Policy in the Formative Years: Indian Trade and Intercourse Acts, 1790–1834.* Cambridge, MA: Harvard University Press, 1962.

———. *American Indian Treaties: The History of a Political Anomaly.* Berkeley: University of California Press, 1994.

Quaife, Milo M. "Jonathan Carver and the Carver Grant." *Mississippi Valley Historical Review* 7 (1920): 3.

Remini, Robert V. *Andrew Jackson and the Course of American Freedom, 1822–1832.* New York: Harper & Row, 1981.

———. *Andrew Jackson and His Indian Wars.* New York: Viking, 2001.

Ritz, Wilfred J., Wythe Holt, and H. H. LaRue, eds. *Rewriting the History of the Judiciary Act of 1789: Exposing Myths, Challenging Premises, and Using New Evidence.* Norman: University of Oklahoma Press, 1990.

Robertson, Lindsay G. "John Marshall as Colonial Historian: Reconsidering the Origins of the Discovery Doctrine." *Journal of Law & Politics* 13 (1997): 759–77.

———. "Justice Henry Baldwin's 'Lost Opinion' in *Worcester v. Georgia.*" *Journal of Supreme Court History* 23 (1999): 50–75.

———. "'A Mere Feigned Case': Rethinking the *Fletcher v. Peck* Conspiracy and Early Republican Legal Culture." *Utah Law Review* 2000 (2000): 249.

Rodney, George Bridges. *Diary of George Bridges Rodney.* National Society of the Colonial Dames of America in the State of Delaware. N.p., n.d.

Rohrbough, Malcolm J. *The Land Office Business.* New York: Oxford University Press, 1968.

Rowland, Kate M. *The Life of George Mason.* Vol. 1. New York: Putnam's, 1892.

Smith, Charles Page. *James Wilson: Founding Father, 1742–1798.* Westport, CT: Greenwood, 1956.

Smith, W. L. G. *Fifty Years of Public Life: The Life and Times of Lewis Cass.* New York: Derby & Jackson, 1856.

Smith, William, Jr. *The History of the Province of New-York.* Vol. 1. Cambridge, MA: Belknap Press of Harvard University Press, 1972.

Sommerville, C. W. *Robert Goodloe Harper.* Washington, DC: Neale, 1899.

Sosin, Jack M. *Whitehall and the Wilderness: The Middle West in British Colonial Policy, 1760–1775.* Lincoln: University of Nebraska Press, 1961.

Spaulding, Oliver L., Jr. "John Pope." *Dictionary of American Biography*. Edited by Dumas Malone. Vol. 15. New York: Charles Scribner's Sons, 1943.

Spaulding, Thomas M. "William Henry Winder." *Dictionary of American Biography*. Edited by Dumas Malone. Vol. 20. New York: Charles Scribner's Sons, 1936.

Swisher, Carl B. *The Taney Period, 1836–64*, vol. 5 of *The Oliver Wendell Holmes Devise History of the Supreme Court of the United States*. New York: Macmillan, 1974.

Taylor, Charles W., comp. *Biographical Sketches and Review of the Bench and Bar of Indiana*. Indianapolis: Bench and Bar, 1895.

Treat, Payson Jackson. *The National Land System, 1785–1820*. New York: E. B. Treat, 1910.

Tucker, St. George. *Blackstone's Commentaries*. Philadelphia: William Young Birch and Abraham Small, 1803.

United Illinois and Wabash Land Companies. *An Account of the Proceedings of the Illinois and Ouabache Companies, in Persuance [sic] of their Purchases Made of the Independent Natives, July 5th, 1773, and 18th October, 1775*. Philadelphia, 1796.

———. *An Account of the Proceedings of the Illinois and Ouabache Land Companies, in Persuance [sic] of their Purchases Made of the Independent Natives, July 5th, 1773 and18th October, 1775*. Philadelphia: William Duane, 1803.

———. *Memorial of the United Illinois and Wabash Land Companies, to the Senate and House of Representatives of the United States*. Baltimore: Joseph Robinson, 1810.

———. *Memorial of the United Illinois and Wabash Land Companies, to the Senate and House of Representatives of the United States*. Baltimore: Joseph Robinson, 1816.

———. *United Illinois and Wabash Land Company Minutes 1778–1812*. Historical Society of Pennsylvania, Philadelphia.

Vattel, Emmerich de. *The Law of Nations*. Edited by Edward D. Ingraham. Philadelphia: T. & J. W. Johnson, 1855.

Warren, Charles. *The Supreme Court in United States History*, rev. ed. Vol. 1. Boston: Little, Brown, 1926.

———. *The Story-Marshall Correspondence*. New York: New York University Law School, 1942.

Washburn, Wilcomb E., comp. *The American Indian and the United States: A Documentary History*. Vol. 3. New York: Random House, 1973.

Washington, George. *The Writings of George Washington*. Edited by Worthington Chauncey Ford. Vol. 2. New York: G. P. Putnam's Sons, 1889.

Webster, Daniel. *The Papers of Daniel Webster. Correspondence, Volume 1, 1798–1824.* Edited by Charles M. Wiltse. Hanover, NH: University Press of New England, 1974.

Weisenburger, Francis P. *The Life of John McLean: A Politician on the United States Supreme Court.* Columbus: Ohio State University Press, 1937.

White, G. Edward. *The Marshall Court and Cultural Change, 1815–1835,* vols. 3 and 4 of *The Oliver Wendell Holmes Devise History of the Supreme Court of the United States.* New York: Macmillan, 1988.

White, Richard. *The Middle Ground: Indians, Empires, and Republics in the Great Lakes Region, 1650–1815.* New York: Cambridge University Press, 1991.

Wilkins, David E. "*Johnson v. M'Intosh* Revisited: Through the Eyes of *Mitchel v. United States.*" *American Indian Law Review* 19 (1994): 159.

Williams, Robert A., Jr. *The American Indian in Western Legal Thought: The Discourses of Conquest.* New York: Oxford University Press, 1990.

Wolf, Edwin, II, and Maxwell Whiteman. *The History of the Jews of Philadelphia from Colonial Times to the Age of Jackson.* Philadelphia: Jewish Publication Society of America, 1975.

Woolen, William Wesley. *Biographical and Historical Sketches of Early Indiana.* Indianapolis: Hammond, 1883.

Wunder, John R. "Constitutional Oversight: *Clarke v. Bazadone* and the Territorial Supreme Court as the Court of Last Resort." *The Old Northwest* 4 (September 1978): 259–84.

Young, Mary. "The Exercise of Sovereignty in Cherokee Georgia." *Journal of the Early Republic* 10 (1990): 43.

INDEX